OVER HERE

An American Expat
In the South of France

OVER HERE
**An American Expat
In the South of France**

by
Randy Lofficier

A Black Coat Press Book

Acknowledgements: Philippe and Bernadette Laguerre, who planted the seed, Kos, Billmon and Atrios who helped it grow, Diane and Evan Todd, for moral support, Cindy Pelter, who speeded our departure, François Lar, who introduced us to the Shire, Jackie Scissors, Scott Rosenberg and the folks at the Gotham Group, especially Peter McHugh, for watching our backs. And last but not least, the citizens of Chalabre, for their warmth and friendship.

Copyright © 2006 Randy Lofficier.
Photos Copyright © 2006 Jean-Marc & Randy Lofficier.

The story continues on our website at www.possumworld.com
More photos can be viewed on the author's site at:
http://www.randylofficier.com

ISBN 1-932983-68-6. First Printing. February 2006. Published by Black Coat Press, an imprint of Hollywood Comics.com, LLC, P.O. Box 17270, Encino, CA 91416. All rights reserved. Except for review purposes, no part of this book may be reproduced or transmitted in any form or by any means, electronic or mechanical, including photocopying, recording, or by any information storage and retrieval system, without permission in writing from the publisher. Printed in the United States of America.

Chalabre as seen from the Château

2004

Wednesday, November 3

How naïve we can be. I wrote in my calendar for yesterday: *Victory Day*. I can't believe I got it so wrong. I'm sure it was another set up. These people are just pure evil.[1]

Still, it's time to look at the bright side of things. JM and I have been talking about leaving L.A. for a long, long time. We just hadn't been able to decide where to go up until now.

If we go somewhere else in the U.S., we'll still be under the evil regime. And, most of the places that are less expensive than L.A. are "red" states. I just don't see us living happily in a red state. We're blue through-and-through. It would be hard to hide my beliefs to that extent.

Plus, my dear friend Raven is a dyed-in-the-wool liberal living in the midst of red farming country. She's miserable there. I don't think it would be all that different for me.

That caused us to think about Canada. Problems with that as well. The left coast of Canada (Vancouver area) is just as expensive as L.A., so that wouldn't help our financial situation any, unless we moved so far out in the boonies that we'd probably never be comfortable.

Montreal seemed the obvious choice. But do we really want to live in a place where people have to get around in tunnels beneath the city for most of the winter? I probably wouldn't mind, but I can't see JM being happy with that.

And, of course, all of these choices have us moving away from something. That seems like running to me. I want us to move *towards* something so that this can be a positive experience.

That led me to what I think was some kind of vision; what my mother-in-law would call a "flash." We need to move to France. It's something we've always talked about doing, but it was going to be a "someday" kind of thing. I believe that "someday" has become "now."

---

[1] And, of course, that was the case. The Republicans stole the 2004 election just as they did the one in 2000. A non-partisan General Accounting Office report has now found that, "some of [the] concerns about electronic voting machines have been realized and have caused problems with recent elections, resulting in the loss and miscount of votes." See *http://www.gao.gov/new.items/d05956.pdf*

I'm going to start doing some research to see if we really can do this, what we can afford and where we should go. Ironically, JM is more skeptical about it than I am. You would think it would be the other way around, given that for him, he's going home.

But, 20 years in our house in Reseda is a long time. We've gotten it all fixed up and nesty. It's hard for him to leave.

Still, as I've told him. Nothing is definite yet. We'll just have to see what turns up.

Thursday, November 4

We called our friend Cindy today. Besides being a good friend, she's the best real estate agent in our area. We've always said that, if we decided to sell the house, the only agent we would trust for the job was Cindy. Before we can make any decisions, we need to know how much the house here is worth, so we can calculate how much we can spend on something in France.

At the moment, I'm only telling people that we're thinking of moving. Better not to totally freak them out. I *did* tell my mother, before the election, that if the Chimp won again, we were outta here. I don't think she thought we really meant it though. To be honest, I don't think *we* really knew that we meant it when we said it. But, it just feels like the right thing to do.

I started looking at French real estate sites to get an idea of what we might be able to afford.

The big "out" is the Var, which is the part of France where most of JM's family lives. We wouldn't want to live in Toulon itself, which is a bit like San Diego, but in the Upper Var, which is mostly small villages, pine forests and grape vines. Unfortunately, it seems that it's no longer hidden and undiscovered. Prices for chicken coops look like you're buying in L.A.! And that's for things that need to be totally renovated.

I checked out the Dordogne region, where our friend Karine lives. That's expensive too, although there are a few places farther afield that might work. We're thinking that we should look out in the country, because that will hopefully be less expensive. And, of course, there are things we'll need to think about, like whether we can get a DSL line or if we'll need to rely on Internet through a satellite dish.

The other regions we're thinking about are in the Ariège and the Aude areas. We have friends who live in Pamiers and that would mean we wouldn't be moving to someplace where we don't have anyone we know nearby. Both places are near the Pyrénées and we think they're still more affordable than some others. I have to be careful though; we don't want to be too high up in the mountains or we may find ourselves totally cut off in the winter. That would be OK if we skied, but since we don't, it's something to avoid.

There are a lot of interesting properties online that have me quite eager to see them "in the flesh." And, we think that's what we're going to have to do. We'll try to get a good airfare to France right after Turkey Day so that we can rent a car and really look at places. No way am I going to buy a property just from pictures on the Internet!

Thursday, November 4

I'm still feeling depressed and bitter about the election. It doesn't seem right that Kerry gave up with no fight at all. I think we all feel betrayed, to be perfectly honest.

Although it's a bit scary to think about such a big deal as moving to another country, at least it gives me something to look forward to, instead of another four years of seeing the Chimp on CNN. I can't even bear to keep the news on right now because it only makes me feel worse.

I also am not ready yet to talk to anyone I know who voted for W. I'm afraid I'll say something that I'll be sorry about later. Better to just keep quiet and not talk politics with them. All my Democrat friends just look shell-shocked and gray.

On the moving front, JM has come up with a wacky idea of pooling our resources with his parents and trying to move to an apartment in Paris that his mother could also stay in after she retires and they move to Toulon. She hates the idea of living in Toulon, so that could mean she'd be staying with us practically *all* the time. I'm going to nip that in the bud. I love my mother-in-law, but I am *not* going to live with her. That would result in murder in a very short time.

Plus, if we do that, he would be forced to find some kind of office job and at our age, that will not be any easier in France than it has been in L.A. For me, moving to Paris has all the negatives of living in Los Angeles and more. I don't want to do it.

Saturday, November 6

I think the "living with mom" idea is over, thank goodness. It doesn't hurt that real estate in Paris is completely crazy. No matter what we can get for our house, it's not enough to allow us to buy a closet in Paris. Even with his parents kicking in something, there just wouldn't be enough to buy anything without taking out a hefty mortgage. That would put us right back to where we are now, so what's the point?

Instead, I pointed out that if we sell our house in Reseda, then buy a much less expensive house out in the boonies, that would leave us with money in the bank and no mortgage. Not enough to live on forever, but at least we wouldn't feel as if we're drowning. Plus, we can keep doing what we're doing and maybe even find some extra work translating or something that would help out.

I think JM realized I was making sense. That's a big relief. I was starting to regret bringing it up in the first place.

I was also able to do some research with Air France and a French government website. We shouldn't have any problem taking Maggie with us. I need to find out if her microchip is compatible with the European system, otherwise she'll need to have a new one put in. Then, she'll need a medical certificate, up-to-date shots, etc. The *big* issue is going to be crate-training her. She's never liked her crate, which she thinks is some type of instrument of torture. If I start working on it now, I'll have a few months to, hopefully, get her used to it. This should be interesting.

Monday, November 8

Several months ago, during the summer, there was absolutely nothing on television. So, I started flipping around and came upon a show on BBC America, called "*Location, Location, Location.*" It's a British real estate program, with these two buyer's agents that help someone find their perfect house. This is *not* the kind of thing that JM and I usually watch. But, boredom will sometimes cause you to do things you wouldn't ordinarily do.

We got hooked. The two hosts, Kirstie Allsopp and Phil Spencer, really know how to boil down what a person really wants and needs. Some of these buyers have been looking for houses for ages without finding anything. It never occurred to us while we were watching that it could ever apply to us.

One of the shows that was particularly useful was one on selling a house. There was a couple that had been trying for months without success. Kirstie and Phil explained that they had way too much stuff everywhere. They needed to clean out and throw out. I remember when we saw it, we talked about the fact that our house looked cluttered.

Well, after a weekend of cleaning up, the couple sold their house the first day it went back on the market.

Our friend and realtor, Cindy, came by today and we told her what we'd learned. She absolutely agrees that that's what we need to do. So, starting today we're getting rid of *stuff*. It's not only a question of cleaning up so that we can sell the house; we need to be brutal if we're going to pack and move to another country. We have tons of things we just don't need, never use, won't miss. In particular, I know there are books we can get rid of. It's kind of overwhelming.

And, of course, we're only *thinking* about moving at this point. It's not definite. We don't know if we can sell the house or find another one that we like in an area that appeals to us in France. It's all still a maybe.

But Cindy wants to put the house on the market the Monday after Thanksgiving. And we want to go to France the day after that for a bit of a *reconnaissance* mission. That's not a whole lot of time.

Tuesday, November 9

The only major problem we've ever had with our house since we've been here has been the roof. I have lost track of the number of times and contractors who have been up there trying to fix it.

The problem comes from the addition, which has a flat roof. From what I've learned, anytime you have a flat roof meeting up with a peaked roof, you are going to have trouble. We have had leaks into our family room (also my office!) ever since day one. We've had everything replaced at one time or another, but still we get leaks.

And, of course, it's always expensive to fix. Somehow, the "guarantees" never seem to cover when it starts re-leaking, because although the water comes in at the same place, it seems to always be coming from somewhere different.

I've tried calling the last roofers to have done repairs, but they never get back to me. So, this time, Cindy has recommended her roofer, Randy, who has always done work for her on the houses she is selling.

Amazingly, his solution seems to be something that can be done in a couple of hours and will not cost us a fortune. All I care about is that when we sell the house, I can honestly say that the roof doesn't leak!

I've also arranged to rent a dumpster to start cleaning out the garage. I'm not looking forward to that, but it's got to be done. I've actually wanted to do this for a long time, but we never got around to it and, honestly, never really had to do it.

I hope there aren't too many spiders in there…

Sunday, November 14

I can't believe how much time all this cleaning up stuff is taking! We get up at 6 a.m., have breakfast and start at it, going until around 6 p.m. Two people really shouldn't be able to accumulate all this stuff!

I think, over the years, that I have had a tendency to be more brutal about throwing things away than JM. He really hates to throw things out. He's not a maniac about it, just always worried that we might wind up needing something.

But, seriously, why did we need to keep ratty picture frames and all that dangerous glass? We should have found a way to dump it ages ago! And, what about the boxes? Most of them are totally useless now for anything. Yes, when you buy a new appliance, you need to keep the box for a while, "just in case," but when you don't have the appliance anymore, shouldn't the box go too?

The problem is, we've got more stuff to dump than space in the dumpster. We're either going to need to rent a new one, or else I need to go and buy some yellow tags at the dump. That's a cool service that the City of L.A. offers. You can buy 25 tags a year for a dollar a piece, then you just have to attach them to trash bags and the regular trash collection will take them away.

I wonder if 25 trash bags will be enough?

Tuesday, November 16

Our friend, Sylvain, is an artist with itchy feet. He never stays anyplace for long and doesn't have a permanent apartment. He does, however, have a storage locker here in the Valley. For stuff that he wants to access on his infrequent trips back to L.A., there has always been our garage.

We've never minded, as there is plenty of space in the garage and we had the whole thing shelved years ago to make it easy to organize all those things you mistakenly keep because you think you may need them someday.

Unfortunately, we need to move before Sylvain is going to be able to make it back to town, and we are not planning on taking his stuff to France with us. Bekins, where he keeps the rest of his belongings, would have come to pick up the boxes, but they were going to charge a fortune to do it. So, we said we would take them over.

Luckily, for a little car, Beanie has quite a lot of space in the trunk, especially when you fold down the back seats. We were able (barely) to get everything inside, although her backend dragged awfully close to the ground.

While we were organizing and moving the boxes into the car, we had a small "incident." One of the boxes had, at one time, contained a bunch of videos. Well, I guess the boxes had been a taste treat for our periodic termite infestations. As we tried to move the carton, it came apart in our hands, leaving a mess of broken tapes and termite goo. I don't know if any of the tapes *had* been important, but now, they're just a pile of trash.

At any rate, all is now safely in the storage locker waiting for Sylvain should he ever need any of it.

With Sylvain's belongings gone, and all of our junk now thrown out, we had plenty of empty space in the garage. That led us to stage two of the house cleaning process. Anything that we absolutely don't need inside for now is getting boxed up and moved out to the garage to make less clutter inside.

One of the things that we're doing is getting rid of a huge part of JM's magazine archives, as well as all our French videotapes. We don't want to just throw these things out, as they could be useful for someone. Luckily, our friend Steve has helped us come up with a solution: there is a University in Oklahoma that has a large media collection.[2] Steve has already donated a large portion of his own archives to them. They are delighted to get JM's collection of magazines as well.

The videotapes, for now, are going to Steve. He will sort through them and eventually send the appropriate ones to the University himself. That's a huge relief. No way were we going to take several hundred VHS

---

[2] The Huie Library, Henderson State University, Arkadelphia, AR 71999.

tapes with us, as we will probably not even bother having a VCR after we move. We've definitely moved on to the DVD generation.

Thursday, November 18

Big disappointment yesterday. We had an appointment with a woman named Julie, who is a professional house cleaner recommended by Cindy. We thought that, once all the sorting, tossing, rearranging is done, that we should have someone come in to do a big cleaning before we start showing the house.

But, she just never showed up. She didn't even give us the courtesy of a phone call. I know people are busy, especially with Thanksgiving coming up, but still, a phone call takes no time at all.

Anyway, I think that JM and I are completely capable of doing the cleaning ourselves. Once the house is emptied out, it will be much easier to clean anyway. So, that saves us probably a couple of hundred dollars. Her loss, our savings.

Then, we went to have lunch with our associate, Peter, at the Gotham Group, a management company in Hollywood. We're going to turn over a portion of our business to them, which leaves us with a foot in the industry while we're living somewhere in France. We've already done some business with them and think that it will be a good match. But, we needed to lay our "wares" on the table, so to speak, so that they knew everything we had to work with. I think it went well!

Saturday, November 20

That's it. We finished! It seemed like we'd never get done. Twenty years lets you accumulate *a lot* of stuff. Still, everything that's in the garage is either going to get sold before we move or it's coming with us. We've boxed all the "personal" stuff that was on the shelves and gotten rid of ugly old furniture that we probably should have tossed ages ago.

Frankly, even if we decide not to move, the house looks loads better this way. Even JM's office looks nicer with a smaller desk in it. Since we stopped having a desktop computer in the front room, we never really needed to keep a desk in there, but we didn't have anyplace else to put it. The whole house just feels bigger and more livable now.

Cindy is supposed to stop by to help us rearrange the paintings in a more attractive way, and then she's going to take pictures to include with the listing. Thanksgiving is next Thursday, and the following Monday, we're officially putting the house on the market. I can't believe we're really doing this.

One thing I've learned in all of the cleaning up, throwing out, getting rid of process: used stuff isn't all that valuable! We sold *a lot* of books. Serious quantities of books. Enough to open a small bookstore amounts of books. And, we really wound up with very little money for them. We won't even discuss the less-than-peanuts that we got for the furniture that we sold. I suppose it was better than paying to have it hauled away, but still.

It makes you think though, that when you buy anything, you should really be sure that you need it, 'cause selling it won't ever make up for what you spent.

Thursday, November 25

How weird. This will probably be our last American Thanksgiving! It's hard to get my mind around that. It's too bad that with all the cleaning, getting ready to get the house on the market and the fact that we're leaving for France next week, we really didn't have time (or energy!) to do anything special.

We used to have big dinners for a bunch of our friends, but everyone is so busy these days. People just don't seem to want to get together all that much anymore. I suppose, in some ways, it will make it easier to leave. We won't feel as if we're leaving all that much behind us.

Still, I made a nice dinner just for the two of us. I don't want to make so much of a mess that it's going to be hard to clean up before Monday!

Sunday, November 28

Yesterday was interesting. We went to LosCon, the big, annual Los Angeles Science Fiction convention. It's the first time we talked about our plans to move to large groups of people. There were lots of our friends and acquaintances there and I think we surprised the heck out of them, to be honest. I bet most of them don't believe we're really going to do it.

Still, there were some people that seemed quite envious that we could even contemplate doing something like this. I think it sounds a bit like a dream to most folks, even if their dream spot isn't the south of France.

Even on a holiday weekend, it's such a hassle getting anywhere around L.A. On Friday, we took a ton of videotapes down to Amoeba Music on Sunset Boulevard in Hollywood. We thought, hey, it's a holiday, traffic should be light. *Wrong!* It was a nightmare. Hollywood is 15 miles from Reseda, it took us *two and a half hours* to get there! I still don't know why it was so bad. The horror, the horror! This, I will not miss. And, people at the convention had the nerve to ask if we weren't going to be sorry to leave L.A.!

Monday, November 29

That's it. The die is cast. Our house is officially "For Sale," with a big sign in the front yard and everything. I bet most of our neighbors are shocked. We've been here for such a long time, we're really fixtures in the neighborhood. Every time I see Lisa from next door, we both get all teary-eyed. Colin and Lisa have been great neighbors, I hope we don't sell to someone they hate.

Tomorrow is the day that all the realtors start coming to look at the house before bringing their clients to see it. I wonder if anyone will be interested? Wouldn't it be embarrassing if no one wants to buy it?

Still. We don't really have to sell if we don't get a good offer, so it's not that big a deal, is it?

Tuesday, November 30

OK. This is so weird. I went out to the hairdresser and when I got back, JM told me that these kind of odd people had come to the house. They tried to get him to come down on the price (really, *not* something that is "done;" they're supposed to talk to Cindy), which he, of course, wasn't about to do. I mean, we just put it on the market *yesterday*! Anyway, despite that, they told him they were going to put in an offer.

Sure. Right. Don't believe a word of it. But, Cindy is on her way over. They actually did it! They put in a full-price offer and want us to sign all the paperwork before we leave for France tomorrow! That is going to put a whole different spin on our trip.

We are going to sign the papers, but leave ourselves an "out," in case we find that the whole moving thing isn't going to work out. We don't plan on buying a house right now, just looking to see if we will be able to afford a house in an area where we want to live. Still, it's nice to know that we can put a deposit down if we do see something we like.

I'm excited, but also feeling a bit queasy. It's happening so fast. And, it's really happening!

Friday, December 3

God, I hate flying to France from L.A.! It's so *looonnng* and so uncomfortable. No matter what you try to do to make yourself comfortable, it never really works. JM is much better at it, because he's good at sleeping on planes, but I've never been able to do that for more than a few minutes at a time.

Still, we're here and that's the important thing.

We did get all the papers on the house signed and put in the various clauses, etc. While we're away, they're supposed to have the house inspected and all that kind of jazz. I hope they don't change their minds. That would be a bummer, now that I've gotten used to the idea of it being sold.

JM's parents, bizarrely, still don't actually seem excited at the thought of us doing this! That really surprises me, because I thought they would be thrilled. Part of it, I'm sure, is that Maman, especially, thinks that there's no actual life outside of Paris. For her, the idea of going to a department like the Ariège or the Aude, is kind of like choosing living-death. What? They have doctors there? I don't think so!

Still, it will be fun telling all of our friends here in Paris what we've decided to do. The weekend should be pretty busy, since today we're having lunch with our friend Frédéric, then dinner with our comic book friends, Stéphane and Olivier (two brothers whom JM can never tell apart) and the "other" Jean-Marc. Then, tomorrow. we'll have lunch with Gil and Isabelle (Gil draws our *Robur* comic series), after which, we're off to a book festival in Sèvres, on the outskirts of Paris. We'll get back in time to change and have dinner with cousins, Jacqueline and Jean-Paul.

Sunday, we'll get up early and drive down to Pamiers, in the Ariège, with our friend Philippe. Philippe, who works for Pamiers' City Hall, and his wife, Bernadette, have kindly offered to let us stay with them while we're property hunting. I'm so excited. We haven't been to the area since 1999!

Sunday, December 5

We're in Pamiers. It was a long drive from Paris. I'm glad that Philippe did the driving, because I'm still jet-lagged.

Seeing our friends over the last few days was interesting: quite a mix of positive and negative reactions. Most people think it's odd to want to leave the U.S., because, for them, it's kind of *their* dream destination. Still, when you explain everything that's going on politically and economically, they get it. They're shocked, actually, because that kind of thing really doesn't get any news coverage in France. No one can believe that so many Americans could vote for the Shrub. I couldn't explain it to them, because frankly, I don't understand it either!

Stéphane and Olivier were very positive about the region that we're going to be looking at this week. They're from Montpellier themselves and their grandmother lives in Tarascon-sur-Ariège, so they know it quite well. They feel we'll be able to find something in our price range and that we'll like the area.

Gil and Isabelle were just negative about the whole idea of moving to France. But, they tend to be a bit on the gloomy side about most everything, so I took it all with a grain of salt. I was a bit disappointed, because I wanted to have lunch at my favorite Chinese restaurant, Mirama, on the Rue St. Jacques, but there's a huge scandal about Chinese restaurants right now, and they wouldn't eat there. I thought that was silly, but, what are you gonna do?

The cousins were actually pretty positive about the idea. They were complaining about taxes though, which for them, are really, really high. But, they have a huge, expensive apartment in Paris and *two* other big properties: one north of Toulon and one in the Sologne, so they get hit big time. Secondary residences in France are taxed at a much higher rate than your primary residence. This will not be a problem for us!

Time to go have dinner and catch up with Bernadette. Tomorrow, it's off to get our rental car and start meeting with real estate agents.

Monday, December 5

This was *not* an auspicious beginning for our search.

The whole day started off wrong.

Bernadette took us to the Hertz representative, which was in a garage in the center of town. Only *it hasn't been a Hertz agency for over six months!* Imagine our shock in seeing the right address, but a Europcar sign instead of a Hertz sign. JM went inside and got the bad news. On the one hand, luckily, they *did* have a car available. On the other, it cost twice what we'd arranged to pay with Hertz by reserving it in the U.S. What choice did we have? We took it. But we weren't happy about it. We'll definitely write to Hertz when we get back home and see if we can't get some money reimbursed.[3]

Then we hit the road, stopping at a *relais routier* for breakfast. That's the French equivalent of a Howard Johnson's on a turnpike. Not vile, but not what you'd call great cuisine. Those places must be the same the world over. We were headed north of Toulouse to the Tarn-et-Garonne region. The agent we were seeing in the town of Lavit had sounded like someone who could look for properties for us, even if they weren't listed with her agency. That turned out not to have been the case.

Unlike in the States, there is no multiple listing service. So, although some properties are listed with several agents, most agents have "exclusive" listings, which you can pretty much only visit by going to them. That means you have to see *a lot* of agents to see a lot of properties. It's time-consuming and frustrating, but that's the way it is, so you deal with it.

We saw several village houses and a couple of farm properties. None of them thrilled us. I think I've decided I don't want a village house. You've got people right next to you and, depending on the village, it can be hard to park. I don't want to leave L.A. only to feel more crowded in someplace else.

We saw one farmhouse in a little hamlet of about seven or eight houses. It had about five acres of land around it, although most of them are currently rented out for exploitation to a neighboring farmer, something that seems to be reasonably common. I quite liked it. It was all on one floor, which was nice, and had a huge adjacent barn, which could be converted into more living/usable space eventually. Plus, it had an enclosed garden right in front, surrounded by trees. I liked that. *But*, and coming from earthquake country, this is a big *but*: there was a huge, structural crack going up the wall in the bedroom. This was in a support wall and looked nasty. Apparently, during the super-hot summer of 2003,

---

[3] Hertz did issue us a refund for the difference in the form of coupons that came in handy later.

the water table really fell and caused some major settling to the house. We were told that the settling had stopped and that the insurance company, as part of the deal, would undertake the work. But when you've lived in L.A., that kind of thing is just way too hinky and scares you immediately. Plus, they wanted far too much money for the property.

And that was kind of our feeling for most of the day. The properties we saw were just much too expensive for what they were. They all needed work and it seemed outrageous to pay such high prices, then also have to pay to renovate a property as well.

We did stop in at another agent in Moissac on the way back to Pamiers and made an appointment to see some houses with her, including one I'd found on the net while looking around. But, JM was very, very depressed on the way home. It didn't help that the weather has been gray and rainy all day, making everything look bleak and sad. He was actually saying we should just give up. But I told him that was nuts! We'd only looked in *one* area, for *one* day! And, it wasn't even the department that we had originally targeted, which is where we're looking tomorrow.

Still, I think he's happy we can get out of selling our house if need be.

Tuesday, December 7

OK, today was a day that will *not* live in infamy! What a contrast to yesterday.

Yes, the weather still sucks. But, somehow, we didn't care. *I think we've found a house!*

We had an appointment at 10 a.m. with the Agence Hamilton in Mirepoix, a smallish market town located just at the Ariège-Aude border. We'd found them online and really liked the look of several of their properties. One of the things that we'd realized early on is that we want a property with "character" and not just a modern "box" like something we could buy in L.A. What's the point of having a house that looks like you could plop it down anywhere in the world and you would have no idea where you were living?

We decided to drive through Fanjeaux, a medieval village in the Aude, on the road from Mirepoix to Carcassonne. I had seen a house there online, and although I hadn't called that agent, I wanted to see if we could track it down. As we were driving there from Pamiers, we felt so much "at home." I can't really explain it any better than that. But the whole countryside, even in the rain and gloom, just appealed to us in a way that the Tarn-et-Garonne had not. There were rolling hills, vineyards, mountains, forests; everything was just beautiful. We were so buoyed up after yesterday. I told JM that I thought we had needed to see the other area though, just so we would know what we *didn't* want.

We had breakfast at the local café in Fanjeaux and then stopped in at the real estate agency in the village. One thing in our favor is that this is not a hot time of year for property buying, so we don't seem to have a great deal of competition. The agent at the Alba agency was lovely and we made an appointment to go back to see her in the afternoon, after we finished with our viewings in the Mirepoix area.

We got to Mirepoix and thought it was beautiful. It's a restored medieval village, with *couverts*, the kind of arcades that make a square around the center of the town. François Lar, the agent at Hamilton, was very nice and really listened to what we said. We had a house that we'd seen on their website that we definitely wanted to look at, but after listening to us, he pulled another property out of his book and we set off.

The first place, the one I wanted to see, was on the road between Montferrier and Montségur. We went through a couple of very unappealing towns, one of them, Lavelanet, was an old industrial center and just looked gray and depressing. Montferrier, which is actually a kind of ski area, totally shocked us. It's in a beautiful setting in the mountains, but they've built these hideously ugly apartment blocks and your first thought is "why?"

The house itself was literally in the middle of nowhere. JM immediately started calling it the "wolves and bears" house. I could see where he got that from. Basically, it's set in a bit of a hollow, surrounded by tall, dark trees. It's part of an old farmhouse that has been converted into three, contiguous houses. Two of them are empty except for in the summer (it was one of those that was for sale) and there was one old woman who lived there full time. That's it. No other neighbors for three or four kilometers. And, it's high enough up in the mountains that you *will* get snowed in during the winter. You couldn't even go out to buy bread or milk without the car. Did I say it was isolated?

Beyond that, it was actually quite small inside; probably a third smaller than our house in L.A. It does have a barn attached at the back, so you could eventually renovate that and more than double the size of the house; but that would be expensive. And, it was quite pricey for what it was, putting it at the very top of our budget without doing any work on it. There was an acre or so of land with it, but that was on a slope and not really usable for much of anything, not even a garden.

I guess it was proof that you cannot buy a house from a picture on the Internet.

Then, François took us to a village called Chalabre. We immediately fell in love with the village. It wasn't like the ones I'd seen in the Tarn-et-Garonne, which were basically straight lines with a road running through them. This reminded us of the *bastide* villages in the Upper Var near Toulon, such as Cotignac. There were four large avenues (*Cours*) surrounding a central *bastide*. There was no main road going through it, so it felt like it was a destination and not just a truck stop.

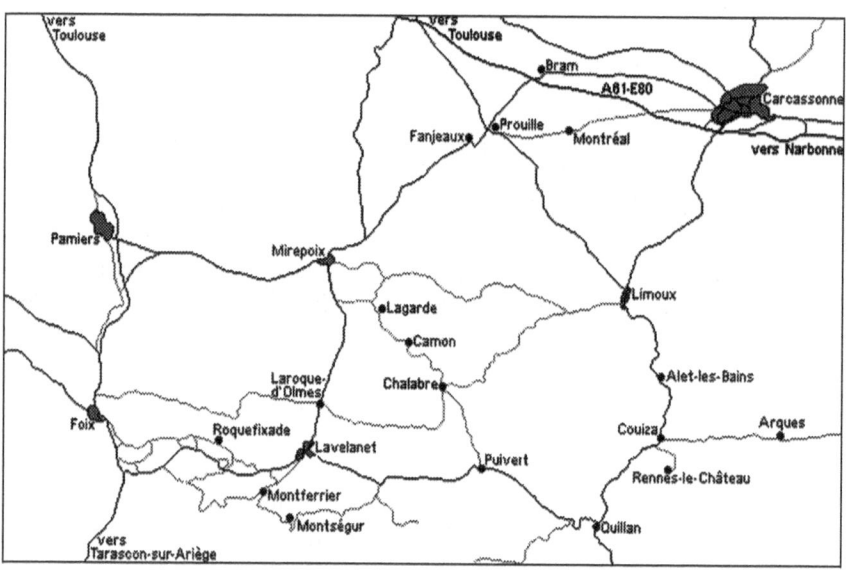

The house that he took us to was on one of the four *Cours*. We liked it the second we walked inside. Yes, it's a bit "tired." It hasn't been redecorated in 40 years. It was over-crowded with furniture and had ugly linoleum and wallpaper. But, it felt "good." Even though it isn't being lived in, it didn't feel cold and damp, which was a good sign.

CHALABRE

An old house with colombages *on the Cours Sully*

Chalabre (pop. 900 winter, 1200 summer) is located in the heart of the Cathar country, in the region known as the Quercorb or Kercorb, also known as the "terre privilégiée" (privileged land) because in 1210 AD the King of France exempted its citizens from paying certain taxes.

Three rivers (the Hers, the Chalabreil and the Blau) meet in Chalabre. There is a covered market, a 12th century church, and the local Château de Mauleon, loated on a hill on the northeast side of the town, overlooking the entire village.

The town center is made up of a small, square-shaped medieval quarter of small streets with the market in its center. It is called a Bastide. *It is bordered by four larger avenues or* Cours, *lined with plane trees, chestnut trees and fountains. Cours Sully is to the south, Cours Raynaud is to the east, Cours d'Aguesseau is to the north and Cours Colbert is to the west.*

South of the Bastide, after crossing the river Blau and to the south and west are the Gardens of Chalabre, along the river Hers.

One of the things that we liked is that each room is on a separate floor, leading off the staircase. So, there are no dark corridors. Every time you go up the stairs to another room, you just can't believe that there is more! It has a garage, a dirt-floored cellar (great for insulating the house) and a huge, double attic. It felt enormous! And, the price was better than anything we've seen anywhere else. *Less* than we were prepared to spend, so it would leave us money to redecorate and do whatever needs doing.

It was actually a bit embarrassing, because we knew we had other appointments, but we loved this house. We decided that we needed to come back to see it another time, and Mr. Lar is going to bring a builder with him so that we can get an idea about the cost of the work that it will need to have done. I can't wait!

After that, we drove back to Fanjeaux, feeling that since we had made the appointment with the other agency, we really had to keep it. We were honest about having found something at a great price in a village that we loved. The young agent took us to see two houses. Both of them needed a lot of work, although the prices were quite low. Still, the big problem for us was that we didn't care for either village.

One of the villages in particular was a bit on the creepy side. All of the houses had the shutters closed, giving you the feeling of being in a ghost town. I guess almost everyone works elsewhere and only comes home at night, which makes sense. But *we* work at home; I don't want to be the only people in an entire village during the day. If we're going to be "home alone," I'd only want to do that in a house where we'd be surrounded by countryside and trees, not blank-eyed houses.

There was a third house that the agent wanted us to see, but we aren't able to get inside until tomorrow. I'm half-tempted to not go, but it seems only fair to be sure of the house in Chalabre.

Wednesday, December 8

We've decided that, just to be safe, we needed to change our train reservation and stay down here an extra day. Luckily, it wasn't that big a deal and we were able to do it pretty easily at the train station in Pamiers.

We went back to the Alba agency in Fanjeaux and saw the house we couldn't see yesterday. That turned out to be a bit traumatic, to be perfectly honest. The house was in Belpech, which wasn't a village that did much for us. But, the house itself was terrific. It was a bit larger than the house we saw in Chalabre and it was in perfect condition. The floors were all original parquet, in great shape. It has six or seven bedrooms (I kind of lost count) over three floors. A large, formal dining room, re-done kitchen (not to my taste, but OK), a large sitting room, a nice-sized courtyard and a large detached garage and storage area.

The downside was that, for all that space, there was only one bathroom and toilet, both on the ground floor. So, either one has to go down several flights of stairs in the middle of the night to use the facilities, or we would have to have at least one more bathroom (and I think two would make more sense) installed upstairs. That would, of course add to the cost.

The biggest problem for us, though, was that we saw it with the couple that owns it, and we fell in love with *them*! He used to be the town baker, but he has had some health problems, which is why they need to sell the house. We felt safe when we left because it was really at the top of our budget and we wouldn't have had any money left over to put in a new bathroom and maybe do some painting/wallpaper removal (what was there was definitely not us!). Then, later in the day, our real estate agent called and told us they had dropped the price by a really *huge* amount so we could buy it!

If only we could buy two houses. But our hearts had been won over by Chalabre and the house we saw there. It needs a lot more work than the house in Belpech, but once that's done, it will have our stamp on it and be entirely to our taste. It's way less expensive than the other house as well, even with the big price drop, so by buying it and doing the work, we'll still be in our budget, I hope.

We had free time during the day before our second viewing of Chalabre, so we met with a kitchen designer in Pamiers. That was a bit of a shock, because he quoted us about 30,000 euros just to do the kitchen and two bathrooms. That seems steep, so maybe we have to revise the way we go about all this renovation stuff. Then, JM looked through the phone book and found a house inspector. I'm surprised to find that very few people here do regular house inspections. But, I know we'll both feel more comfortable with one that tells us what shape the house *really* is in.

We went back to Chalabre and had a drink in the café that is only a few doors down from the house, then we went and took another look. The builder that Mr. Lar had found for us met us there. We started to speak to him in French, but were surprised to find out that he was British and didn't actually speak French!

His name was Chris, and we liked him quite a lot. We spent almost two-hours looking around, going from room to room, taking pictures, discussing all our options, etc. Chris thinks it will cost about 50,000 euros to do all the work, we may not do everything at one go though. We'll just have to see. The good news is that he thinks the house is in fabulous shape and that the price is an excellent deal. We told Mr. Lar then and there that we wanted it, so tomorrow morning we're going to his office to make the official offer! I can't believe that we've actually bought a house in France! Won't everyone in L.A. be surprised when we get back?

The Cours Colbert in Chalabre

A small side note: we didn't want to have Bernadette hold dinner for us too late, so we decided to eat on our way back to Pamiers. We found this terrific restaurant in Mirepoix, called Le Commerce. There was practically no one else there and we had the best meal. The weather has remained cold and rainy, but they served a four-course dinner for under 20 euros, which included an amazing vegetable potage. I would have been happy with just that. Sylvie, the lovely waitress who served us, actually knows Chalabre very well and had lots of good things to say about it. So, we came away feeling as if we've made the right decision.

I hope the owner takes our offer tomorrow.

Thursday, December 9

OK. That's it. We've just bought ourselves a house! I feel exactly the same way that I did 20 years ago when we bought our place in Reseda. Excited and scared spitless all at the same time!

My mother-in-law, who has not been wild about the idea of us moving out to the "boonies," suddenly did a complete turnaround last night! We told her about the house and she started saying it was "miracle," which of course totally cracks us up. We're definitely pleased about things, but I don't know if I would go that far. Still, she called us about 15 times, to make sure that we knew how important it was to lock in the contract for the house. Kind of like she thought someone else was going to suddenly swoop in at ten o'clock last night and buy it before we could this morning. We told her not to worry. It's not L.A. after all!

We got to Mirepoix at around 9 a.m. and called the owner of the house, who lives in England. She accepted our offer after a bit of negotiation, and we've tentatively set the date for closing for the end of January. That basically gives us less than two months to get back to L.A. and actually sort out the biggest move either of us has ever made!

When I moved to California from Philly, I didn't really own much of anything, so it wasn't a big deal. JM came to L.A. with a suitcase. Again, no biggie. But we're moving our entire house! There's so much to sort out despite having done all that cleaning and throwing away. The logistics of the whole thing is a bit overwhelming, especially when looking at it while we're still sitting here in France and can't even begin to get started.

Still, I know that we'll manage. We always do.

Once the "big" event of the day was done, we spent the rest of the time site seeing a bit around the area. We had lunch in Carcassonne inside the Cité, which is the medieval portion of the town. It was a bit nostalgic for us, because we've gone there on vacation several times, and always loved it. But the idea that it is now going to be "our" city is almost mind-boggling! How does a place go from being a vacation destination to home? Wow.

Afterwards, we visited Limoux, which is the next larger town to Chalabre, at about 18-miles away. It was hard to tell what it was like on such a short drive around, but it looks kind of interesting and I'll look forward to exploring it further.

Then, we went back to Chalabre and walked around. It was still pretty quiet there, as the weather has been nothing to write home about. But we still felt good about moving there, which is a positive thing, I'm thinking. We took a bunch of pictures, but I'm kind of sorry that we didn't buy a digital camera before coming over. I'm worried that the throwaway camera that I bought won't really give us a good idea of things when they're developed.

Ah well. It's a small thing. Tomorrow, we head back to Paris.

A street in Old Chalabre

Saturday, December 11

Yesterday was a loooong day! We got up at some ungodly hour to take the train from Pamiers to Toulouse, then from Toulouse to Paris. We got home after lunch and showed Papa the map of where we're moving.

This is the weird part: when he saw where Chalabre was located (JM, by the way, is incapable of remembering the name of the town and keeps referring to it as Chabrol!), he said, "Oh. It's right near Esperaza. Your great-grandmother lived near there." Apparently, there's another little nearby town called Rouvenac, and JM's grandfather used to spend his summer holidays there. The world really is a small and weird place. Both of these towns are less than ten miles away from Chalabre!

After spending a few hours at the apartment, we went to meet our friend Thierry at the Gare de Lyon, then went to spend the night with him and his family just outside of Paris. We had a great time. We really love Thierry and his wife Catherine, and it's just a shame we don't get to see more of them. I wonder if that will change when we are actually living in France?

We came back to Paris this morning, then spent a great afternoon with our long-time friends Jacques, Yves and Henri. As usual, Maman made way too much food. I think it really surprises everyone that we're doing this. No one ever really believed we'd actually come back to France to live. I'm not sure we ever truly believed it either!

Still, as nice as all the visiting was, I'm eager to get back to L.A. and start the whole process of moving. There's just so much to do.

Monday, December 13

Our bags are packed and we're getting ready to have a last family dinner here in Paris before heading back to L.A. tomorrow morning. It's an early flight (aren't they always?), so we've ordered a cab for 6:30 a.m. We'll be at the airport too early, because we always are, but I feel better that way than worrying about being late.

Yesterday, friends of my in-laws came over for afternoon tea and today; we did a few more preparatory errands. First, we went to the bank to talk about handling buying the house. In theory, we won't need a loan, but we will have to move money from the sale of our house in L.A. over here and want to do it the easiest way possible. It's always good to know your banker in advance of having actual business to conduct.

Then, we went over to the Prefecture de Police for JM to find out what he needs to do to replace his old French driver's license. He got one right before moving to L.A. in 1978, but it was a temporary license, because he'd gotten a medical exemption from the military (which was compulsory at the time). He tried to renew it in L.A., but they made him take a physical and he passed out in the middle of it, freaking out the doctor. He never wanted to take it any further and just let the thing lapse. He's hoping that if he just files for a replacement, they'll give it to him with no physical this time.

There were so many people going into the Prefecture that it was a bit of a zoo. After finally getting to the right office and waiting in line there, we found out that he needed to go to the local police station and make a declaration of loss, *then*, he would have to apply again at the Prefecture. However, for some arcane reason, they didn't want him to do *that* until after the beginning of the year. I think they may be changing the licenses or something.

We did get the documents we needed at the police station, but the rest is going to have to wait until we get back. Not a long time to wait, after all.

Next stop: LAX!

Thursday, December 16

I can't believe we have to make that flight again in something like a month's time! I think I'm getting too old to sit in a plane for 12 hours at a stretch. I wish they would just knock us out when we get on and wake us up when it's time to get off. Or else we just need to get so rich we can fly first class in sleeper seats!

Maggie was sure happy to see us when we picked her up at the kennel. Little does she know that a big adventure lies ahead for her. I hope that she won't find the next few weeks too traumatic. I *know* it's going to be traumatic for her humans as well, so we'll all be in it together at least.

I've already started making calls to look into the cost of moving. The big problem is that most companies seem only willing to give estimates, then they charge afterwards, based on the weight of what you move. This is not good for people like us who own mostly books. That's going to kill us if they put them on a scale. Luckily, I seem to have found one specialist, international moving company, Rinkens, who will give us a price based on the quantity of stuff, not the weight. We'll get them to come out and look at what we have so we know if we've got to get rid of even more than we have already.

Shock and awe continues amongst our friends. I don't think any of them expected us to come back and say we were actually going to go ahead with this move. I think they all figured we would have changed our minds. And, even the ones who thought we'd go through with it didn't think we'd do it so fast.

Personally, I don't see what the big deal is. Why is it different then deciding to sell our house in Reseda and buy one in another section of L.A., or in another state? A move is a move, isn't it?

Sunday, December 19

We had breakfast with our friend Diane yesterday, and dinner with Terry and Paula. I think Diane is really taking this whole moving thing hard. She says she wants to spend every Saturday she can with us until we go.

I do admit that seeing our friends brings home the one part of this that is difficult: leaving so many people behind. Still, it's not as if, under normal circumstances, we see that much of anyone. This must be the first time we've had dinner with Terry and Paula in months, for example, and they only live 20 minutes away.

It will be interesting to see how closely everyone really keeps in touch once we're gone. I know they all mean to do it now, but it's so easy to get into the habits of daily existence and move on to new friends and social outlets. Will people still remember us once we're 6,000 miles away?

No time to dwell on all that though. We have lots and lots to do before we can go anywhere. For example, we need to set up a garage sale. The problem is that it's six days to Christmas, then there's New Year's, then we're running out of time! We've actually been planning to have the mover's come around January 15; maybe we're being overly ambitious?

Wednesday, December 22

We met a lovely lady this week. She's a friend of Cindy's and actually only lives two blocks away. Her name is Kathy, and she and her partner do a lot of yard sales. Cindy thought she could help us get ours together. She really did give us some great tips and suggested that we might be better off trying to sell certain of our items through want ads rather than in a yard sale. I don't know though, it seems awfully complicated. How are we going to get it done before we move?

Meanwhile, our social life has been a whirlwind. Suddenly, people we haven't seen for years want to get together to have meals and find out about the move. As busy as we are, it's a relief not to have to cook in the chaos that is our house. Between getting rid of all my little appliances and moving things that I need to sell out into the garage, it's gotten a little complicated in the kitchen. At least I don't have to pack anything. The movers will do all that, so I can at least have access to dishes until we're ready to go.

It's been fun though, getting to see people like Gerry Conway, who we lost touch with over the years. It's really a shame to realize that there was so much time wasted with not seeing friends when we could have enjoyed each other a lot more.

One day this week, we're going to sneak off and play hooky for the afternoon though. What with one thing and another, we haven't been to a movie in ages. We want to see *The Incredibles* before we leave!

And, we'll drive out to Hemet to see Mom and Dad. That will be the saddest thing for me, of course. I know I don't have any choice and we'll stay in touch by phone, but I will really, really miss my Mom.

Our House

At the Place de la Bastille in Paris

2005

Tuesday, January 4

Happy New Year to all!

Yes, it's a new year and our adventure draws ever closer. Kind of freaking me out, to be honest. We had what at first seemed like bad news, but now turns out to be good news.

First, the seller of our new house in Chalabre has pushed the closing date to February 17 or 18. We were a bit concerned about that, because we were going to close on our L.A. house around January 15. Then, we had to figure out where to stay. JM's parents bought a new apartment in Toulon, and our original idea was to fly to France, then stay there for a month until we could move into our new house.

But, Papa called and said he wasn't sure if dogs were allowed in the building. That turned out to be a false alarm, but in the middle of panicking, the buyers of *our* house asked if we could change the closing date to the end of January. That was actually perfect, since we'll be able to stay in the Hôtel de France in Chalabre from February 6 until we move into the house. We'll get to know the village and be on hand if we need to meet with builders or things like that.

And, to be honest, we feel a lot more comfortable having these extra two weeks. We *could* have done everything, but it would have been tight. In particular, I don't know how we would have had time to arrange the yard sale. Right now, we're leaning towards either January 15 or January 22. I think we'll have to see what the weather holds, because at the moment, it's been pretty sucky. Lots and lots of rain.

However, Randy the roofer seems to have been a bit of a miracle worker! Despite all the rain, not a drop inside the house after 20 years of almost constant watery headaches! At least I feel that we were honest when we said our roof doesn't leak!

I called to talk to our friend and vet Gayle this morning. There's paperwork that needs to be filled out for Maggie before we leave. While we talked, I struck a deal with Gayle for her and her significant other, Steve, to buy our plasma screen TV. At first, we wanted to take it with us and get a converter for it. But, the more I thought about it, the more I realized that it might wind up with us moving the darned thing, then it not working after all. What would we do then, with a hugely expensive piece of junk that we wouldn't even be able to get rid of. No, better to sell it here and buy a new one with the money we get.

The electrical appliance issue is actually a bit of a heartbreaker. I have so many little appliances that I use all the time, but which will be too complicated to use when we move. Even though I can get transformers for them, anything with a motor, for example, just won't work properly with the different cycle of the current, even if the voltage is stepped down. So, food processor, vacuum cleaner, etc., all have to find new homes. Most of the things like that I'm giving to friends. I know I won't sell them for enough money to make it worthwhile, so better to give them away where they'll be appreciated.

The other big issue of the day was visiting with our accountant, Jackie. He's been our accountant for 20 years, as hard as that seems to be believe! We needed to find out if we could make an arrangement with him to handle all of our U.S. financial business for us, as it will be pretty complicated to manage that long distance. Luckily, he sees no problem, so that's another little worry out of the way.

Another hassle we've been dealing with has been Terminix. We've had a termite contract with them for years, and they did a fair amount of work repairing termite damage that we had before we got the problem under control. Suddenly, during the termite inspection that we needed to sell the house, they "discovered" unrepaired damage! How can that be when *they* were the ones we paid to repair it in the first place?

JM has done a fair amount of screaming into the phone over this. Clearly, something is wrong here. But, we're over a barrel. If the damage isn't fixed, we can't sell the house. The guy from Terminix had the nerve to say we signed off on the work. Well, yes. It was under the house. We heard them hammering and sawing and doing all kinds of noisy house-repairy kind of things. No way were we going to crawl under there afterwards to look! We just assumed they did what they were paid to do.

Finally, we came to a compromise solution and split the cost of repairs with them 50-50. I still think something's not quite kosher, but we need to get this process sorted out.

It's amazing anyone survives moving.

Sunday, January 9
Last night was the annual Twelfth Night Party at our friend Len and Christine's house. It was a great opportunity for us to say good-bye to a lot of folks all at one time. Once again, everyone said we should stay in touch, but, seriously, we weren't in touch all that much now, except for the occasional party.

Looking around the room, I realized how many people we've come to know in L.A. over the years. It's amazing. You'd think that as writers working at home we'd be pretty isolated. And, I suppose we are, since we don't go out all that much. But, damn! We do know a lot of people! I wonder when we'll see any of them again?

Sunday, January 16
Well, yesterday and Friday were quite the experience. We decided to have the yard sale this weekend, because the weather was gorgeous and who knows how long that will last in an El Niño year!

JM and I are not yard sale people. I don't really enjoy pawing through other people's junk, and I tend to just give away or throw away my own junk. But we had so much stuff, that it seemed just wrong not to try to find it new homes.

We spent most of the week tagging prices on things. We put an ad into the *Daily News* and thought we had prepared ourselves. Well, not really. The first big shock was that people showed up at our door two hours early! I was still in my PJs and hadn't even had a cup of coffee yet! What on Earth possesses the Yard-Sale-Zombies? It's something that is way beyond my comprehension. These were clearly not "needy" people either. Just older women from the neighborhood who didn't want to miss out on any "good" stuff! And, as if I didn't have enough of my junk out there, they asked if I had anything else!

Clearly, Friday morning is primetime for the aficionados of these types of things. I guess people don't work or something, because we were really pretty packed. I couldn't believe the things that sold first, either. For example, a box of old phone cords and electric cords that didn't belong to anything was totally snapped up in a matter of minutes.

The other thing that was weird for me, was that no matter what price I had put on something, people wanted it for less. Five dollars? No, I'll give you three! And, the people who drove up in Mercedes and were obviously well heeled, were the ones who bargained the hardest. I guess it's no surprise that they have enough money for an expensive car.

At one point, we had decided to sell our kitchen chairs. They are really old and kind of ratty looking, but after sitting in them for two days, we decided we needed to keep them, because they are really comfortable. Besides, I couldn't bear selling them for two or three bucks a piece.

In fact, there were a ton of things we wound up not selling after all, because it was just so annoying to see people bargaining down the prices on our life. I had a bunch of teapots I wanted to sell and JM made me keep them, because people were just so damned cheap.

I didn't mind when folks who clearly didn't have a lot of money came with their kids, and the kids were looking longingly at some of the stuffies or other toys we were selling. I often just wound up giving the kids the toy they wanted, because I knew it would be loved. But, when someone who was clearly not in need tried to buy a practically new toaster oven for three dollars instead of ten, I just took it and gave it to our friend Diane, who had come to spend Saturday's freak show with us.

And, it *was* a freak show! For all of the normal looking people who showed up, there were a bunch who, honestly, creeped me out. There was one guy in particular, who had clearly never cut his toenails in his life. He was wearing shorts and sandals (it *is* January, even if it is Southern California!) and he had toenails that had to be three inches long! They could've qualified as deadly weapons in some states.

Anyway, surprisingly, almost everything went. The bits and bobs that are left over we're giving to our neighbor Kathy to sell at her next garage sale. As hard as it is to believe, the only things left in our possession are the few pieces that we'll give to friends at the last minute, when we don't need them anymore (that coffee maker is staying as long as possible!) and what we're taking with us. The clean up and clear out process is over.

Thursday, January 20

We've had a couple of interesting encounters with people over the last few days and weeks. It's surprising how many of them have told us how "brave" we are. I guess there were quite a number of folks who said they would leave the country if the Shrub stole another election, but of course, most of them didn't mean it. The fact that we not only meant it, but also are actually *doing* it, seems to be relatively unusual.

Whether this means anything in the greater scheme of things or not, I don't know. But it is nice to think that there are those out there who admire us. Of course, in our minds, the braver thing would have been staying and trying to survive in a country that we no longer feel we know.

And, there's the economic side of this as well. Writing is a wonderful thing, but not so much if you want to eat. We do make money at it, but not enough to continue living in a place as expensive as L.A. So, for us, we truly felt as if we had no choice but to move. Are we doing the right thing, moving to a small village where we know no one in the south of France? I don't have a clue. But staying in L.A. was definitely the wrong thing for us at this time in our lives.

Tuesday, January 25

Exactly one week from today we will begin our new life in France. I can't believe that it's already happening.

The movers are coming on Saturday and I have a hard time believing we'll be ready, but I know that somehow, we will be. I know that I'll feel better once we've got everything packed though. And, to be honest, I know I'll feel *really* better once we're landed safely in Paris and gotten Maggie through customs.

Wednesday, January 26

I started packing suitcases today. The hard part is figuring out what we're going to need until we have the furniture, etc., delivered to the house sometime in May. It seems that there is *a lot* that falls into that category.

Now, we need to decide if we really have to have all that stuff with us. I hate to spend money to buy something that I already own if I don't take it with me.

How on Earth do people who move frequently do it? I suppose that's part of the problem for us. We've been in this house for 20 years and swore we wouldn't move again. Guess we shouldn't swear anymore.

I keep going down the lists we made of what has to be done before we go. I think we've been pretty efficient in getting it all done, but who knows? We might suddenly find ourselves in Chalabre with the horrible realization that we've forgotten something of vital importance. Well, we'll deal with that if it happens.

Meanwhile, I've made it official and opened a French Internet account with Wanadoo. That way, we'll be able to get online as soon as we're in France.

Friday, January 28

What became of Conservatives? [4]
by
Dr. Paul Craig Roberts

I remember when friends would excitedly telephone to report that Rush Limbaugh or G. Gordon Liddy had just read one of my syndicated columns over the air. That was before I became a critic of the US invasion of Iraq, the Bush administration, and the neoconservative ideologues who have seized control of the US government.

America has blundered into a needless and dangerous war, and fully half of the country's population is enthusiastic. Many Christians think that war in the Middle East signals "end times" and that they are about to be wafted up to heaven. Many patriots think that, finally, America is standing up for itself and demonstrating its righteous might. Conservatives are taking out their Vietnam frustrations on Iraqis. Karl Rove is wrapping Bush in the protective cloak of war leader. The military-industrial complex is drooling over the profits of war. And neoconservatives are laying the groundwork for Israeli territorial expansion.

The evening before Thanksgiving Rush Limbaugh was on C-Span TV explaining that these glorious developments would have been impossible if talk radio and the conservative movement had not combined to break the power of the liberal media.

In the Thanksgiving issue of National Review, *editor Richard Lowry and former editor John O'Sullivan celebrate Bush's reelection triumph*

---

[4] Dr. Paul Craig Roberts was Assistant Secretary of the Treasury for Economic Policy during 1981-82. He was also Associate Editor of the *Wall Street Journal* editorial page and Contributing Editor of *National Review*. This article is © 2004 Dr. Paul Craig Roberts, was published at:
http://www.vdare.com/roberts/041126_conservatives.htm
on November 26, 2004, and is reproduced here by permission of the author.

over *"a hostile press corps." "Try as they might,"* crowed O'Sullivan, *"they couldn't put Kerry over the top."* There was a time when I could rant about the *"liberal media"* with the best of them. But in recent years I have puzzled over the precise location of the *"liberal media."*

Not so long ago I would have identified the liberal media as the New York Times *and* Washington Post, *CNN and the three TV networks, and National Public Radio. But both the* Times *and the* Post *fell for the Bush administration's lies about WMD and supported the US invasion of Iraq. On balance CNN, the networks, and NPR have not made an issue of the Bush administration's changing explanations for the invasion.*

Apparently, Rush Limbaugh and National Review *think there is a liberal media because the prison torture scandal could not be suppressed and a cameraman filmed the execution of a wounded Iraqi prisoner by a US Marine. Do the* Village Voice *and* The Nation *comprise the "liberal media"? The* Village Voice *is known for Nat Hentoff and his columns on civil liberties. Every good conservative believes that civil liberties are liberal because they interfere with the police and let criminals go free.* The Nation *favors spending on the poor and disfavors gun rights, but I don't see the "liberal hate" in The Nation's feeble pages that Rush Limbaugh was denouncing on C-Span.*

In the ranks of the new conservatives, however, I see and experience much hate. It comes to me in violently worded, ignorant and irrational emails from self-professed conservatives who literally worship George Bush. Even Christians have fallen into idolatry. There appears to be a large number of Americans who are prepared to kill anyone for George Bush.

The Iraqi War is serving as a great catharsis for multiple conservative frustrations: job loss, drugs, crime, homosexuals, pornography, female promiscuity, abortion, restrictions on prayer in public places, Darwinism and attacks on religion. Liberals are the cause. Liberals are against America. Anyone against the war is against America and is a liberal. "You are with us or against us."

This is the mindset of delusion, and delusion permits no facts or analysis. Blind emotion rules. Americans are right and everyone else is wrong. End of the debate.

That, gentle reader, is the full extent of talk radio, Fox News, the Wall Street Journal *Editorial page,* National Review, *the* Weekly Standard, *and, indeed, of the entire concentrated corporate media where noncontroversy in the interest of advertising revenue rules.*

Once upon a time there was a liberal media. It developed out of the Great Depression and the New Deal. Liberals believed that the private sector is the source of greed that must be restrained by government acting in the public interest. The liberals' mistake was to identify morality with government. Liberals had great suspicion of private power and insufficient suspicion of the power and inclination of government to do good.

Liberals became Benthamites (after Jeremy Bentham). They believed that as the people controlled government through democracy, there was no reason to fear government power, which should be increased in order to accomplish more good.

The conservative movement that I grew up in did not share the liberals' abiding faith in government. "Power corrupts, and absolute power corrupts absolutely."

Today it is liberals, not conservatives, who endeavor to defend civil liberties from the state. Conservatives have been won around to the old liberal view that as long as government power is in their hands, there is no reason to fear it or to limit it. Thus, the Patriot Act, which permits government to suspend a person's civil liberty by calling him a terrorist with or without proof. Thus, preemptive war, which permits the President to invade other countries based on unverified assertions.

There is nothing conservative about these positions. To label them conservative is to make the same error as labeling the 1930s German Brownshirts conservative.

American liberals called the Brownshirts "conservative," because the Brownshirts were obviously not liberal. They were ignorant, violent, delusional, and they worshipped a man of no known distinction. Brownshirts' delusions were protected by an emotional force field. Adulation of power and force prevented Brownshirts from recognizing implications for their country of their reckless doctrines.

Like Brownshirts, the new conservatives take personally any criticism of their leader and his policies. To be a critic is to be an enemy. I went overnight from being an object of conservative adulation to one of derision when I wrote that the US invasion of Iraq was a "strategic blunder."

It is amazing that only a short time ago the Bush administration and its supporters believed that all the US had to do was to appear in Iraq and we would be greeted with flowers. Has there ever been a greater ex-

ample of delusion? Isn't this on a par with the Children's Crusade against the Saracens in the Middle Ages?

Delusion is still the defining characteristic of the Bush administration. We have smashed Fallujah, a city of 300,000, only to discover that the 10,000 US Marines are bogged down in the ruins of the city. If the Marines leave, the "defeated" insurgents will return. Meanwhile the insurgents have moved on to destabilize Mosul, a city five times as large. Thus, the call for more US troops.

There are no more troops. Our former allies are not going to send troops. The only way the Bush administration can continue with its Iraq policy is to reinstate the draft.

When the draft is reinstated, conservatives will loudly proclaim their pride that their sons, fathers, husbands and brothers are going to die for "our freedom." Not a single one of them will be able to explain why destroying Iraqi cities and occupying the ruins are necessary for "our freedom." But this inability will not lessen the enthusiasm for the project. To protect their delusions from "reality-based" critics, they will demand that the critics be arrested for treason and silenced. Many encouraged by talk radio already speak this way.

Because of the triumph of delusional "new conservatives" and the demise of the liberal media, this war is different from the Vietnam war. As more Americans are killed and maimed in the pointless carnage, more Americans have a powerful emotional stake that the war not be lost and not be in vain. Trapped in violence and unable to admit mistake, a reckless administration will escalate.

The rapidly collapsing US dollar is hard evidence that the world sees the US as bankrupt. Flight from the dollar as the reserve currency will adversely impact American living standards, which are already falling as a result of job outsourcing and offshore production. The US cannot afford a costly and interminable war.

Falling living standards and inability to impose our will on the Middle East will result in great frustrations that will diminish our country.

So far, I've written about the daily travails of getting ready for our move, however the above article has made me want to explain more on the "why" of our move. Paul Craig Roberts neatly encapsulates the emotions we've been feeling in the last couple of years. Those of us who proudly wear the label of "liberal," or "progressive," which I think more aptly describes many of us, no longer feel that we are welcome in much of this country.

Perhaps some believe that it is a cop out to leave and that we should just stay and fight. But do we have to be here to do that? I think that remaining involved and voting in elections as an expatriate is just as valuable.

Sure, if we were here, we could hand out leaflets at the mall and organize with other Dems, but I don't think I have the energy for that right now. It is clear that there is still a large group of Americans who are willing to support hatred and ugliness. I find it exhausting to listen to them and prefer to live someplace where I'm not faced with their terrifying world view on a daily basis.

Am I an ostrich? I don't think so. I am a proud American who sees her country driving over a cliff and can't find the power to make it stop.

What a day! We finished packing the suitcases (except for the last minute items like the toiletries and the computers and attendant bits). It's amazing though, we've got *eight* cases! Granted, two of them are pretty small and three are mostly blankets wrapped around a few pieces of equipment that we're taking, like a cool international DVD player that plays just about anything from any country in the world, but still!

Of course, Diva Maggie has her own suitcase: an entire duffel bag filled with food and various other items of interest to the well-traveled Border Collie. I can just imagine what customs will think about that if they open it. Hopefully, there's nothing in there that they think we shouldn't be bringing in.

Our living room now looks like a luggage store. I'm so grateful that our good friend Diane volunteered to help us get our stuff down to the hotel at the airport. No way is all of it plus Maggie, her crate, our carry-on bags and humans going to fit in poor little Greenie Beanie (our Toyota Echo). I hope we find porters at both ends to help us in the airport. I'm planning on keeping Maggie in her crate until we're out of Charles de Gaulle airport, so we're definitely going to need help in Paris.

It's good to have it done though. I feel less worried about being ready on Saturday now. Tomorrow is Maggie's final pre-flight check at her Auntie Gayle's (our vet), last trip to the Post Office and UPS, then we're done. Now, if only escrow on the house closes with no further hitches we'll be ready to start our new life.

Saturday, January 29

In 12 hours, the movers are scheduled to arrive! Miraculously, we're ready for them.

Cindy confirmed that the buyer's loan funded today and escrow will definitely close on Monday, so we're on target to actually pay for our new house in Chalabre.

The day has not gone entirely according to plan, however. First, we woke up to a very weirdly-colored sky. As day broke, instead of getting lighter, suddenly things got darker and we had a heck of a storm! Of course, it was just in time for me to take Maggie over for her pre-flight check up and I had large, wet paw prints all over the back seat of the car, plus, traffic was even worse than usual.

An hour or so later, when JM and I set off to the Post Office to mail out a package to ourselves in France, I realized I didn't have the Post Office box key. I came in to look for it without success, so JM came to look too. Neither of us could find it, so at this point I'm guessing it's either packed somewhere or lost forever.

Now, Maggie was starting to get very anxious by this time and when JM went out the front door, she did something she never does and ran out after him, making it clear that she was *not* coming back inside and wanted to get in the car. We gave in and took her, figuring that if we made an issue of it, she'd only get more upset.

The final weirdness came at dinnertime. JM was looking for yet one more thing that shouldn't have been packed, but clearly had been. He grabbed a suitcase which unfortunately banged into an antique, cast iron, table mirror that I've had since I was about 12. In spite of it being wrapped in bubble pack, the base snapped off when it hit the floor. Really bad luck, because it must just have hit at the wrong angle. On the good luck side, the mirror itself didn't break, so I'm guessing there won't be seven years bad luck. I was really upset at the time, but now I think JM is more bothered by it than I am. He insists that we pack it in the suitcases and find someone to repair it right away.[5]

Still, if that's the only thing that breaks during the move, we'll be in good shape

---

[5] The mirror was indeed satisfactorily repaired by a local French artisan, as reported later.

Sunday, January 30

Yesterday was quite a day. We got up at 5:30 a.m. so that I could do several loads of final laundry, we could go out to breakfast and get the last little items packed, not to mention throwing out anything that we *didn't* want to take, like the trash!

Our dear Diane came over at 8:30 a.m. bearing coffee (bless her heart), then helped us load suitcases into her car. I don't know what we would have done without her. Once we'd loaded Maggie's crate into *our* car, there was only room for two of the eight cases we're taking with us. It would have been a nightmare to get to the airport otherwise.

The movers showed up at 9:30 a.m. and started packing everything at 10 a.m. They were simply wonderful! I have to thank Rinkens for sending Moses and his great crew. I've never seen anything like them. They packed *everything*, even the furniture! It was all on the truck (barely fit too) by 5 p.m. Then, JM and I kind of wandered around the empty house and got all teary-eyed. Twenty years, and now it's over. Tomorrow the house won't belong to us anymore...

We're staying with our friends Terry and Paula and their good dog Charlie. The only surprise is that Maggie is not being nice to Charlie at all! They play and are sweet most of the time, but if poor Charlie comes over to me for a head pat, she makes a nasty little "yip" and sends him packing. He looks so crushed when she does it. I've never known her to do this before and I figure it's a combination of jealousy and anxiety.

Hopefully, that behavior won't continue. We need to be nice to the new French dogs we meet.[6]

Monday, January 31

Last night was great! We had a wonderful send off dinner with our friends Terry, Paula, Diane and Evan. Everybody laughed and had a great time and Diane and Evan even brought a bottle of *Blanquette de Limoux* for a toast. Too bad JM and I don't drink.

Maggie was really mean to poor Charlie, getting an evil gleam in her eye every time he came close to me. I'm happy to say she was much nicer to him today and even gave him little doggie kisses at one point while I was petting him.

---

[6] Sadly, Charlie crossed the *Rainbow Bridge* far too early, later in the year (due to cancer). We miss sweet boy Charlie...

However, Maggie's saga does not end there! This morning, I got up early and let the dogs out back before I took a shower. When I got back to the bedroom, JM said, "I think there's a problem." The Diva had found a mysterious source of poop and had rolled around in it! She came proudly into the house to show her daddy how pretty she was and *yuck*!

She was simply covered in the stuff. I had to grab her and drag her into the shower for an *impromptu* bath. She wasn't thrilled, but I have to say that she's now looking all lovely and fluffy to meet her grandparents on Wednesday.

We drove down to the hotel this morning and half-an-hour later the tow truck showed up to take Greenie Beanie away for her long sea voyage. I called Eike at Rinkens and was astonished to discover that our things are due to arrive in Marseille on March 5! That's really amazing, since I was expecting it to take close to twice that long.

Now, we're just hanging out, doing some email and working a bit. Diane is bringing our luggage by in a little while then we'll have to find a dog-friendly place to eat dinner: not easy in L.A. Still, everything seems to be going according to plan: Air France has confirmed that all is well for our reservations as well as Maggie's. No problem for the extra baggage, which we can pay for at the airport. The hotel shuttle will take us to the airport at noon and we'll have the hardest part for JM and me: watching the airline take Maggie away in her crate. We're all going to suffer for the 12 to 15 hours over that one.

Tuesday, February 1

It's just after 9 a.m. We're leaving for the airport in less than three hours! It's hard to believe that the day is finally here.

Maggie is all dressed in her Anxiety Wrap, which I think will help her cope with the flight. I definitely feel that it helped her with the move on Saturday. She was super calm and unperturbed despite all the strangers and weird noises. Right now, she's sound asleep under the desk as I type. I hope she stays this calm for the rest of the day (unrealistic of me?).

Strange to think that tomorrow at this time, we'll still have *five hours* of flying to go until we get to Paris! If all goes well, I'll write my next blog from there.

Wednesday, February 2

Believe it or not, I'm sitting here typing this at 2 a.m. in our hotel room in Paris. Yep, jet lag has kicked in big time.

I've got quite a *résumé* of events for today, which turned out to be a really *big* day for all of us.

First, I need to really tip my hat to the Radisson at LAX. I don't know if all of the Radissons are as pet-friendly as they are, but they have certainly won our loyalty. Everyone we met there was very sweet to Maggie, greeting her, petting her, including her. In fact, when we went to get something to take out at the coffee shop, they even offered to let us sit in their lobby area with her to eat, which I thought was really wonderful of them.

After eventually eating breakfast at the lobby bar, we went up to our room to wait until it was time to go to the airport. Maggie was quite aware that "something" was going on and didn't want to eat or anything. Finally, after a last minute irritation with Cingular Wireless, we ordered a bellman and took off.

The shuttle dropped us at the Delta/Air France terminal and JM went off to find a Skycap while I took on the task of loading the Diva into her crate. She did not want to go, I can tell you that. Funny how a place of safety can become a prison if you look at it in a different light. However, I finally succeeded in getting her inside. JM and the Skycap appeared and we loaded crate and massive pile of suitcases on his trolley and went inside.

Clearly, we needed to pay for extra luggage. However Air France was terrific. I told them we were moving back to France and their ticketing agent was very kind. She charged $50 less for Maggie than I had been told (three times) it would cost; also, she counted the heaviest of our suitcases as our free allowance and didn't charge us at all for one of the other bags. So, we probably saved about $150 on the overall cost.

The next part was not so good, however. TSA insists that you remove the dog from the crate, which is incredibly stupid, because they shouldn't insist that she go in there before they check the crate in the first place! I did that and went back to the Air France counter to finish up while JM and the Skycap took the luggage for screening. Of course, as usual, Maggie was the hit of the place with ticket agents climbing out from behind the counter to make a fuss over her.

After her crate was x-rayed, we had to put her back inside. Well, at that point she *really* didn't want to get in! The obdurate TSA agent insisted that I leave the crate on the luggage cart, which put it about ten inches above the floor. So, there I was, on my hands and knees on the floor of the terminal trying to force a struggling, terrified, 50-pound dog into a little crate that she didn't want to get into and which was up in the air! I begged him to let me put it on the floor but he refused, saying, "We do it this way everyday." I took my life in my hands to say, "Well, that's nice, but I don't!" Finally, I did manage to push her inside and had to watch her panic-filled eyes as they wheeled her away.

The next several hours were nerve-wracking as we worried about whether she was OK and if she would get on the plane OK. When we finally boarded Flight 065, I asked several of the flight attendants to check on whether she'd been boarded or not. I received confirmation and was able to take off with that worry out of my head. However, I was very nervous during the 11-hour flight, wondering how she was and couldn't totally relax until I saw her again in Paris.

We actually arrived at a different terminal than we had used in December, which turned out to be a good thing. In December, the dogs that were on our flight were put on the luggage conveyor belt, but in this terminal, they delivered her on a cart directly to the baggage handling office and then paged me that she was there! I loved that, because I was much less worried about her that way. I ran over to greet her and she looked *so* happy to see me. My original plan had been to leave her in her crate while we were in the terminal, but she so wanted to come out that I relented. It turned out fine. She wasn't the least bit frightened of all the people and luggage and followed along with us happily.

JM had to push four carts of luggage by himself! I would stay with the carts while he took one to a "relay" stop: first the baggage office, then customs, then the shuttle, so the stuff was never left alone at all. Customs asked to look at the paperwork from the French Consulate that we were repatriating and that was it. In fact, at no time did anyone, except the Air France check-in desk, ever even look at Maggie's paperwork or check her microchip or rabies certificate. So, it was all a bit of a waste, really. Still, better to conform and not need it, then not have it and be asked for it!

When we got out of customs, the van from Paris Connection was waiting for us. They're a great company, a husband and wife team from Scotland who opened up their tour company in France four years ago.

You can find them at their website [7] if you need an airport shuttle or a tour guide. They're lovely people and very helpful to their clients.

At any rate, we got into Paris easily and came straight to our hotel, the Ibis Opera-Bastille, which we chose because it accepts dogs, is reasonably priced and is within walking distance to the family. Our room is small but comfortable. Did I tell you that our room is small? Once poor JM dragged all the luggage up here, it doesn't leave much walking around in room, but for less than 100 euros a night, I really have no complaints.

While JM was doing the luggage thing, Maggie and I waited down in the lobby watching over the cases. She was quite the hit with everybody. She was still in her Anxiety Wrap and looked very chic, kind of like Mrs. Peel in *The Avengers*. I can see that she's definitely going to help us meet new friends in Chalabre.

Since Maggie's Buddy Bowl was still in her crate, I took her over to see if she wanted a drink, and the poor baby! She was so dehydrated and thirsty, I doubt she'd had anything to drink at all since she left us in the morning. I suppose she just didn't think about it, even though her bowl was in there with her. She was probably just too scared. I tried to limit how much she drank at a time, because I didn't want her to get sick. I think it took her most of the day to really catch up on liquid intake.

After getting to our room we immediately went back out and bought a new French cell phone. That's turned out to have been a really useful, cost-saving purchase already.

Of course, Maggie is coming with us on every errand that we do and I couldn't be more impressed with her behavior. It's as if she has been doing all this her whole life! I think I need to ask our good friend Raven to design her a t-shirt that says *"Born to be French!"* For the first time in her life, she walks like an angel on her leash with no pulling. When we sit in a café or restaurant, she lays down under the table, watching the world go by. Just a real joy!

After a nap, we finally took Maggie to meet her grandparents. They were totally won over, making a huge fuss and feeding her *filet mignon* and *crêpes*! Maggie took one look at my mother-in-law, Arlette, and immediately saw that she had a slave for life. I better never leave her with them or she'll be too fat to walk!

The only hiccup in the whole day was a call from the company which was supposed to be wiring the funds from our house sale. Appar-

---

[7] http://parisconnection.fr/

ently, because the money arrived from the escrow company and not from us, they couldn't send it to us! It's all part of the wacko regulations put in place to keep anyone from laundering money or funding an "evil" organization. However, what it really does is keep normal people from accessing their own funds!

All I can tell you is that we had to jump through hoops in the middle of the night, making phone calls, faxing documents, making more calls, etc. What a nightmare. JM was so stressed that, at one point, he nearly walked out into traffic! The biggest problem was that all the other solutions we found for getting the money would have meant huge delays and risked our not being able to pay for our new house on time. *Horror!*

Without dragging it out, finally today, the issue was resolved and the funds sent, so all is well again in Possumworld.

Celebrating my birthday in Paris with Maggie

Thursday, February 3

Today is my birthday! I'm not sure if I should celebrate or hide.

Anyway, after the supercharged events of the night, it was impossible for us to get back to sleep until almost 5 a.m. We used the time to do email, rearrange our luggage to make the room more usable, take showers, etc. So at least it wasn't wasted time. We were finally able to fall asleep and didn't wake up until 8:30 a.m., which was perfect. We took Maggie down for her first French *petit déjeuner*.

Since we're in a hotel that caters to "furriners," it's got a great breakfast buffet with ham, cheese, cereal, etc., added to the usual coffee and croissants. Of course, I scored some ham to bring up to the room to give Maggie afterwards. I have some scruples, not wanting to be too obvious in feeding my dog on the 6.50 euros that we paid for breakfast!

Even though by that time, the money issue hadn't been resolved entirely, we were feeling confident enough to go to the bank to discuss all the necessary bits of starting a new life.

It was so weird. I guess it's all starting to feel *real* now because of doing these kinds of mundane tasks. One thing that we looked into was insurance of various types. I don't know if it's the fatigue or what, but at one point, JM and I looked at each other and started laughing rather hysterically. Our health insurance is going to cost us around $50 a month, as opposed to the $700 a month we were paying in L.A.! Our homeowners' insurance will be $200 *a year* instead of something like $1,500 before. Auto insurance is only slightly less, but that's because we don't have any driving record here. We're going to see if whether getting a letter from State Farm explaining our years of no claims or tickets will help any.

Finally, we had my birthday lunch which was the culmination of my birthday wish. We sat in a restaurant with Maggie at the table, all of us feeling completely content and at peace. What a wonderful way for us to start our new life.

Friday, February 4

I had a wonderful compliment last night. We were having dinner and the waiter raved about my French, which was so nice. He told me that I have almost no accent at all and bet that in six months I'd sound like a native. Totally made the rest of my birthday celebration perfect (well, that and the fabulous chocolate concoction served with both ice cream *and crème anglaise*).

We're still waking up at 2 a.m. then going back to sleep for another couple of hours at 4 or 5 a.m. We really want to get over that before Sunday if possible, because there's a long drive ahead of us and falling asleep on the *autoroute* would not be a good idea.

However, JM and I both noticed that Maggie seems to be getting over her jetlag today. She's sleeping a bit less and seems perkier. It's hard to put your finger on it, but it's one of those things that everyone with a pet will understand. You just *know* that they feel better.

We did have a bit of *Sun* today, which was great, although it fooled us Californians into thinking we could go outside without coats, which may not have been the smartest thing we ever did. By the time we came back from our afternoon walk, the humans were both freezing and seriously in need of some hot chocolate in the hotel bar.

Not a huge amount to report today, as we took it easy, had lunch with a friend, worked a bit and rested. Tomorrow will have more interesting things to report, I hope. And, of course, Sunday we're driving "home!"

Saturday, 5 February

Sorry that I've been off-line for a couple of days. We used up our wi-fi access in Paris on Saturday afternoon, then spent all day Sunday driving and weren't able to connect again until Monday evening our time. So, lots of catching up to do.

It was mostly a quiet day except for some family stuff which would be terribly boring for anyone but us! However, there was one cute moment.

As many of you may know, the French national pastime is going on strike and demonstrating in the streets. Usually, this is reserved for pleasant spring days, but sometimes the various groups feel incensed enough to bear the brunt of the nasty weather and march in the winter.

Saturday was such a day. The workers were basically demonstrating in favor of the 35-hour work week, which they're afraid the government is trying to take away.

At any rate, since we were taking Maggie to her grandparents for afternoon tea, we dressed her up in one of her Christmas bandannas (thank you, Connie Carstens!). Of course, we *had* to put her in a red one. One of the things about my in-laws apartment is that it's generally on the main route of most demonstrations: halfway between the Place de la République and the Bastille. Since we were staying near the Bastille, we had to go right past this one to get to their place.

Maggie hated the noise, of course, but we got a couple of cute pictures of her wearing her red bandanna in solidarity with the unions, who are often (or at least used to be) supporters of the French Communist Party.

Maggie demonstrates her solidarity with the French workers

Sunday, 6 February

We got up bright and early on Sunday morning to start the next leg of our journey. We had breakfast at 6:30 a.m., then walked to the Gare de Lyon to get to the Hertz office.

I had reserved a mini-van in Los Angeles, but the Paris office told me that what I had reserved was actually a mini-mini-van. We were really afraid our luggage wouldn't fit, so had to move up to the next size. I've rented a lot of cars over the years, but this was absolutely, without question, the worst vehicle I've ever driven. It was a Peugeot 807 and I can't imagine who designed it. Normally, I like Peugeots. In fact, we had a Peugeot 206 in December that was really fun to drive. But this thing was a beast!

Because the Hertz office is in a big tower, the cars are parked in an underground lot. You get a ticket to get out of the parking lot and have ten minutes to get down to the right level, find your car, figure out how to get it started and get out of the parking lot. Normally, it's plenty of time. However, the Beast didn't wait before causing me trouble. No way could I find the hand brake! I couldn't even get the thing out of its parking spot. I had to get out, find the interphone that connected me back to the Hertz office and ask them where it was. It was on the left-hand side of the driver's seat on the floor! Who would ever think to look there?

I should have taken that as a sign, but we managed to get in, check things out and barely make it out of the parking lot before the ticket expired. Then, I had to drive back to the hotel, past the Sunday flea market and find a place to park so we could load up.

Thinking that if we left Maggie in the car the two of us could more easily bring down the bags together, we went into the hotel to check out. That's where the first little hiccup occurred. Despite the fact that we'd paid cash for breakfast every morning, they had charged us an extra 13 euros a day for it! In spite of all the really good experiences we'd had at Ibis, this wasn't one of their shining moments. They had a real problem trying to recredit those 51 euros back to us. It took forever, and in the meantime, poor JM had to bring all the luggage down on his own while I stood there trying to get the bill straightened out. Strike two of a really long day.

At last, we'd paid, the luggage was outside and we were loading the Beast. It took me ages to figure out how to fold the back seat down. Even after doing that though, there was barely enough room in there for everything. At one point, we even had to seriously consider leaving Maggie's crate behind. Still, after playing with it all in a Rubik's cube fashion, we did manage to load it all inside. Of course, I couldn't see out the back of the Beast, but thank goodness for side mirrors.

We were able to hit the road just before 9 a.m. We got out of Paris with only one wrong turn that put us onto the autoroute heading east instead of south, but luckily that only cost us about five minutes of driving time.

We were definitely right to leave the driving for Sunday morning. There was much less traffic than if we'd left during the week, which, given the reduced visibility of the Beast, was a blessing. After about two hours of driving, we decided to take a rest stop break. The snack bar didn't allow dogs, so JM stayed outside with Maggie and took her for a walk while I went inside to take care of business and get a coffee from the hideous coffee machine. Every one of those machines in the universe makes vile coffee, but at least it was caffeine.

Then, back on the road we went. The rest of the drive was relatively without incident. One interesting note was our lunch, which we had at a rest stop in the Corrèze. It was a cafeteria-style restaurant and was really decent for food eaten in less than ideal conditions. Certainly it beat any fast food I've ever had on a U.S. highway by way more than a mile!

I didn't switch driving tasks with JM because I didn't think he'd be comfortable driving the Beast. On top of that, at one point we wound up having a really strong crosswind, which made it incredibly difficult to hold it on the road. All in all, that made for a very long, tiring drive.

Entering Chalabre

We got off the autoroute in Pamiers and drove towards Chalabre. What a strange feeling it was to be coming back less than two months after we had left with the realization that we were driving home and not on vacation. It was really the first time that it hit us. On top of that, the weather was crystal clear and we had a magnificent view of the Pyrénées, with their snow-covered peaks, standing majestically over everything. What a spectacular site and we're living in their shadow. In spite of being tired, it was incredibly moving.

At last, at 5 p.m., we pulled into Chalabre where, with no visibility out of the back of the Beast, I managed to park. JM got out and went to check in. That was the third strike of the day: the hotel was closed up tight! Eeek!

We sat around for a few minutes, then went across the street to the nearest cafe to find out if some disaster had struck since we'd checked on Wednesday that our reservation was good. The locals thought that everything was fine, but that the family went out on Sunday afternoon if things were quiet, but we should expect them to return around six o'clock.

JM wound up talking with Violette, one of the villagers. She had only moved here a few years ago and had nothing but good to say about the village and its citizens. It was quite reassuring, really.

We stayed sitting in the car till 6:30 p.m., still no sign of anyone at the hotel. We really weren't sure what to do. Finding another place to stay in Mirepoix (20 kms away) wouldn't have been a problem, but we would have been really stuck because of the luggage. We needed to turn the car in at 8 a.m. Monday morning and then we wouldn't have been able to get all our luggage *back* to Chalabre! Finally, the hotel's employee appeared and told us that they never opened before 6:30 p.m. on Sunday night. About five minutes later, lights came on inside and we knew all was well.

It turned out that JM had spoken with Didier, who is the chef (an excellent one) but he hadn't told his wife, Marielle, who runs the hotel side of things! So she had no idea we were coming and Didier hadn't remembered to tell us not to bother getting here before 6:30 p.m.!

Still, all ended well. We took the largest room that they had, which was also on the first floor, and settled down. To make things simpler, we took the room as "*demi-pension*." That means that for an extra, fixed charge over the room rate, we get breakfast and dinner. The dinner is what's known in France as a "menu." That means three courses set out by the chef, usually with no choices. It works out well, because instead of doing what most of us do, which is to always eat the same things, it means you get a dinner picked for you by someone who knows what he's doing!

I have to say that although Didier may not be the best at taking messages, he's a terrific chef, so we're quite happy with the arrangement.

Oh, and a big surprise! In a courageous move for any French restaurant, no one is allowed to smoke in the dining room! What a fabulous bonus.

The Hotel de France

Monday, 7 February

In spite of everything, we were still feeling jetlagged. I'd found the alarm clock before going to bed on Sunday and ambitiously set it for 6 a.m. We actually wound up waking up at 5 a.m.

Marielle and Didier take Monday off, so they don't cook or fix breakfast. However, they kindly made us a breakfast tray with hot coffee, tea, milk, orange juice, croissants, bread, jam, butter, honey and little cakes and set it in front of our door before they went to bed at 2 a.m.! The coffee, etc., was in thermoses, so it was nice and hot when we were ready for it.

We showered, ate, walked Maggie and set off on the road at 6:45 a.m. Once again, the Beast lived up to its name! I don't know if it was because it was a diesel, or because it was a beast, but I could not get it to drive! It felt like I was riding a bucking bronco or something. As soon as I put it into first gear and tried to ease my foot off the clutch, it shivered and sputtered and tried to stall out. To make things worse, it was pitch black and raining ice. I had no idea if I could get the Beast to drive well enough to make the 50 km trip to Salvaza, the Carcassonne airport, where we had been told we *had* to be by 8:30 a.m. if we didn't want to pay another 180 euros for renting the Beast for an extra day!

So, tense and pissed off, we shuddered onto the road.

Let me say that during the day, the road between Chalabre and Limoux, which we have to take to get to Carcassonne, is stunning. One of the most beautiful roads that I've ever driven. At 6:45 a.m., in the pitch dark morning, when icy rain is pelting down and you are driving a car that is threatening to stall out every few minutes, it is terrifying. There are hairpin turns, sheer drops into a river, and on this day, piles of snow from the last storm. We would suddenly enter banks of thick fog that made it almost impossible to see. I couldn't wait to hit a "normal" road!

Luckily, as the Beast warmed up, it drove better and was less threatening. Still, I wanted to be rid of it as soon as possible. We stopped in Limoux for its last drink. I haven't mentioned it before now, but what a gas guzzler! Diesel is less expensive than unleaded, but the damned Beast still wound up costing us about 120 euros in fuel! You couldn't pay me to own one of those things. Between the extra cost of renting a larger car, putting JM on the rental agreement as "second" driver and the fuel, we probably spent over 400 euros getting from Paris to Chalabre. I don't think we could have done it any other way, but it was a shocking expense, nevertheless.

At last, we drove into Salvaza. It's a tiny place and the only airline that uses it is the Irish carrier, Ryanair. At 8 o'clock on the dot, we parked the Beast and walked up to the Hertz office, only to find it closed! They don't even open before 9 a.m.! We didn't have to rush and drive in the dark and ice after all.

Luckily, the chef at the airport restaurant took pity on us and opened early to make us "second" breakfast (just like hobbits!). Maggie, on the other hand, didn't seem too thrilled to be back in an airport! I think that she was afraid we were going to put her on another airplane.

When the Hertz office opened, the people there were very nice and we got a great little Opel that will be perfect for the next month until Beanie arrives from her sea voyage.

After getting rid of the Beast we came back to the hotel and decided to try out our Internet connection. We discovered that the hotel's phone system isn't compatible with our modems, so we couldn't use our dial-up account! Luckily, technology allowed us to find a solution later in the day.

Off we went to have lunch in Mirepoix with our real estate agent, François. He told us that the seller of our house was upset because he'd sold the house so quickly! Still, things seem on track for the signing of the papers on the 17th or 18th. We're meeting with the notary tomorrow (Wednesday) and should have a better idea of things then.

Monday is market day in Mirepoix. Parking was a little difficult because of that, but we found a decent spot and got to see some of the market, although it was actually closing down for the day. What we saw of it looked wonderful and I'm sure we'll be heading back to check it out more closely.

Lunch was at Le Commerce, which is both a hotel and restaurant. We'd already eaten there in December and the staff remembered us and the fact that we were moving to Chalabre. I loved that. The food there is excellent and amazingly reasonably priced. The 11 euro menu was: a tray of various salads, quiche lorraine, veal stew with homemade pasta, and a dessert or cheese. Maggie enjoyed the bits of veal stew I fed her under the table.

After our delicious meal, we set off for Pamiers to resolve our Internet issues at France Telecom. We had decided to get a PC card so that we could connect over the cellular network. The salesman at the Telecom office tried to talk us out of it, since we'll be moving into our house in about two weeks and will have DSL put in. "It's too expensive," he told us! But, we explained that sometimes you just have to bite the bullet. Besides, it will give us a bit more liberty when we travel around the country, enabling us to stay on line, even if we're not at a hotel with wi-fi.

Back home to Chalabre to test the connection and everything worked according to plan. Of course, two-and-a-half days of email took a while to download, but eventually it did and all was well.

Because of our delicious lunch, we didn't need much in the way of dinner and stopped at one of the local markets. JM went inside to get a couple of things while I stayed out with Maggie. The checkout clerk was great and very impressed to find out that Chalabre now had two resident comic book writers!

That's been the great thing about the last few days. Absolutely everyone that we meet in the town is very warm and welcoming. They seem genuinely glad to find out that we're settling here and are not at all stuffy about strangers.

The day ended with a quiet snack in our hotel room, a final walk around town with Maggie and deletion of several hundred emails trying to sell us vi*gra!

Tuesday, 8 February

Finally we catch up to today.

Breakfast at the hotel isn't served until 9 a.m., so we had a couple of hours to shower, do email, walk Maggie, etc. We were excited because we were having a first meeting with our new architect, Bruno Geli, at 9:30 a.m.

While we had breakfast, Didier and Marielle told us where some of the important local shopping places were for buying gas, etc. It's amazing what you don't know when you move to a new place!

Then, Bruno got here to talk about work on the house. He was a bit disappointed that we weren't going to be able to get inside the house for a look. But we had to explain that we don't want to rock the boat until the papers are signed. Still, we were able to describe what we want to do and talk about budgets, schedules, etc.

Unfortunately, it may be a couple of months before he can get started on the big work of doing the kitchen. However, he's going to at least get us started with an electrician and hopefully doing the floors, tearing down the separation wall in the bedroom and stripping the wallpaper. We can live without a finished kitchen for a couple of months as long as the rest of the work is done or at least underway.

The funny bit was learning that Bruno had lived in Santa Monica for a couple of years in the late eighties! So, we all got along great and really communicated well. We all walked over to at least look at the house from the outside, and he told us that it definitely looked solidly built, which was good to hear.

While we were walking around town, another local came over and asked me about Maggie. His name is Christian and he had his little daughter Shawna with him. Then, he went to get his dog, who is a beautiful Belgian Shepherd. He and Maggie looked great together and she seemed to really like him. It's quite clear that Maggie is, once again, turning out to be a terrific asset. She makes it so much easier for people to approach us and talk. I think we're going to be happy here, and we have to thank Maggie for making that happen more quickly.

We resolved a couple more little problems today. First, we reorganized our hotel room. If we're going to be living and working in it, we really needed to be able to *find* things! We still have a mystery on our hands. We're positive that we packed certain things, and no way can we find them! Our last guess is that they're in the one box that we sent on ahead. We'll be getting it from our friends in a few days, and if they're not in there, they've clearly disappeared into the ether.

On a more prosaic note, we figured out how to get our laundry done! There isn't a coin laundry in town and the only one we've found so far was in Pamiers, which is about 40 kms away. It seems kind of silly to go that far. However, there's a lady in town who does washing, drying, ironing, alterations, etc. Her prices are quite reasonable. At first, I felt uncomfortable at the idea of having someone else do my laundry. But, on reflection, it seems to make more sense than driving 40 kms to do it myself. So, until we have a finished kitchen, I guess I'm not going to do any laundry at all!

So that's all the news that's fit to blog from Chalabre today.

Wednesday, 9 February

We met with the local notary, Maître Duchan, this morning. His office is on the "outskirts" of Chalabre. It took us ten minutes to walk there instead of the usual five to get anywhere else. Coming from L.A., we're used to always counting extra time, so we arrived half-an-hour early.

Maître Duchan is very nice, somewhere in his early forties I would guess; a local who took over his father's business after he retired. So, he knows the place very, very well. We got along great and I'm sure we'll see more of him as time goes on.

We spent about an hour going over the various documents that we needed to deal with. It was interesting, because some things are very similar to buying real estate in California, while others are quite different.

For example, there was a termite report. Apparently, there are no termites in Chalabre, although some have been found in Limoux, 20 kms away. The climate appears to be different enough here to have kept them at bay, although they will probably make their way here eventually.

There were, however, some other wood-eating beasts in the house. We'll definitely need to get those treated right away. Luckily, it seems as if the infestation is pretty minor, but still, you want to deal with it as soon as possible.

There were also asbestos and lead reports. The asbestos in our house seems to be confined to the ugly linoleum and one or two older pipes. Since we were going to deal with those things anyway, it's not a problem. Apparently, having the asbestos in things like that is not a problem where the house needs to be tented or anything to get rid of it. Still, I think it means that we will not be able to be in the house while they're ripping up the flooring. As for the lead, like almost everywhere in the U.S., it's in old paint on the windows. Since we don't have any children, we don't have to really worry about that either. Although we'll probably have the windows repainted at one point or another.

The most important thing to come out of the meeting, however, is that the final papers will be signed on Thursday, February 17, at 4:30 p.m., and the house will be ours! We have seven days from today to change our minds. I can't see that happening, but it's the reason we can't officially close before the 17th. The seller does not have seven days to change her mind, which was reassuring to both of us, who always worry about something going wrong.

The Chalabre Post Office (right)

We walked back to town, just missing the post office by a few minutes. Most things here close between 12 p.m. and 2 p.m. for lunch. I know in L.A. that would drive people crazy, because everyone does their errands at lunchtime. I don't mind it though and we'll learn to work our lives around it. We always have when we've been in France for visits, so it shouldn't be a big problem.

We had a delicious sandwich in the hotel bar for lunch, then worked for a couple of hours before going out to finish the day's errands. We did our first visit to the post office, where we introduced ourselves and had a nice chat. I think that's the thing that I like most here. Everyone has time to chat when you go to do business. It's a leisurely pace to life that is extremely refreshing.

After, we went back to the little supermarket, where the clerk remembered us from the other day. He helped me pick out samples of local apples to try. We're apparently in prime apple growing region and there were a large number of varieties from which to choose. I love that.

One of the two pharmacies in Chalabre

Then, I decided to try my luck at the pharmacy. I needed to get my migraine prescriptions filled and I haven't gone to a doctor yet. The pharmacist had helped me with a problem with my ears yesterday and remembered me and the fact that we were seeing the notary today. He asked how things were going with the house.

He looked at what I've been taking, looked them up in his book, made a phone call and ordered them for me tomorrow. He was very apologetic about the cost, which, of course, is actually less than half of what my co-pay was in L.A., so I didn't mind at all. Once I'm signed up with social security and a *mutuelle*, they'll be totally covered.

But the best part of the day was our visit to the Château! We hadn't been able to do that in December, because of the weather. Maggie loved it. Lots of grass and trees on the walk. There's an old horse that lives there. I don't think she's ever seen one of those before. I'm pretty sure she thought he was a giant sheep. She got into her best border collie, head-down, tail-down crouch and gave him the eye. I'm pretty sure she wanted me to let her go and round him up, but I resisted her efforts.

When we came back to the hotel, she just curled up for a nice nap. She's probably dreaming about having steak again for dinner.

Thursday, February 10
Last night finished up pleasantly, with us spending a long time talking to Didier and Marielle in the hotel bar. There were no other guests in the hotel and the last bar clients had left, so we were able to have a nice chat.

I think we surprised them by telling them they were being written about on this blog! I read what I'd written about them and they seemed to get a kick out of realizing that they were now known by invisible netizens around the world.

Didier is waiting for France Telecom to come and install their DSL line. We've convinced him that he should make sure he gets wi-fi access for the hotel guests. I know it would have made our lives a lot easier.

Once they're all set up, I think they want to set up a Hotel de France-Chalabre website and JM has offered to help them. Chalabre will soon be taking over the world!

We decided that our task for the day was to get insurance for the house. We need to have that in place before the transfer can officially take place. If we don't have our own insurance, then the insurance of the seller would carry over. But, we really felt we wanted to take care of it on our own.

When we were in Paris last week, Mme. Andersson, our account representative, had given us quotes from the BNP, which besides being a bank, also does insurance. We thought it would be better to deal with an insurance agent in town if we could, since if we ever need to make a claim, it seems to make more sense to deal with someone locally. So, we went to Groupama, which is on the Cours Raynaud, just a few houses down from the hotel.

Once the house was taken care of, we talked about the car and health insurance issues. It seems we should wait until we sign up with Social Security before even thinking about getting a *mutuelle*, which makes sense. Also, the car is going to be a little complicated, as we already knew. We'll probably need to get just liability and maybe theft to cover it temporarily until it passes all the steps to get its very own *"carte grise,"* the French equivalent of getting a Californian pink slip.

After the insurance issue was dealt with, we decided to head to Carcassonne to get JM's lost driver's license replaced and to talk about me getting a French license. We stopped in a small village between Limoux and Carcassonne for lunch. It was OK, but certainly not the best meal we've ever had. Didier really stands above the crowd in our opinion.

We easily found our way to the Prefecture de Police. Since we had Maggie with us, I had to wait outside while JM went in to deal with the *administration*. When we'd tried this in Paris in December, it had taken ages just to get inside the Prefecture. Then, another 30 or 40 minutes of waiting in line at the Driver's License bureau, only to learn that they weren't issuing new licenses until after the second of January, because the European Community was changing them.

I don't think I waited outside for more than 15 or 20 minutes before JM was back. He had had a really pleasant experience with the woman in charge and just needed to get a photocopy of his identity card and a stamped, self-addressed envelope at the post office. He'd also learned that there was no way for me to get an exception on getting a French license. Only eight U.S. states have reciprocal agreements with France for exchanging licenses. California, sadly, is not one of them. So, it looks like I'm going to have to study the French driving code and take a test. I can drive with my California license for a year, so I don't have to rush into anything at this point.

When we got back to the Prefecture, JM was only inside for five minutes before coming out and telling me it was all taken care of. They'll send him his new license when it's ready.

One of the things that struck us was how nice it is doing any of this kind of thing here. In Paris, they're always so rushed and everyone is a bit stressed. Here, every time we go into a post office, the Prefecture or a bank, people are pleasant and laid back. It makes dealing with things much nicer when the people who are handling matters aren't nasty to you.

We are still short of plug adapters for some of our electric cords, so we thought we'd look around downtown Carcassonne to see if we could find any. No luck, but we happened to see a real estate office and couldn't help but look in the window at the properties on offer to see if there was anything we would have rather had. Human nature! The answer was a definite "no!" We really felt we'd gotten a good deal on the price, and we didn't see any pictures that made us regret our decision.

While we were looking, a man with a six-month old retriever puppy walked up so that Maggie could say hello. He was one of the real estate agents and pointed to a house in the window that he'd just sold. It was comparable to our new home, but was about 25,000 euros more! When we told him that we had bought in Chalabre, he was very complimentary, saying what a great town it was, etc. He also told us where to go looking for the best mushrooms! Of course, I'm not sure if I'll be brave enough to eat mushrooms I gather myself unless someone who knows what they're doing comes with me.

We're trying to figure out if it's Maggie, or if we've been lucky, or if it's this area, but so far we've been really blown away by how nice people have been. More than that, by how approachable they are. I know that in most cases it's just surface friendliness, but that's a great start to real friendship.

Finally, after giving up on finding adapter plugs for today, we gratefully left the big city to return to our beautiful countryside. I realized how tired I am of driving in crowded places after living in L.A. Sure, by L.A. standards, Carcassonne is nothing. But, after only a few days here in Chalabre, it was more than I was in the mood for.

As we drove home looking at the beautiful vineyards and rolling hills, we really felt at peace. We took a couple of little tiny lanes and found a beautiful lake that we can't wait to go back to in the spring. I think that watching the seasons unfold here will be an incredible trip. It's still a bit like being in a dream.

Friday, February 11

We went shopping today.

That wasn't our original plan, of course, which was to stay in our room and work all day. But we decided we needed to find the branch of our bank that is in Pamiers and, while we were there, we figured we might as well go looking for things that we'll need when we move into the house next week.

The drive to Pamiers was fantastic. The Pyrénées looked more spectacular than ever, the snow on them was shining in the sun. It was hard to believe that we've got that magical site to look at any time we want!

A small weirdness when we got to the outskirts of Pamiers though. The police had the *route nationale* closed off. We still don't know why. We had to make a massive detour to get back to town, which we didn't really mind. We're getting into a very relaxed mindset here, not taking these little interruptions in our day too much to heart.

Finding the bank proved relatively easy. Then, we had a coffee in the Café Havana and walked around town for a while. Maggie is getting very good at this stuff, staying by my side, not pulling and usually not suddenly crossing in front of me to trip me. She didn't seem the least bit fazed by the cars going by right next to her in the narrow streets, which is great progress.

Then, we headed off to find the Conforama outside of town. We'd actually passed it when we'd taken the detour in the morning. However, we had a little bit of a problem finding it again from the other direction. We made it eventually, just in time for it to close for lunch.

Now, in L.A., that would have driven me nuts, because I would have driven through horrible traffic to get somewhere and knew that there was even more horrible traffic awaiting me on my return. But here, we just decided to find a place to have lunch ourselves!

We had the most "American" of our experiences since being here, because the Conforama (which is a bit of a combination between a mini-Ikea and a Circuit City) is in a big, outdoor shopping center, not a mall, *per se*. Part of the center is an actual mall though, which has a Carrefour as well as a bunch of other stores and restaurants. The Carrefour is the equivalent of a Target or Wal-Mart, but with food as well as all the other kinds of things. I can see us going there once a month or so to get non-food items that will be hard to find at the little markets here in town.

Although you can take dogs into a lot of places, food stores are not one of them, so JM sat on a bench with Maggie while I wandered the Carrefour to find a few items that I needed. Then, we went looking at the food choices. One end of the mall had a cafeteria and the other one had a brasserie. The cafeteria actually looked more appealing, but with Maggie, our bags, etc., it looked too complicated to try and maneuver around getting food. So, we walked back to the brasserie. Not a great choice to be honest. It wasn't bad, but it wasn't particularly good either. The service was actually the worst we've encountered since being here, including in Paris and on the autoroute. They weren't rude, just incredibly indifferent. Still, it gave us a place to hang while we waited for the Conforama to open again.

At a bit after 2 p.m., they did just that. They also don't allow dogs, so we left Maggie in the car while we went shopping.

Again, Conforama is not the high end of things. But it's got well-priced, serviceable goods. The people were very pleasant and they seem willing to negotiate prices if you're buying enough stuff. We checked with our friend Philippe from Pamiers and they have a good reputation around here.

We were able to get a foldout couch/bed that we will certainly be able to use even after our furniture arrives. We also bought a small computer desk and a couple of chairs, so we'll be able to work and sleep. We need to either find a friend with a van or else we can rent one from Conforama to bring the stuff home, then take it back to them afterwards.

Most interestingly for us, though, was being able to look at a bunch of kitchen appliances as well as kitchen cabinets, etc. I think we'll be able to go back there after we've signed for the house and place an order for a stove, washer, dryer, fridge, dishwasher and television set all at once. The nice young woman we talked to felt they'd make us a deal on such a large order, so hopefully we'll be able to save some money. That stuff they'll deliver as well.

Then, like Ikea, they sell kitchen cabinets, etc. We saw something that we liked and, while not the high end of the line, will be perfectly serviceable and attractive. I think I can make compromises in some areas so that I can get exactly what I want in others.

We drove home feeling that we'd be able to buy what we need and still stay within our budget, which was a bit of a relief, since we'd been worried that we would have to spend way more money to be happy with the kitchen. Now, I can concentrate on finding floor tiles, etc., to make things look the way I want.

As always, it felt good to come home to Chalabre. We're excited about getting our house next week, but we'll also miss living in the hotel. I love coming home and being able to talk with Didier and Marielle. They have lots of good tips about doing things in the area and they're both just really sweet people.

In fact, I found out something fun today! Chalabre has a Carnival in April! Everyone gets dressed up in disguise and goes around the town dancing. It sounds fantastic! I can't wait to see it. Of course, JM says that he thinks they're building a wickerman outside of town!

Also, Limoux is the Carnival capital of the region. Every Sunday for three months, there are different groups that dress up and go around the town. At the end, all of the groups go around the town together! It sounds like something that we shouldn't miss, so maybe we'll check it out this weekend.

Sunday, February 13

We got back too late last night for me to write my daily entry, so I'm playing catch up today.

We had our first disappointment Saturday morning. It was market day in Chalabre. Maybe it's because we're in February, but we were sorry to see that our market was not up to our expectations. First, no one uses the lovely covered market place in the center of the village. I suppose it's really too small for the way people do things today. A lot of the food vendors have large trucks with their stock laid out on display cases inside, so it wouldn't be possible to have them in the covered market.

The other surprise was that the market actually takes place right outside our door on Cours Colbert! Talk about convenient. But I guess we need to remember not to park in front of our house on Friday nights if we want to use the car on Saturday morning.

There were very few vendors. One butcher van, two vegetable stands, one lady making veggie galettes that looked and smelled very good, one van doing rotisserie and the few other vendors really looked like they were mostly selling used clothes and similar items. I guess we'll be going to the market in Mirepoix or Limoux for now. I need to research the days that they have theirs, although I know at least one of Mirepoix's days is Monday.

The covered market

There were very few vendors. One butcher van, two vegetable stands, one lady making veggie galettes that looked and smelled very good, one van doing rotisserie and the few other vendors really looked like they were mostly selling used clothes and similar items. I guess we'll be going to the market in Mirepoix or Limoux for now. I need to research the days that they have theirs, although I know at least one of Mirepoix's days is Monday.

I did stop back by the Vival, which is a local mini-mart, and picked up a few apples and other items. I have to say that their produce is really of an excellent quality, so I don't mind at all buying things there. Since we're in prime apple growing territory, the apples are just wonderful around here. We've been eating a few a day, which is a habit we plan to continue.

After working in our room for a couple of hours, we headed out to find somewhere to have lunch. We found a place that we're determined to go to frequently: Le Munich. It's on the road to Pamiers in the village of Rieucros and, bizarrely, is an Alsatian restaurant! Yesterday was cold and damp (weather which continues today) and it seemed the perfect time to sample a *choucroute*.

For anyone not in the know, *choucroute* is an Alsatian specialty of various sausages and other meats with a large serving of sauerkraut and boiled potatoes.

The Munich does an absolutely wonderful meal! Their sausages are fabulous, some of the best we've ever tasted. Many of their products are delivered twice a week from Alsace, so they're definitely authentic. They also make their own apple strudel, which was just heavenly served with a bit of vanilla ice cream. I can see we'll have to be careful not to go there too frequently though, or we'll both have to buy bigger clothes.

After lunch, we drove on to Pamiers to see our friends Philippe, Bernadette and their son Mikael. They have an adorable little Bichon Frisé named Layla, and we were impatient to introduce Maggie to her. We were surprised to see that they also have a "boarder," a yellow lab named Melba who belongs to a friend of theirs. Melba is staying with them for a few weeks.

Luckily, all three girls seemed to get on well. Layla, who is about the size of either of the other dogs' heads, doesn't seem to be aware of her size at all and joined in all the fun. However, Maggie still seems to be feeling a little insecure and after a while did not want Melba coming near either JM or me, the same way she acted with Charlie Dog in Woodland Hills. I suppose we'll never be able to tell her she doesn't have to worry. Perhaps after we're all settled into a real house again, she'll calm down about that kind of thing a bit.

Bernadette and I left the boys and went out to visit Lapeyre, which is a bit like the kitchen/bathroom/window section of Home Depot in the States. It turned out to be a worthwhile visit, because I think I've found the kitchen that I want to put together from their various catalogs, including the tiles for the floors.

JM and I need to go back and talk to them tomorrow to discuss the best way to proceed. We don't know if we should consider letting them install the kitchen and master bath if they can start before our architect, or just buy what we want from them and let Bruno handle finding the workers to put everything together. It's all going to depend on time and budget, especially budget!

We spent the rest of the afternoon and evening with Philippe and Bernadette, which is always fun. We reminisced about how odd it was that Philippe had written to JM out of the blue about six years ago, which is probably what put this whole move of ours into motion. We would never have come to this part of France if we hadn't already visited them here and knew that we had friends in the area. Another case of the Internet being used as a force for good.

After dinner, we drove back home. We're still marveling at how, even though we are driving a farther distance, it still takes less time than going anywhere in L.A. on most days. It's so peaceful and beautiful driving the roads, even at night. And, of course, I need to get used to keeping my eyes peeled for deer! Quite a change from keeping my eyes open for a traffic jam.

Today the weather was just not fun at all. We decided it was a perfect day to stay inside and work, which we've been doing since this morning. We had a quiet lunch in the hotel bar, where I had another of my interesting conversations with Marielle. I tried one more dish that I always said I wouldn't eat. And, I had a small glass of Muscat (a sweet wine) with my meal. I figured I didn't have anything else to do today, so it would be interesting to see if I got a migraine or not. So far, so good. I'm determined to be as open-minded about trying new things as possible now that we're living here. It's difficult sometimes not to stick to old routines. But what's the point of doing that when you've changed everything else about your life?

Monday, February 14

Snow!

Last night, when we went to bed the weather was foul. An icy rain was falling and the wind was howling. We took Maggie out for her last walk of the night and everyone cracked up because we finally broke down and put on her raincoat from L.A. We knew people would find it funny, but she really, really was miserable in the weather and we thought at least that way she wouldn't get quite as wet.

When we woke up, the rain had clearly turned to a dusting of snow overnight. Nothing big, but it looked quite pretty.

Since today was Monday, the day the hotel is "closed," Marielle had left us a breakfast tray outside our door before they headed off for a day of sightseeing with friends. We ate, then decided to head out to Mirepoix to see the market, then on to Pamiers to talk with the kitchen/bath company a bit.

By the time we got down to the car, it had *really* started to snow! But the roads seemed fine, so we decided it would be OK.

Outside of town, the snow was starting to stick to the ground and the trees. It started to turn into a bit of a blizzard. I wasn't sure about continuing, but JM said to keep going, so we did. However, at Mirepoix we realized a couple of things. First, walking around the outdoor market would *not* be fun in the snow. Second, if we did go to Pamiers, we had no guarantee that the road back to Chalabre would be passable when we got back. As far as I can tell, there are no chains in the rental car, and even if we had them, I have absolutely no idea how to put them on.

So, instead, we stopped at the Super-U that we get to just when we enter Mirepoix. It's a big supermarket and we thought we'd pick up some supplies to eat at the hotel.

Luckily, French supermarkets have all kinds of wonderful goodies, and it was more of a problem choosing than finding something. The Super-U has a terrific cheese department, so we headed there first. In December, we had tasted a wonderful local cheese and we found some of it and had the cheese lady give us a nice chunk. Then, we went to the deli section. I'm always astonished by the wide variety of salamis and different kinds of ham that one sees here. Even the things that are in commercial packaging are usually of a great quality. However, the one thing I don't usually like to buy in supermarkets is bread. You're almost always better off at the local *boulangerie* for that.

We also thought to pick up some inexpensive cutlery, paper plates, etc. After all, we'll still need to be using those things once we move into the house.

When we got back to the car, the snow was a bit lighter and we probably could have gone on to Pamiers, but we had one big errand back in Chalabre and were eager to get on with it. The roads were relatively clear, but everything on the side of the road was covered in snow and looked just beautiful.

After putting things the "refrigerator" or more accurately, on the ledge outside our window, we headed over to Cours Colbert to introduce ourselves the seller of our house! She had arrived in town last night and said we could come over to meet.

It was weird going back inside the house after not seeing it since December. I was worried that I wouldn't like it anymore. But we still got the same good feeling about it and were able to see beyond all of the furniture and weird wallpaper to what our life will be like when we've made it ours.

We were also concerned that we might not get on with Mme. Poole, who will be living next door to us at least part of the time. However, we seemed to get along fine. She likes our ideas of what we want to do to renovate the place and had actually wanted to do many of them herself, but her late mother had objected at the time and she wasn't able to carry them out. She agreed that we could return tomorrow with our architect to take measurements and take a good look around. We parted on excellent terms, which was a big relief.

Back in our room we enjoyed our picnic feast. Diva Maguy (Maggie) shared our ham and even ate all her kibble, then had some cheese. Now, Maggie really doesn't usually like cheese, but this she really gobbled up. She really is quite the little food snob, is Maggie. The other day at the shopping center, she absolutely refused to eat the ham from the mediocre *croque-monsieur* I had ordered, whereas she eats just about everything Didier cooks and gobbled up the good quality ham at lunch today. What can I say? She knows quality when she smells it.

Didier

After working for a couple of hours and dealing with yet one more annoying banking problem (resolved), we decided to go out for a drive. At first we were going to try once again to go to Pamiers, but after having been thwarted twice in that endeavor, it just seemed like too much of a hassle. Instead, we chose to head towards Puivert, which is another medieval city about 10 or 15 kms away. It's up a bit higher in the mountains and it had had quite a bit more snow than we had in Chalabre. Everything was simply stunning to see. We really felt as if we were driving through a Currier and Ives print. We stopped to walk Maggie in a grassy spot by the side of the road and I'm not 100% certain that she was as enamored of it as we were. I think she wonders where her California Sun has gone.

We spent the rest of the evening in our room, finishing off the remains of our picnic and working, then a final walk around the village before coming in for the night. We're really starting to get excited about being in our own space by the end of the week. It will be wonderful to have more than one room in which to live again.

Tomorrow, we confront the French administration in the form of a visit to the local Social Security representative. That should prove to be an interesting experience.

Tuesday, February 15

Today was our day to confront French Social Security, which, unlike in the U.S., is the medical insurance system and *not* retirement.

Everyone in France has to have medical coverage and what you pay, and which particular organization you pay to, is based on your profession and income.

Since JM did work in France for a while before coming to live in California, he was a part of the system long, long ago. I've never lived here so I am not. In theory, because we're "authors," we will eventually be covered the AGESSA which is a complicated acronym (the French love those) for author's social security "*caisse*." However, because we have not as yet earned any income in France, we don't qualify for our first year. So, instead, we're going to be covered by what's known as the CMU, which is the basic Social Security for people who don't earn any money.

We need to provide one year's worth of income tax returns, and then our premiums will be calculated on the difference between our income and their minimum salary level. We made *very* little money in the year that they are requesting, so my guess is we'll be paying a very small amount for our first year.

Social Security covers about 70% of the medical costs, so then you take a complementary insurance plan, or *mutuelle*, to cover the difference, which for us we've already calculated to cost around $60 a month. We can't do any of this until after we officially own the house tomorrow afternoon. Then, we can fill out the paperwork, get the photocopies that we need and go back to see our local Social Security rep, M. Bonnet, who comes to the village once a week.

We had a nice lunch with our local notary, Maître Duchan. It was quite interesting, because JM and I found out some differences about the way issues of marriage and inheritance work here in France. We'll need to do some paperwork there as well, just to make sure that we're both protected in case of something horrible and unthinkable happening. Of course, eventually, the conversation turned to U.S. politics, which is always interesting while, at the same time, being depressing.

At around 3 p.m., Bruno Geli, our architect, came by and we went back to see our new house. Mme. Poole is really very nice and we all wound up having a great afternoon.

There is a fair amount of work that needs to be done, but most of it is decorating. However, there are still some structural things that definitely need to be taken care of. Knocking down the wall in our master bedroom shouldn't be too complicated, although the pipes for the radiator run along the top of it, so that will probably require some planning. Also, the floor in the master bath and bedroom slopes pretty heavily, which, considering that the house was built in 1840 (that's a definitive date now), is not too surprising. I've checked with other friends who have old houses and that's a pretty common problem. We may need to do something about that, especially for the bathroom part, otherwise it will be hard to put in a shower, and new fixtures.

The biggest headache (literally) is the door to the first floor bathroom. Seriously, did a hobbit put it in? It comes just to the height of my forehead. Even though I *know* it is there, I banged right into it again yesterday. I thought I'd given myself a concussion. I've suggested closing off the door that currently exists, we can put in a new door by giving up the walk-in closet in the guest bedroom/library. We don't really need that closet anyway, and we can put a normal height door in without it being too complicated.

We've definitely changed our minds about sealing off the fireplace on the ground floor. It does take up a large part of the wall for the new kitchen, but *wow,* is it a terrific fireplace! Mme. Poole has been using it since coming to town on Sunday and it heats up practically the whole house all by itself! We sat in front of it, talking and drinking tea, and were all so cozy I couldn't believe it. Maggie just curled right up and went to sleep as if she'd been living there her whole life. I have the feeling we'll be using it all the time. It does, however, mean we have to seriously rethink the kitchen design.

Bruno hopes to have the plans for all the work drawn up in three weeks or so, then we can start interviewing subcontractors. So, that means no actual work will get done for at least a month.

When we woke up this morning, we found that it had snowed much more during the night. The ground is covered and everything looks like a postcard. I'm going to go out after breakfast and take some pictures. However, I'm not sure if it's going to snow more today or not. It looks a bit as if it might. Our plan for today was to go and visit France Telecom in Carcassonne to get things rolling for our phone and DSL, but I don't think I want to chance the road between Chalabre and Limoux today if there's a lot of ice on it. We'll have to play it by ear, I guess. I'm definitely going to have to get snow tires and chains for Beanie when she arrives.

Wednesday, February 16

Despite the snow on the ground this morning, we decided we would head out to do our errands. It's interesting to drive in this weather, because a few kilometers of distance seem to mean huge differences in the weather conditions.

Chalabre is at about 1,200 or 1,300 feet, so we get more snow than they do in the areas that are more in the plains.

We drove to Pamiers first to do some banking. There were some snow flurries but nothing on the ground. Then, we headed to the outskirts of Pamiers to pick up some catalogs from the home improvement store. There, the parking lot was a mass of slushy ice and snow, and it was only about 6 kilometers from the center of town.

Since it was still not even noon, we figured we might as well go to Carcassonne to talk to France Telecom about our phone and DSL connections. On the way, we stopped in the village of Montreal to have lunch.

It was a cute little restaurant called the Auberge des Dominicains and was actually almost packed, which is always a good thing. I was surprised to see what a young crowd of people were there, including the owner. I couldn't help but wonder where they all worked in the area, because it was about 15 kilometers away from Carcassonne and I couldn't imagine anyone driving all that way for lunch when they work in an office or somewhere.

At any rate, one of the best things about the restaurant is that they greeted Maggie as if she was a human guest, which I always think is a positive sign. The owner has a Brittany Spaniel named Pepsi, who also seemed to be quite taken with Maggie. The two of them were playing and having a great time. The owner said we had to come back so that Pepsi could see her new friend!

Then, we drove on to Carcassonne and found the telephone store. The lady who helped us was also a dog fan. She has a Sheltie and wants to get a Border Collie, so she was asking all sorts of questions about Maggie. Do you see a pattern here?

It turns out that rather than making things more complicated, having Maggie with us actually opens doors and makes things better. People start out by being warm and friendly, so we don't have to break down any barricades.

All went well on the ordering end of things and we will have an official land line telephone installed Monday morning. Then, we should get our DSL installed a week to ten days later. We need to find out what speed they can provide as, right now, depending on your location, France Telecom offers up to 8 MB, which is just amazing. I have the feeling though, from what other people have told us, that we'll probably only be able to get 2 MB, which is still great, especially after using this horrible cell phone card connection.

By the time we left Carcassonne, the snow was starting to fall again. I wanted to take the long way home, but JM convinced me that we should try the road through Limoux, which is much closer. The problem is that between Limoux and Chalabre, the road is extremely winding and goes up very high in altitude. It's completely beautiful and stunning in good weather, but can be a bit on the terrifying side when the weather is bad.

Today was a terrifying kind of day. Although in general the roads around here seem to be plowed pretty quickly, not all of the parts of the road get the same attention. There were parts of the Limoux road that had not seen anything resembling a snow plow and with the snow falling and wind blowing, as well as the fact that the temperature in some places was down to several degrees below freezing, it was not a ton of fun. JM declared himself impressed with my driving, but I was white knuckled for a good bit of the time. Skidding on black ice could have taken us over the edge of a steep drop a few times, which really wouldn't have been a lot of fun.

Still, we made it home safe and sound and I was glad to park the car and come inside.

Around 6:30 p.m., Marielle called us from downstairs to say we were expected for an aperitif. We had no idea who could be expecting us, so down we went. It was Mme. Poole! She said she had missed seeing us today and so had taken the chance on dropping by.

That really made our day. We all hit it off really well and I know that we'll get along fine as neighbors when she's in the village. I'm guessing that she feels relieved as well, because I think she was worried about what kind of people would buy a house to which she is obviously still very attached emotionally. We invited her to join us for dinner tomorrow night to celebrate signing the documents for transfer.

While we were in the bar, Violette, whom we'd met on the Sunday we arrived, stopped in with her son, Anthony. We chatted a bit, then Mme. Poole left and we headed upstairs to work until dinner. There were a fair number of people in the restaurant tonight. When we finished eating and were coming up to the room, everyone wanted to talk a bit and play with Maggie. Violette and Anthony were having dinner as well, so I went over to talk a little more. It made us realize how lucky we were to find a place like this to live. After only being here for a week, we already feel as if we're being accepted as members of the community. I have to admit, it's a very good feeling.

The only dark cloud on my personal horizon is that I'm suddenly feeling as if I might be getting the beginnings of a sore throat. So many people that we know are sick right now, it's been hard to stay away from them. I hope I'm just imagining things because I'm tired. Being sick would not be convenient!

Friday, February 18

We are *Home Owners*!

Yesterday afternoon we did it. We signed all the papers and now officially own our new home in Chalabre. We're going to start moving in today.

When we got up yesterday morning, it had snowed even more heavily overnight. If you didn't need to drive in it, it was really beautiful to look at. I took my camera out after breakfast and took pictures of the village in its blanket of white. As soon as we have a normal speed Internet connection, I'll load them onto our website.

We stayed in the hotel for the rest of the day working, until it was time to go over to meet Mme. Poole at the house. We're so pleased that we've all hit it off, because this has been a difficult experience for her and I think it helps to have us come over there to talk a bit. She's only had a week to do what JM and I took over a month to do in Reseda, and we'd only lived in our house for 20 years. Her grandparents lived in this house and her parents never threw anything away in all their years living there. So, it was filled with memories as well as being a difficult thing for a single person to clear up on their own.

We all walked over to the Notary's office together, then went back to Cours Colbert to celebrate with a fire in the wonderful fireplace and a cup of Ovaltine! The funniest part was that. as soon as we were back in the house, Maggie insisted on being let into each and every room! She went up the steps, stood at a door, walked around the room, went up to the next level, etc. Then, she happily went back down to the living room to settle near us and the fire. I do believe she knows that this is her new home. We were all fascinated.

The rest of the afternoon passed quietly in conversation, then we all came back to the Hotel de France to celebrate with dinner.

JM and I are feeling very lucky to have found this wonderful village. I know that I feel that we've made the right choice in coming here.

Now the hard work of getting the house set up begins.

Sunday, February 20

Today is Sunday. I didn't have time to write anything yesterday, so there's a lot of catching up to do.

On Friday, we started bringing our bags over to the house. Nicole was waiting for an antique dealer to come and take some of her furniture. Our friends Marielle, from the hotel, and Vincent, a really nice local bloke who does beautiful home restorations, came over with us to have a look around.

Marielle convinced me that two of the pieces in the house: a bookcase and a buffet in the kitchen, were actually beautiful old antiques that just needed some restoration. I felt that we should keep them, because they really feel as if they belong in this house. Eventually, I'll have them refinished and put the buffet in the dining room to store dishes and the bookcase in my office.

Then we all took a look around. Both Vincent and Marielle were wowed by the plasterwork on the ground floor ceiling. It was all done by Nicole's grandfather, who was a master plasterer. Apparently, we've got the only house in Chalabre with ceilings like this.

As we looked around the house, Vincent was very kind to share the benefit of some of his knowledge about house restoration with me. He has very graciously offered to consult on any questions we might have, even though he's totally booked up for the next three years and can't do any of the work himself.

In particular, he thought the estimates we had for the terrace/attic were outrageous. That made me feel much better, as if it's something that we can hope to realistically accomplish if we get the plans approved.

After helping Nicole move a few more things into her house, she and JM went over to the *Mairie* (town hall) to see about getting a couple of extra dumpsters in front of the house and to find out who to contact about changing the water over to our name.

The Mairie de Chalabre

Then, JM, Maggie and I took off for Conforama to pick up our fold-out couch, desk and chairs. We finally got to stop at the *Poulet sur le Toit* (Chicken on the Roof), which does some kind of barbecued chicken. I'd wanted to stop there because the name cracked me up.

Well, it was interesting but not particularly good. Very little actual chicken on the chicken! It was even hard to come up with pieces to share with Maggie.

Still, it was pretty fast and on the way. We got to Conforama just before two o'clock, when they open after lunch.

When they brought out the bed, any hopes we had of bringing our stuff home in the rental car were quickly dashed. It might have worked if we had a roof rack, but without it, no way.

So, we rented their little truck for 39 euros for two hours (they actually gave us two-and-a-half for no extra charge, because we had to drive so far). They loaded it and we set off. All in all, except for the total lack of any suspension, it was better to drive than the Beast we drove down from Paris. Maggie got to sit up front, which I think she liked, and we made the first leg of the trip back to Chalabre in under 40 minutes.

Unloading was not overly fun, but we managed, then got back into the *camionnette* and headed back to Pamiers. We did the whole round trip, including unloading, in under two hours, which was pretty impressive.

Then, we headed over to Carrefour to buy a few things for the house. We didn't have a one-euro coin on us, so we couldn't get a shopping basket. Although I understand the reasoning behind it, which is to keep people from leaving their carts all over the place, it's still kind of annoying.

At any rate, we managed to get a few things, then headed back home again. We unloaded them into the house, even getting to leave the now-hated dog crate here. We were too tired to try setting up the couch, so went back to the hotel for our final night.

Saturday, it snowed again. When I took Maggie for her morning walk I brought the car back to the hotel so it wouldn't get blocked by the market in case we needed it. We had breakfast, then started to bring the rest of our bags over.

At first, even with the snow, we did it on foot. I started unpacking while JM went back for more. However, after a while, the snow was falling heavily enough that we decided to load the car with the final bags and drive over. That was it. We were moved out of the Hotel de France, our home for the last two weeks and finally installed in our new home on Cours Colbert.

Snow in the Rue du Presbytère, behind our house

We had a nice picnic lunch with Nicole, put together our rather complicated bed, and then the Sun came out! How nice to see a blue sky for a change. We all decided to take a walk over to Nicole's garden on the outskirts of the village, then walked along the river Hers for a bit.

It was a great outing. Maggie saw a few more friends, and as usual, someone stopped me to ask all about her. I took the opportunity to praise the benefits of rescue dogs.

We got back home and Marielle called to tell us that we'd left Maggie's bed at the hotel! The horror. JM went right over to get it. Although, to be honest, she didn't use it last night, choosing instead to sleep on the rather hideous orange couch in our room.

Nicole showed me the ropes on how to run the heater, the hot water tank, the various door locks, etc. Then we decided to go out to dinner. It was snowing rather heavily by then and we even had lightning and thunder. I didn't even know you *could* have lightning and thunder in a snowstorm.

We wanted to drive to Rieucros to have a choucroute at the Munich, but when I started trying to drive, the car was sliding all over the place. It seemed a rather foolish thing to attempt, given the circumstances, so I reparked the car and we all walked back to the Hotel de France for another of Didier's great meals.

Ten minutes after we sat down, the snow stopped and pretty much melted away. I guess we could have gone out after all, but I think we made the right decision.

We were all exhausted by the time we got back home, so it was straight to bed. We slept the first night in our new house! It was quite warm and cozy; in fact, too warm and we had to turn the radiators down during the night.

This morning, I got up walked Maggie and went to buy croissants for breakfast. Then, we decided the suitcases *had* to go. So, we started unpacking as much as we possibly could. I even hung things up in a closet, what a novelty. Now, our room is pretty much luggage free, something that I'd almost given up hope of ever seeing again.

I took Maggie over to the Hotel so I could have a coffee, damn my caffeine addiction, and found out that Vincent is now in bed with a cold or the flu.

When I got home, it was clear that Nicole's cold has gotten worse and I worry that she has bronchitis. We wanted to try for the Munich again at lunch, but she really wasn't feeling up to going out. JM and I didn't want to leave her, so I went and picked up some supplies at the Vival. We may try again tonight, although it started snowing again this afternoon, so I don't know what will happen by later on.

Now to hope that neither of us gets sick. Although at least if we do, we're all snug in our own home, which will make it much easier to bear.

Tuesday, February 22
Sunday was a day spent mostly at home. Nicole was feeling very poorly and the weather didn't make it overly tempting to drive around. We had snow in the morning, then it stopped around lunchtime, but by

dinner it was coming down pretty heavily. We still haven't been back to the Munich for a choucroute!

However, as evening rolled around, Nicole felt better and we wound up getting a pizza from Stella Pizzeria, which is right outside our backdoor. Nothing could have been easier. During the winter months, she's only open Thursday through Sunday for dinner, but it's still darned convenient. We have a *"carte de fidélité,"* which means we get a free pizza for every ten we buy. Such a deal!

The snow stopped and I took Maggie out for her before bed walk. It was just gorgeous. The snow was all crunchy underfoot and the air had that wonderful, fresh snow smell. We both had a wonderful walk. Other people in town were also out walking and those of us who had braved the cold and snow had a special smile for each other, as if we knew something that all those folks still inside did not.

When we got up Monday though, the snow had fallen even more heavily during the night. It was up above ankle height and Cours Colbert wasn't plowed. This was all rather dramatic, because Nicole had to get to Carcassonne for her flight back to England. A friend from the village had promised to take her, but he chickened out when he looked at the road. We said that we would drive her.

France Telecom had promised to send someone out to install our telephone line. But, looking at the weather, we were pretty sure they wouldn't make it. We were wrong. At five minutes after 8 o'clock, they appeared. Very impressive. In less than an hour, holes had been drilled, wire pulled and we were connected to the outside world! The installation crew was a crack up. It was like being in a Marcel Pagnol story: the older, crusty guy and his incompetent apprentice. Maybe we'll write about them one day.

We still have to find out when our DSL will be installed though. I can't wait.

The rest of the morning was spent moving the last bits of what Nicole wanted to keep over to her house next door, then we hit the road.

That was an interesting trip. None of the road between here and the *route nationale* to Mirepoix had been plowed or salted. There are some pretty windy bits too, especially between Camon and Lagarde, where the forest keeps the Sun from ever hitting the road. I basically kept in second gear the entire way. The 20 kilometers to Mirepoix that I usually drive in 20 minutes, took us 45 minutes. Still, we made it with no incident of skidding. We figured that the best bet was to stop and have lunch at Le Commerce before continuing on to Carcassonne.

Now that we've been there several times, everyone recognizes us. I think Nicole was surprised by that. Sylvie, whom we've talked to each time we've been there, also knew Nicole. She used to run the Café de la Paix here in Chalabre and also worked at the refreshment stand in Puivert.

Sylvie was able to give us an end to something that had happened on Saturday night. When we'd tried to go out to the Munich and instead wound up back at the Hotel de France, we had a fright. What we thought was an oil tanker came barreling into town and turned onto the Puivert road at top speed. With the icy snow, we were sure he was going to slam into the corner of the building and take us all out in a ball of flame.

It turns out it was a *milk* tanker. The guy who drives it has a horrible reputation. The tanker goes to the local dairies to collect the milk production. This guy drives like a maniac, taking the roads at high speed, never slowing down and never getting out of the way of on-coming cars. All the people in Puivert know about him and are terrified. As soon as we described what had happened to Sylvie, she immediately knew what the truck was. We love the idea of the mad dairy truck driver.

The only slightly upsetting thing happened when I walked into Le Commerce with Maggie. The hotel's dog had been joined by two other dogs who attacked her! One was an old German Shepherd and he didn't hurt her, but it scared us. We'd never had anything like that happen before. Being the good girl that she is, Maggie didn't fight back, which probably helped her to not get injured. Of course, everyone was upset and apologized profusely. It turns out he's a very old dog who belongs to the owner's daughter, and he was just boarding there for a couple of days. He's a bit aggressive to other dogs because he was feeling insecure, I guess.

We had a wonderful meal, as always at Le Commerce, then set out for Carcassonne. Amazing what a difference of a few kilometers makes. There was no snow whatsoever for most of road between Mirepoix and Carcassonne. We laughed when we realized how weird it must have sounded to the Ryanair people when Nicole asked if her flight was still scheduled for the afternoon.

We made it to Carcassonne in good time, dropped Nicole off, all feeling a bit sad, then JM and I headed back to Mirepoix to buy some household essentials like cleaning products, coffee, etc.

We got a headstart on cleaning, then tried to make dinner. I found out that the oven didn't really get hot enough to cook anything, so we had one more picnic meal, then just kind of crashed for the night.

This morning was our day to head back to the local Social Security office. We turned in our file and should be officially insured in about two weeks or so. Then, we went over to the Town Hall to check on various things. We met the Mayor and the employees of the Mairie. They seemed pleased that there were new people moving to the village who were going to be living here all year round instead of just having vacation homes.

Next, it was back to the Groupama office to sign the insurance contract on our house and get things underway to insure Beanie when she gets here sometime after March 5. Our insurance agent also paints, and we wound up buying one of her pictures.

We got things underway with the local plumber, stopped at the post office to sort things out with our mail, dropped laundry off with Solange and realized that we had done a day's worth of L.A. errands all before lunch.

Now, we're waiting for the *Compagnons d'Emmaüs* (kind of like the Salvation Army) to come by to pick up the last of Nicole's things from the house. It will be pretty empty here then, but it will enable us to feel that we're really getting underway with the renovations.

Friday, February 25

Where to begin! This has been a more than hectic week, made worse by sporadic Internet access; a problem we've now resolved.

The Emmaüs guys finally came to take the furniture. Unfortunately, we totally filled their truck and they couldn't fit everything in, so they have to come back next week for the rest.

After they finished, we decided to take the relatively awful espresso machine I'd bought back to the Super-U in Mirepoix. They have their return policy posted at the door, which states that they do this as long as it's within eight days.

Even though stores here do this, indeed they *have* to do this, many of them are still a bit unclear on the concept. Denise, the lovely lady at the customer service desk, had no problems with it at all. The machine was all there, nicely wrapped in its packaging, etc. However, the store manager, whose personality bore an uncanny resemblance to Basil Fawlty, was not so obliging.

I said I would take a higher-priced machine. However, the only thing they had was a Krups Nespresso. I hadn't wanted something that could only use pre-packaged coffee "dosettes;" however, I had heard good things about the Nespresso and agreed. What I didn't realize at the time was that you can only get the Nespresso dosettes from Nespresso. If I had, I could have avoided some unpleasantness.

I thought I should buy some extra coffee to go with the machine, and of course, they don't sell any Nespresso at the Super-U. Basil's Manuel (another store employee) said that I should just buy one of the other brands of dosettes and that they would work fine. I wasn't convinced, but took a package anyway.

When I got back to Denise, she assured me that they *wouldn't* work, as she has a friend with the machine and knows. She called the Basil, who insisted that they would. He told me that they sold those machines all the time and no one ever complained. I suggested that they look into getting the right coffee, then I would come back and buy the machine.

Basil got pretty nasty at that point. He complained that I'd "used" the other machine and he'd "graciously" agreed to accept it if I took another machine. I explained that I wouldn't have known it didn't make decent coffee if I hadn't used it. Finally, after getting close to having his head explode, he agreed to reimburse me.

I later found out that he has quite a negative reputation around here. The final little moment came when I saw "Manuel" carefully tape up the box of the machine I'd bought and put it back on the shelf without any notice that it had been used. Beware the Super-U!

Finally, we finished and decided to drive to Rieucros for a choucroute. We got to the Munich only to discover that it is closed on Monday, all day, and for dinner on Tuesday and Wednesday nights. Really no luck at all. Instead, we headed back to Mirepoix for dinner at Le Commerce.

On Wednesday, we had an appointment with Bruno the architect and two of the contractors whose names Nicole had given us. That wound up being a rather depressing day. The first contractor told us that we would have to move out of the house for three months while he did the work! I did not like that one bit. The second contractor was an electrician, but he didn't inspire the least bit of confidence in us.

We were really feeling upset, because it became clear that much of what we hoped to do we will not be able to do. I do not want to move into a *gîte* for three months after just getting settled here. Not to mention that the money for living somewhere else would be far better spent on this house than on accommodation.

Marielle came for a visit in the afternoon, which was nice and cheered me up some. Then, Christian Drouin, a local plumber who already knew the house and who does work for Marielle and Didier came to give us an estimate. It was like sun coming out from behind the clouds. We talked a lot about what we wanted to do and he recommended several other contractors in different fields with whom he worked. He thought the idea of us moving out was ridiculous and didn't see any reason why we would have to.

Christian is busy until June, but we've decided that we'd rather wait for him then attempt anything else. He told us he would bring the others to see us on Thursday. Also, he suggested that we get our appliances and he would connect the washing machine so we could actually start to live a normal life.

That got us to realize that we'll just have all our furniture, etc., delivered as soon as it gets to Marseille. Since we'll be doing all the work a bit piece-meal, we'll be able to move from room-to-room as need dictates. The workers will probably start in the kitchen, so we can go in and out through the back door without ever needing to come into the big room until it's finished.[8]

We felt much better doing the work this way. It's a compromise on the one hand, but it also makes things look a little more manageable. We decided to walk over to the hotel to have a sandwich and tell Didier and Marielle.

The two of them kindly offered us dinner on them, which we thought was just a lovely, and unnecessary, gesture. We're so lucky to have met the two of them.

Dinner was delicious, of course. But how could it have been anything else. The surprise of the evening was meeting a trio of diners at the next table. Lizzie, Coral and Peter, expat Brits who live in the nearby village of Rivel. We all started talking when JM got a phone call from L.A. It was one of those moments when people really hit it off and we

---

[8] As you'll see, this was a definite case of *naiveté* on our part! If I've learned one thing from this whole experience, it's not to count your contractors before they're hatched!

talked for several hours. They invited us for apéritifs on Sunday and we all walked over here to show them the house.

It was interesting seeing it with other newcomers. One of the things we hadn't realized was how lucky we were to have central heating in an older house. We've kind of just taken it for granted. They all declared that we'd gotten quite a deal, which made us feel really good, not that we needed outside validation, but it's always fun to have.

A successful Wednesday, after all.

Thursday we had an appointment with Michelle at Conforama to discuss kitchen appliances. I already knew what stove I wanted, but the rest was a bit of a mystery. It's fun buying all new appliances, but it's also somewhat daunting, because they have so many "features" and gadgets that you don't know what you need and what you don't! For some strange reason, we wound up buying everything in either Ariston or Whirlpool. It wasn't planned, it just worked out that way. Then, we got our big "treat," another 42-inch plasma screen TV to replace the one in L.A. We didn't get a Sony this time though, since it would have been 1,000 euros more! I also bought an espresso machine. And, yes, it was a Nespresso. Except this time, Michelle explained that you had to buy the pods from Nespresso by mail or Internet.

They made us a very nice deal for buying everything from them and we also bought another table to use for eating until we get our furniture. Like Ikea, you have to put all their stuff together, so we loaded in the boxes and set off for Carrefour to get a few items before heading home to build.

We had lunch at the cafeteria at Carrefour and, once again, the Diva lived up to her name. She totally refused to eat the food from there. To be honest, I didn't eat it either, so I can't really blame her.

At last, we got home and put together our table. Then, we opened up the desk we'd bought from Conforama last week so we could put that together as well.

There was a fatal flaw in *that* plan. The desk came with an amazingly large array of pieces. When we looked at the instructions, it became clear that there was no way we were ever going to manage to build it ourselves. It needed a drill, a hammer and various other tools that we just don't have. So we bravely tried to get the pieces back into the box (no easy task!), taped the plastic back on with duct tape (how would we survive without that?) and loaded it back into the car. Then, we set off back to Conforama. Luckily, it's a beautiful drive, or I think it would have been annoying.

After the Super-U experience, we were prepared for an argument. But, no. They were astonished about the need for equipment. Apparently, it's very unusual for their items to require any outside tools. Without question, they gave us a credit and we went back inside the store to find a replacement.

We decided we'd be better off with a coffee table that would be more useful in the long run, and figured we should look for one that was simple! No more drawers to build.

Unfortunately, the table I really liked looked a bit complicated. The salesgirl in the furniture department went to her computer to find out how complicated. She came back and told us that she knew what good clients we were (I guess there aren't that many people who buy a whole household's worth of appliances in one morning!) and we could have the already built table from the store! What great news. No more little bits to figure out!

They helped us load it into the car and it was back to Chalabre to meet the "team." Christian had told us they'd be here at seven, so we had just enough time to make it back before they got here.

What a wonderful group of guys they turned out to be. They're full of good ideas and suggestions and they understand our situation, so that they won't suggest things that are too expensive. The painter, Joël, said he would come back this morning to take measurements, then they'll all give us estimates.

We went out back to Stella Pizza for dinner where we had a bit of a surprise. Because of the big purchase at Conforama, JM's credit card is blocked until next week! It's a safety feature on the debit cards here, which I suppose makes sense, but was a bit embarrassing because we didn't have any cash! The pizzeria said we could pay today, but we remembered that still had our U.S. cards, so paid them that way. Phew! What a way to start getting a reputation.

This morning, Joël showed up as promised. We wound up really hitting it off with a great conversation about books and history. This is an amazingly interesting village, filled with eclectic people. It's easy to see ways to do things in the future that will be good for the community. In fact, this morning, the idea of starting up a small bookstore came into the conversation. Who knows? Maybe once we're settled we'll look into doing that.

So, there you have it. It's now Friday evening and we've actually spent the day working!

Amazing. A routine is starting to set in.

Saturday, February 26

All of my recent blogs have been about the actual day-to-day events of our new life. I haven't really had time to reflect on what it all means to me. I thought I would take that time now.

This has been an amazing experience for us emotionally. For any of you who watch *The Gilmore Girls*, it feels as if we've moved to the French version of Star's Hollow. This is a real, quirky, wonderful community, which, unlike what I feared, is very open and welcoming to newcomers.

Now, it's possible that if we didn't speak French we might have had a slightly more difficult time. But I do think that the people of Chalabre are, in the main, delighted to have new residents come to town, no matter where they're from. Of course, when we tell them that JM's great-grandmother was from Rouvenac, which is about 5 kms away, they always seem pleased at the return of a child of the region!

One of the things that I just love about life here is that everyone says hello to you whether they know you or not. I think that for most anglo-saxons, that's a weird thing. In the U.S., we're used to not looking at each other when we walk on the street. We certainly don't say hello to strangers without a good reason! Here, if you are walking down the street and someone is coming towards you, if you don't say "*Bonjour*" or "*Bonsoir*" or something, you look like a snob! No one would dream of walking into or out of a store without saying hello or good-bye to everyone in the place, even if it's in a general kind of way. By the third or fourth time you've seen the same person on your meanderings through town, you're bound to stop and chat. Then, voila! you've made a new acquaintance or even a friend.

In L.A., JM really didn't talk to people all that much. Here, the atmosphere has somehow allowed him to blossom. He loves going out and meeting the villagers for a bit of gossip. It's impossible for either of us to go out for a "quick" errand, because we always run into someone with whom we have a chat. For people who work at home, it's a terrific thing.

No sense of loneliness or isolation at all. Even going to pick up milk is a social event.

I never thought of myself as a "country" person, but since being here, have realized that that is really what I am. I feel totally at peace with this new lifestyle. I've always been weird about bugs and germs and things, but here, I don't seem to worry about any of it. I go down into the cellar to get wood and don't even think to worry about looking for spiders! We have no refrigerator and I just keep things in the garage without worrying about whether they're cold enough (they are!). I don't worry about whether a restaurant has an "A" health certificate (there are none posted), just about whether the food tastes good.

While we were driving back from Mirepoix, we pulled over to the side of the road to get out of the car and look at the stars. You can't see the stars in L.A. 90% of the time. Here, the sky is velvety black and the stars are bright and crisp. It was -3 C (28 F) but we didn't feel the cold, all we felt was wonder at the beauty of all this.

I do miss my friends in L.A., but I don't miss life in L.A., which was a different thing. I know that if I'd had to drive back twice in one day to a store that was 30 miles away, I would have been in a horrible mood. Here, I didn't mind because the drive itself is a pleasure. There is always something beautiful to see on the way, whether it's the snow shining on the Pyrénées or a crane standing in a pond.

I'm not sure what twist of fate brought us here, but it is one to which I will be forever grateful.

Monday, February 28

Yesterday was mostly quiet. We went for an aperitif at the home of our new friends Lizzie, Coral and Peter, who are British expats living in Rivel, the next town south of Chalabre. Lizzie's place is just beautiful. It's the old *café* and has been wonderfully restored. It shows that we've got a long way to go with our house!

We had a great time sitting around and talking. Maggie was completely in love with Lizzie's Springer Spaniel, Dylan. I've never seen her act like such a flirt! The two of them were licking each other's ears and faces, petting each other with their paws, etc. Such behavior from a middle-aged lady like Maggie!

Lizzie

Peter

Florence, Lizzie's other dog, a black lab, took it all in stride, using the infatuation to keep Dylan and Maggie out of the way so that she could hit us up for snacks and pats!

We came home and fiddled with computer stuff for the afternoon. I tried to set up our DSL connection, but I don't think the line is totally "live" yet, so I suppose we'll have to wait for the technician to come on Thursday. Too bad.

The Café Rives *in Rivel*

Last night, we put one of the DVDs that Raven and Ian have been recording for us into my computer and watched television for the first time. It wasn't bad, although what we have that passes for furniture leaves a lot to be desired. We could have gone upstairs and watched in bed, but the fireplace is downstairs and that's a powerful draw!

In fact, when we got up this morning, not only was it really, really cold (-9 C or 15 F), but it had snowed again overnight and there were between two and three inches on the ground. I took Maggie for her walk, then bought bread and made breakfast. Afterwards, I walked to the post office. I have to say that I was pretty darned cold by the time I got back. We did bring the warmest clothes we have, but I suppose California warm and Pyrénées warm are two separate things.

Still, everyone here says that this has been an unusual winter, so maybe we won't have to worry about it next year.

This being Monday, the hotel is closed. Normally we just picnic all day, but with the cold, I really didn't feel like eating only cold food for lunch. Instead, we drove over to St. Colombe and had a very nice lunch at Chez Esmé, which everyone has been telling us to do. We were the first there, so we scored a table right in front of their fireplace!

Then, this afternoon, one of our electricians, Stéphane Montoro, came by. He went through every room taking notes about what we wanted where and says he'll have an estimate by the end of the week. He seems to think it will be considerably less than what we had thought, which will be very nice if it turns out to be so.

Speaking of the Montoros, this morning, when I was out walking Maggie, I ran into one of our "regular" morning dog people. We started talking and I was surprised that he knew so much about us. It turns out he's the father of Manu Montoro, our mason! It just goes to show how small a community this really is. No secrets here!

We had planned to go to Pamiers tonight to visit Philippe and Bernadette, then stop and have dinner at Le Commerce. However, everyone in town is saying that the road between Camon and Lagarde really isn't good today. Considering how cold it has been all day, I would doubt that any of the snow or ice has melted at all, so we decided we'd better not go after all.

Instead, I went out to pick up a few things, and to try and eat something hot, I'm going to attempt to bake potatoes in the fireplace. I've got aluminum foil and hope, so we'll have to see how it goes. Tomorrow,

Conforama is supposed to deliver our appliances, so I'll have the means to really cook for the first time in a month.

Wednesday, March 2

We have a television!

In fact, we've got not only a television, but also a whole slew of appliances. Several of them are sitting in their boxes in the soon-to-be kitchen, awaiting their moment of glory.

Yesterday, the Conforama van pulled up on schedule with two deliverymen and all our goodies inside, well almost... As they were unloading the washing machine, I thought it looked unfamiliar. And, indeed, it wasn't my washing machine at all. The number was one digit different from the one I bought and the stockroom clerk had pulled the wrong thing, so they're coming back tomorrow with the right one. Then, Christian will come over and hook it up for us so I can actually do my own laundry. Ah, the things that sound exciting after several weeks of living out of suitcases.

The fridge was a bit tricky. I bought the tallest one that would fit in the current kitchen and they were doing really well except for the hideous neon light fixture that hangs down from the ridiculously low ceiling. However, impressively, they did actually manage to maneuver everything into place. JM and I thought that we'd have to move the buffet out of the room but it fit without needing to do a thing. It was with a small tear in my eye that I emptied my low-tech non-fridge in the garage to move our food upstairs to where it is a bit more accessible.

I thought I would be cooking by now, but nope. The cooker comes ready to use city gas, not bottled gas. Some mysterious bit called an "injector" apparently needs to be changed first. Why, I don't know, but since I'm basically afraid of gas, I don't want to mess with it. The service tech is coming Monday to set everything up, so it's cold cuts until then. Not that that's suffering here. At the deli counter at Carrefour today I had trouble choosing what to buy. Who knew there were that many different kinds of ham?

We did set up the television today, although that was a bit stressful, because JM and I are not all that strong and it was a bit heavy, but we managed to do it without breaking anything, so we're happy. Tonight, we get to watch Raven and Ian's DVDs on a real television!

Last night, we had dinner with Bernadette, Philippe and Mikael. Melba, the yellow lab was back after a weekend out, and Diva Maggie doesn't let her get away with a thing! During dinner, Maggie chased poor Melba out of the kitchen and if she tried to come back in, Maggie was out from under the table in a flash, giving the poor girl the eye in her best Border Collie manner. No way was Melba going to take a chance with that!

Little Layla, the Bichon Frisé, does not get the evil eye, so she was happily hanging out in the kitchen with the rest of the pack. I wouldn't have put up with her being chased away in her own house.

Today was calm. We went to Pamiers early so that I could get my new bankcard. I feel all official, since I don't have to use JM's credit card now when I go out shopping. Now, it's just like in L.A. I carry all the money and pay for everything so JM doesn't have to even carry his wallet. It's kind of satisfying, really, to find ourselves falling into a normal routine.

Of course, there are plenty of differences. In L.A., JM hardly ever stopped working long enough for a long lunch break. I wonder if that will continue once we're eating at home more often? We also took a break in the afternoon to wander over to the Gamm Vert, a home and garden store near the post office, to look for an electrical extension. Usually, I was the one doing that kind of thing, but it was nice to do it together. Also, to stop and check on if Marielle was feeling better, drop the photos I took of the Vival off for them, etc. It makes the day seem fuller and richer.

Another small incident that shows how nice things are here. I was looking for a knife so we could cut open the television box. I had just walked out the door and our baker-neighbor was just parking in front of the house. He asked how things were going and I mentioned my search. He offered to lend me one of his! I thought that was just so nice of him. I really love this town.

Thursday, March 3

A red letter day here in Chalabre. We got our DSL! Woo hoo! That also means we were finally able to update the pictures on our website

It feels so good to be back connected in a normal way and not fighting over the telephone line again. We're using wi-fi, so we have to take one of the computers upstairs to see if it will work through the stone walls. No bets on that one, I'm afraid.

Our other interesting bit of the day was going back to the Community Center, this time to meet with the person who handles subsidies for doing house repairs. If you have a house that's older than 15 years (no problem there!) and you don't make a lot of money (sadly, no problem there either!), the government will help you bring your house up to current code for things like electricity, window replacement, plumbing, etc. We need to fill out a dossier, then we'll hopefully get a bit of extra money to do the things we need done. Excellent news.

Our beautiful sunshine seems to have disappeared again. We may get a bit more snow tonight, although nothing like what they got up north over the last few days. The *autoroutes* actually shut down to truck traffic, which only clogged them more so that nobody could use them. Not a really great idea.

Still, I don't care. It's beautiful here no matter what the weather. It will be easier when the appliances are hooked up so that we can cook in the house and not have to worry about eating out all the time. But, slowly, slowly things are falling into place. Conforama came back today with the right washing machine and hopefully, Christian will come and hook it up today or tomorrow.

Oh, I made an interesting discovery. I kept wondering why my back hurt. Then I realized! The kitchen sink, the table in the kitchen and even my new stove, are all made for *Hobbits*! They're at least six inches lower than where everything was in L.A. I stopped in to talk with Solange at the Pressing about it. She's very tall too, and she told me that they've had everything in their house raised higher. I told JM that we'd have to ask Manu to put the stove on some kind of platform, otherwise I wouldn't be able to cook.

Tonight, we're going out for pasta, then back home to watch more *Daily Show with Jon Stewart*! Thanks, Raven and Ian!

Friday, March 4

Well, last night wound up being a little more exciting than we planned!

We had decided to go out the backdoor to Stella Pizza for some pasta bolognaise. As we got to the door, we noticed a flashing light outside. "How odd," we thought. When I got the door opened, there was a huge firetruck parked right out back and smoke was pouring from the first floor above the pizzeria! Madame Stella was standing outside with a neighbor, looking a bit in shock.

Apparently, the chimney for the upstairs woodburning stove had caught on fire. The chimney sweep had given it a clean bill of health only a month or so ago! Guess that proves there are no guarantees in life.

Clearly, there was no pasta in our future for last night, so we headed over to the hotel and one of Didier's wonderful creations. I swear I've never tasted better vegetables in my life than what he makes. I'm trying to talk him into writing a veggie cookbook, but he's too modest.

While we were sitting and eating, the local fire siren went off again and we saw another firetruck race by. I don't know where that one was going. Pretty scary stuff and a good reminder that you can't get complacent with these old chimneys.

Today was cold and grey with periods of snow flurries. Nothing serious but not the kind of day to make you feel like wandering around. Instead, we've stayed in working most of the time.

Emmaüs did come by in the afternoon to take the last remaining things that they couldn't fit two weeks ago, so that was nice. I don't think they really wanted all of it, but they took it to be helpful, which we appreciated.

When I was taking Maggie for her afternoon walk, I saw Madame Stella and asked how things went after we left last night. The upstairs room where the fire started is a total loss and the large, beautiful dining room is also destroyed, probably by water damage as much as anything else. She's going to carry on baking pizzas for take out though, so we'll order something for tonight to help her feel more "normal." Amazingly, she thinks she can open the small dining room next week sometime.

It really was lucky that if it had to happen, it happened when it did. Her son sleeps above the room that burned and he might have been trapped in there if the fire had hit later in the night. So, while there was damage, it was only to things and not people. That's the important bit to remember.

Once again we saw how this community pulls together in times of need. No one is anonymous here. I know that for some people that would be a negative, but I consider it one of the true gifts of living here.

Sunday, March 6

It's Sunday and I just walked in from the Patisserie with a beautiful apricot tart that is still warm from the oven! It smells so good, I don't know how we're going to resist eating it before we take it to lunch with Lizzie, Coral and Peter!

Our bakery

Food is the subject of the day. Yesterday, as we were driving to Carcassonne to extend the contract on our rental car until Beanie arrives, we started talking about the differences between French and American food.

In America, food looks beautiful and lasts for a long time in the refrigerator. However, it is all a bit on the bland side. Here, sometimes the produce isn't as perfect, but it has an enormous amount of flavor. Also, there are so many different kinds of a fruit or vegetable from which to choose, and each one has a different taste and texture.

I noticed, for example, that at the Gamm Vert, they're selling seed potatoes for spring planting. There must have been 10 or 15 different varieties there. When I mentioned it to JM, he said he remembered how his grandfather had very specific likes and dislikes about the variety of potatoes he used. Then, we talked about how good the potatoes that I'd cooked in the fireplace the other night had tasted with only a little bit of butter and salt. The potatoes themselves had flavor. When I made baked potatoes in L.A., I always had to doctor them with all sorts of things to make them good. These needed so little to be excellent.

When did the beauty of a fruit or vegetable become more important than its intrinsic quality and flavor?

After we left Carcassonne, we drove home through Limoux, then Quillan and Puivert. It was getting late, so we were looking for a restaurant to have lunch. Because of the season, there are still a lot of places that are closed. We saw a couple of pizza places, but weren't tempted, since we do have Stella's whenever we want pizza. Then, we saw a sign for an auberge in Nebias, a small village near Puivert. We stopped there and they were open.

What a find! It's owned by a husband and wife, he's originally from India and she's originally from Vietnam. He was an engineer at Aero-Spatiale and she was a nurse, then two years ago they decided to follow their dream and open an Auberge! It's all home cooking using fresh ingredients, organic when possible. Normally, you call in advance and request what you want to eat, then she cooks it for you. Yesterday, she had prepared a navarin of lamb and spring vegetables, which was excellent.

We talked more about the nature of food quality. It's true that you can't compare fresh food with stuff that has been sitting on a market shelf for several days. The carrots and potatoes in the stew were rich and bursting with flavor. It made me even more impatient to start cooking again. I just can't wait to start using the wonderful produce that is available here.

Monday, March 7

Oops.

Yes, that's the by-word for today. We're still in the midst of our cold spell, which is not due to change until at least next week. No big snow, but temps down at freezing and below, with a nasty windchill factor to boot.

We went out to pick up a few things in preparation for being at last able to cook tonight (I hope) and were seriously chilled to the bone on our return. We had lunch, then JM noticed that the house felt a bit chilly, which is pretty unusual. He checked and the radiator was cold.

That normally doesn't happen. I went down to the garage and checked on the fuel tank. Yup, *big oops*. We ran out of oil!

We're both surprised that we ran out that fast, but I think that's because we need to get the thermostat fixed and also because, for the first week we were here, the heater had been turned up pretty high.

We cut it back and also turned the radiators in the rooms we're not using way, way down. Still, it was running almost non-stop for that first week, and I think that burned a lot of oil.

Since it's only 1:30 p.m. right now, we can't call for more oil. We'll have to hope that when we get through at 2 p.m. that they can make us an emergency delivery this afternoon or we're going to be very, very cold tonight.

Luckily, we can build a fire while we're downstairs, but that won't help us in the bedroom at night. We'll just have to see what happens.

I knew I needed to keep an eye on this, but it just slipped my mind. I won't let that happen again, that's for sure.

Still, the house is well-insulated, so even though it's not warm, it won't get freezing either. And, we'll have the added benefit of cooking a hot meal if all goes well. Nothing fancy, but hot and that's what counts right now.

Speaking of cooking, I find it really hard to get out of a French supermarket.

There are so many interesting food choices that I just want to wander the aisles and stare. It is almost impossible to make a decision, because I want to try everything! Even the pre-packaged meals and desserts all look appetizing. I'm sure as time goes on I'll find brands I like and others I dislike, but right now I haven't reached that stage.

I didn't want to buy too much until I'm positive that I will be able to cook, so I wound up with a potatoes au gratin/ham dish for dinner and a frozen lasagna. With JM, lasagna is *always* a safe choice!

Add cheese, bread and dessert to either of those and we'll be happy campers. Plus, I picked up some soup that looks like it will be good. I'm always satisfied if I can have soup. I like to make my own, but without pots and pans that will be a little challenging for now.

Think good, warm thoughts for us. More details to come.

Time for a quick update.

The repairman came to change the mysterious parts that make my stove work with butane instead of city gas. However, he asked where the pipe and connector were. "Don't those come with the stove?" I asked naively. Apparently not. We would have to connect them ourselves. Uh oh...

More "uh oh" to come. The stove has an electric ignition for the gas, which most stoves do these days. We could just plug that in, right? Nope. Coming out of the back of the stove is a wire that has to be hard-wired into a plug! "It's easy," says the sadly misinformed repairman. By the time he left, he was looking seriously concerned about our capacities in dealing with anything as complicated as a gas cooker.

We walked over to the Gamm Vert (quickly becoming our favorite store!) and got the mysterious pipe and connector, then came back prepared to connect them to the bottle of gas. Another slight hiccup in the process occurred. We needed a wrench, which of course we didn't have! So, back to the Gamm Vert, where I'm now a regular.

Home again and somehow we managed to connect everything, but we couldn't light the stove. Concerned lest we blow ourselves up with gas and an open fireplace, JM ran across the street to the handy mechanic who also sells bottled gas. Small villages are very convenient for these kinds of things.

The nice mechanic came over and checked our gas connections, which we'd amazingly done correctly. However, the gas bottle was empty. Ah ha, a fatal flaw in the plan! Once we put a new bottle on, everything worked great, although with matches instead of electrical ignition.

So, now I can honestly say "I'm cooking with gas!"

Tuesday, March 8

I'm going to try this again. I just uploaded today's blog and it disappeared!

The thrust of the whole thing is that we've got *fioule*! Which is also known as oil.

Strangely, as we were waiting for the delivery truck to come, the people whom we'd initially tried to call, suddenly showed up at our door. Why they came, we don't know.

But at any rate we couldn't take oil from them since we had already ordered it from someone else. We may never know the answer to this one.

Last night wasn't too horrible after all. Mme. Drouin, the wife of our plumber, loaned us an electric space heater, which took the chill off of our bedroom. Of course it was wonderful down by the fireplace. But the rest of the house was pretty chilly this morning when we got up.

I spoke with my friend, Karine, in the Dordogne. She tells me that in the ten years they've been in their house, they've never heated the bedrooms! I think they're super-human, seriously!

We had to let the *fioule* sit for two hours before we could light the heater. When we finally did that, there were a few minutes when we weren't sure it was going to work. But it finally made its *Vwoosh* noise and took off. Now, the radiators are feeling toasty. In fact, I just took off my top sweater layer.

The other nice thing that happened today was that Stéphane Montoro, the electrician, stopped by to put a plug on our stove so that we can use the automatic ignition. Much easier than throwing matches into the oven and hoping for the best.

I was actually able to cook (well, heat up) dinner last night and lunch today. I'm going to be reduced to that for a few weeks until my pots and pans arrive.

Apparently, the container with Beanie and the rest of our worldly goods did *not* leave Houston last month, but only left last *Thursday*! That means it will be two more weeks for the ship to arrive, then another week for our belongings to be delivered. Luckily, we extended the contract on the rental car, so we should be OK for a while.

This heating up stuff isn't too bad, given the quality of what I've found so far in the supermarket. We had a *gratin dauphinois* with ham (potato casserole) that was amazingly good for something you buy out of a supermarket. I've eaten worse in restaurants in L.A.

Tonight, I may doctor some soup that I bought, serve it with cheese, bread and dessert. Or, I have a frozen lasagna to try. I know what JM is going to want to eat! He has a lot in common with Garfield.

I'm going to try to get out to one of the open markets now that I can cook at least a little bit. I'm dying to try some fresh produce.

Wednesday, March 9

Today was a very quiet day. We went to Pamiers in the morning to do some shopping and I almost couldn't drag myself away from the Carrefour!

JM sat on a bench outside the store with Maggie while I went inside. I'm much better at food shopping when I'm on my own, because I love to wander the aisles and look at everything. JM gets a bit more impatient, because he doesn't understand why I need to take so long!

As always, I was simply amazed that the types of things that are available here, which are so different from what we find in U.S. markets. There's a really wide range of foods, which, in the States, would be considered "gourmet" specialty items, but here are just average supermarket food.

I'm talking about things like patés, cheeses, delicatessen, regional specialties, etc. Almost any one of them would have either sent me running all over L.A. to find, or I would have had to special order online.

Another thing that I like is that portion sizes are a bit smaller. I always found it difficult to buy things for just two people that wouldn't either cause us to overeat, or leave leftovers for far longer than I would feel like eating them. It's much nicer to buy something that we can eat in one meal, or even two, than something that we have to look at for three or four days when we're tired of it. Less waste as well. (And less "waist" too!)

The dairy aisle never ceases to amaze me. The quantity of different desserts, yogurts, etc. is simply mind-boggling. I don't know why no one does anything like these in the U.S. Other than pudding cups and yogurt, there just isn't a lot to choose from. Here, there are *parfaits*, creamy things in all kinds of flavors like rum raisin, biscuit, light chocolate, dark chocolate, white chocolate, caramel, coffee; just about any kind of thing that you want. Yogurts come in a wide variety of flavors, textures, fat content, styles. It would take me most of my life to try them all.

Then, there is the butter: dozens of different kinds of butter from each area of France. Salted, unsalted, partially salted, various fat contents, easily spreadable. It goes on and on.

I don't think I can do more than touch on the cheese, of course. There are, of course, more pre-packaged cheeses than you can shake a stick at. Then, there is the counter where the nice ladies make suggestions and cut your cheese to order. I'm grateful that it's all much more affordable here than it was in L.A., where everything was imported. Because if not, we'd be breaking our budget on cheese alone.

I'm going to have to see if I can take some pictures to share with you. You really do have to see it to believe it.

The Château de Chalabre

Thursday, March 10
Today turned out to be absolutely beautiful.

After lunch, JM and I decided we needed to go out and just *be* in the Sun. We headed out with our camera and Maggie, with no goal in mind but to simply enjoy.

First, we walked around town, taking pictures of Chalabre under the sun, something that we haven't really been able to do before.

Then we took the car and decided to head towards Limoux. But first, we drove up to the Château to get some pics from there.

During the summer, the Château does medieval re-creations, so they have a stable and horses for jousts, etc. I don't know if the majority of the horses live there all year round or not, but there is a very old, retired horse that hangs out in a paddock next to the Château. Today, a very sweet pony joined him.

While JM went to take pics, I took Maggie over to see the horses close up. She seemed quite fascinated, but was well behaved. The horse was not completely sure about our presence and, although he sniffed my fingers, decided to back off a little bit from the Diva. However, the pony seemed to be fascinated by our presence and came up from the far end of the paddock to see what we were doing.

One of the horses kept at the Château de Chalabre

Now, he wasn't all that much bigger than Maggie, and I think at first she thought he was a funny-smelling, weird dog. The two of them actually sniffed noses, which was really cute.

Then, I think Maggie realized he was *not* a dog and decided he needed to be watched for herding potential. She planted herself outside the paddock and just stared. I tried to take her back to the car and she just lay down and wouldn't budge. Eventually, reluctantly, she came along with me.

Back in the car, we just started driving through some of the small back roads in the area, exploring. It really is astonishingly beautiful here. We would drive from totally dry ground and, suddenly, around a curve, unmelted snow was everywhere.

We wound up at Lac Montbel, and were blown away by how large and gorgeous it is. I have the feeling that the whole area must be pretty heavily overrun by tourists in the summer, but looking at it under the sunlight today, I can't say that I really blame them.

MONTBEL

Lake Montbel

The village of Montbel

Lake Montbel is an articial lake created in 1985, which serves as the main drinkable water reservoir for the nearby city of Toulouse (over 1 million population).

Chalabre and the neighboring villages get their water from local sources. The side of the lake opposite to the last picture features a beach, boats and facilities for diving, sailing, surfing and canoeing.

The old village of Montbel still sits on a hill overlooking the lake.

Friday, March 11

One more step on the road to normal life today: our washing machine is hooked up! I'm typing this to the gentle sound of clothes getting clean. It's a good sound.

We also got a cool new wireless thermostat, so we should be using less heating oil as well. The heater totally turns off when it reaches the right temperature, whereas before, it ran almost constantly, which can't have been good.

Last night, our mason, Manu, came by to discuss the various issues he needs to deal with. He's going to come over in about two weeks to see if the stone in the downstairs walls is in good enough shape for us to be able to have them show. I would love that if it were the case. He also had some really good ideas for the kitchen, which makes me eager to get started on remodeling. Still, I need to be patient.

I think that doing all these jobs slowly is really going to work out well. First, we get to know the artisans with whom we'll be working and second, it gives us a chance to think about what we really want, without making rushed decisions that we'll regret later.

Tomorrow, the roofer is coming to look at the skylight and see if it can be repaired or if it needs to be replaced. He's also going to consult on the bathroom door height problem, which is the work that will be the most complicated to do.

I'm getting used to doing things differently than I have been for the last 20 years, and that's not a bad thing. Slowing down, simplifying, enjoying life, these are all benefits of this new existence.

Sunday, March 13

The weather seems to have turned to spring here. Both yesterday and today were just beautiful: cold in the morning but delightful in the afternoon. It seems to have brought everyone out of hiding.

Our market was bigger and busier than I've seen it before, both with more merchants and more buyers. I wound up finding all kinds of thing that I needed for the kitchen from one of the stands. Then, I bought a beautiful rotisserie chicken and some vegetable fritters for lunch. It was all excellent.

On the house side of things, we had a small problem with our long-awaited washing machine! When I started my second load of laundry Friday night, it started to leak! But our wonderful plumber, Christian, came by on Saturday and tightened one of the connections which had come loose because it was too close to the wall.

Also, another roofer/carpenter came by to look at our skylight and help work on the ever-present first floor bathroom door problem. The more people we have trying to figure it out, the better off we'll be.

After our delicious chicken lunch, JM and I walked up to the castle to visit the horses. Maggie managed to scare the ponies, who now don't trust us at all. Not that I blame them, she was looking particularly wolf-like during our visit.

Our friends Philippe and Bernadette came over to have dinner with us at the hotel. But before that, Bernadette and I had time to walk around the village and I finally paid a visit the small fruit/vegetable/cheese store and bought some amazingly good cheese along with farm fresh butter! Heavenly.

This morning dawned even more beautiful than yesterday. It was warm enough to go out with just a sweater and no jacket! I couldn't believe how great that could feel after the last month of cold and damp.

Our British friends, Lizzie, Coral and Peter, picked us up and we all went to Rieucros for a *choucroute* at the Munich, where we're now considered regulars. That's one of the things I love about living here, getting to know the people with whom we do business and bringing them new customers.

After lunch we drove through the countryside and were blown away, as usual, by the beauty of this region. The sky is a crystal clear blue, the Pyrénées are majestic, the rivers that crisscross the area are flowing and clear. It is also fishing season and the trout fisherman were out in force. I don't know if they were catching anything, but they sure looked like they were having fun.

We capped off the afternoon sitting in Lizzie's garden, soaking up the sun. It really does feel as if spring is right around the corner and I'm so looking forward to seeing how things change as each season fulfills its promise.

Monday, March 14

The gorgeous weather continues. We opened windows and shutters wide today to let the fresh air blow through the whole house. It got up to 15 or 16 degrees C (about 70 F) in the afternoon and the bakery had to close the blinds to keep all their newly prepared Easter chocolate from melting!

Our nice plumber, Christian, stopped by this morning just to check on whether our washing machine was doing okay. We talked about my new idea for redoing the kitchen and he has offered to loan me some tools so that I can actually attempt to refinish the antique buffet myself! JM remains unconvinced about that, perhaps because he has heard my screams when I've injured myself with various kitchen implements over the years...

Then, at lunchtime, Stéphane Montoro, the electrician, appeared. He had finished the estimate for the electrical work, which actually came in lower than we had anticipated. The even better news is that his current job is going on hold next week, so he can get started working on things here! I can't believe it, we may actually have modern electricity!

The final "house" thing was the carpenter coming to measure the garage door. He thinks he'll be able to install that in ten days or so. That should have it done by the time that our furniture arrives, which will allow us to store things in the garage if we need to. It all seems to be falling into place.

The nice weather has brought everyone in town out to wander and do their errands. It makes us all feel like visiting and chatting, probably because no one really wants to go back inside. It made me really hope that we will eventually come up with the money to do our roof terrace. I just keep thinking about how glorious it would be to sit up there with my laptop, writing this blog in the sunshine and warm breezes.

An interesting side note. One of my American friends went to her local DMV to get a picture ID. They wanted *six* pieces of identity before they would give it to her! Who *has* that many pieces of ID? Everyone in France is always complaining about the bureaucracy, but it seems to me that it's nowhere near as bad as that. JM wanted a new ID card at the town hall today, and he only needed a certified copy of his birth certificate, some pictures and a form he had to sign. Piece of cake!

Something else I've been meaning to mention. There's a great book I read several years ago. *Cultural Misunderstandings: The French-American Experience* by Raymonde Carroll.[9] I found it hugely informative and helpful in understanding how two cultures can look at the same thing so differently. Really a worthwhile read.

Tuesday, March 15

We are officially part of the system! We stopped by the Community Center to find out if there was any news from Social Security, and lo and behold, we have been approved!

It will be several weeks before we get our *"cartes vitales"* which will be our individual medical cards, but we have an officially stamped piece of paper, so that if we need to go to a doctor, we can. We haven't received a bill yet, but I'm sure that will come sooner or later.

Once again we were struck by how pleasant it has been dealing with the *administration* in the area. The nice man who comes once a week to deal with Social Security issues always seems so eager to help us; it's a real pleasure dealing with him. Of course, I know that there are both good and bad bureaucrats, but we've been particularly lucky on this front. Maybe it's the water?

Speaking of water, I think I'm going to disappoint our plumber. I called an *ébéniste* which is someone who restores wood. He's coming next week to look at the two pieces of furniture that I need refinished. I just don't think that my skills are up to working on 200-year-old antiques of that size. If I'm going to do this kind of thing, I think I should start small. Not to mention that it would probably take me close to 200 years to finish them!

His name is Gabriel Chevalley, and I met him at the Hotel de France last week. He's got a good reputation and I like him a lot. Of course, I have no idea how much doing that kind of thing might cost!

---

[9] Still available at Amazon.

I committed my first *faux pas* today. I put out my yellow recycling bin and first, M. Martinez from next-door came over to tell me that it wasn't the right day. A little later, I went over to the butcher's across the street and Didier (yes, another Didier!) mentioned it to me as well. I figured I had better move it before I created a village incident! One of those differences with L.A. that I hadn't counted on. There, people leave their trashcans out for days at a time and no one says a word.

Still, it seems to have been a small thing and I'm now in line with the neighbors. Crisis averted!

Thursday, March 17

I've got to get used to thinking metric!

Yesterday, I decided I wanted to *really* cook, not just throw together dinner from prepackaged ingredients. So, I went across the street to the Boucherie du Kercorb and got a beef roast. It was a filet roast and cost 26 euros for a kilo. At first, I thought it was really expensive, until I started doing the conversion in my head and realized that it actually only came to about $11 a pound (using cost of living as opposed value of the dollar), which is an incredible bargain for filet by L.A. standards.

I also picked up a few potatoes, some fabulous *crème fraîche*, farm fresh butter and more cheese at our local vegetable/cheese shop.

With that, I was able to make a potato gratin: thinly sliced potatoes, lardons (chopped bacon), *crème fraîche*, whole milk, garlic, chives, salt (but *fleur de sel* which is amazingly good) and some cantal cheese. Baked that in the oven for about an hour-and-a-half, then rubbed more *fleur de sel*, garlic, *herbes de Provence* and olive oil on the roast, which I cooked for about 20 minutes on a 500 degree (F) oven.

I know I shouldn't say this about my own cooking, but it was a fabulous dinner. I need to go across the street to tell Didier how much we enjoyed that roast. I can't stop thinking about the leftovers we're going to have for today's lunch.

I'm now getting eager for my kitchen things to arrive, because I will be able to do much more cooking once I have the appropriate tools.

Speaking of metric, we had a funny moment with our electricians. We were looking at the placement of the plugs we need to put in the bedrooms and JM pulled out the American tape measure, because of course, we'd measured all our furniture in inches, not centimeters. The electricians were quite surprised, because they'd never had occasion to run into the American measurement system before. I think they were fascinated by the differences.

Today was also my first attempt as a French teacher! Strange, I know, but it worked out that way. Our British friend, Coral, doesn't yet feel comfortable speaking French, so I've offered to help. I still remember how awkward I felt when I was first learning. I think it might be easier for her to speak with someone who has "been there, done that," and who understands the things that are difficult to learn.

It went pretty well, although on this first day, we did speak more English than French! Next week, I'll try to be better about pushing the French-envelope. Still, I hope that Coral got something useful out of the experience.

While she was here, we did a few small errands in the village, one of which was visiting the flower shop. I've been admiring the beautiful cups and glasses that she has in her window. Today, I found out that Lily hand paints them herself. They're really stunning and quite reasonably priced for all the work that goes into them. I've got my eye on a set of coffee cups, but I'm feeling too guilty to buy them right now.

Friday, March 18

We had our first encounter with the French medical system today. Only it wasn't for us, it was for Maggie!

Yesterday, we went to Limoux to pick up a package. Some of the companies here use a system called *Relais Colis*. They've got a network of stores that act as delivery points for purchases. The idea is that you find one that's near where you live or work, then you don't have to worry about being home to receive a package or have a neighbor take it in for you. Quite clever, really.

We hadn't had time to walk around Limoux before and we quite liked it. Lots of nice stores, including a great pet store with a selection of more natural foods that I can try with Maggie. We walked around for about 45 minutes, then came home through the beautiful mountain road between there and Chalabre.

When we got into the house, Maggie went to her usual spot under our work table and napped until it was time for dinner. When it came time to eat, she couldn't stand up! She couldn't put her left hind leg down on the ground and actually collapsed, poor little thing! I wound up partly hand-feeding her. Eventually, she did manage to stand, but it clearly was uncomfortable.

I took her for a short walk, and surprisingly, after she walked for a few minutes, she seemed to feel better. But once we were back in the house, as soon as she lay down then tried to get up again, the problem was clearly still there.

So, this morning we called a vet in Lavelanet who had been recommended to us by our British friends in Rivel. It turns out that poor Maggie has sciatica! I certainly sympathize, having had it on and off myself for years. I think that last week, when she got out of the car and slipped because her leash was tangled up and JM hadn't seen that in the dark, she must have twisted her back. It just took several days for the sciatica to kick in.

Now, she's on anti-inflammatories for a few days and we're supposed to try to keep her from going up and down the stairs. This is not popular at all. And, tomorrow we're supposed to have lunch at Dylan and Florence's house. I don't know what to do: leave her home or take her along and keep her on her leash the whole time. Neither is the ideal solution, I'm afraid.

Still, in an effort to give her gentle exercise that wouldn't make things worse, we took a quiet walk around town this afternoon, picking up ingredients for dinner and getting sympathy from one and all. I'm sure the warm temperature outside is good for her back and the sunshine is good for all our morales.

Sunday, March 20

Today's theme is contrasts and gratitude!

We set out early this morning to drive to Perpignan, which is on the Mediterranean coast. We took the back roads, which is the best way to go anywhere if you're not in a hurry. The countryside still continues to blow me away with its beauty. I never get tired of discovering a new road or small village.

That being said, discovering Perpignan was not a particular success. First, the weather there was much cooler than it had been when we left Chalabre. It was barely 50 (F) there when it had been around 60 (F) here. Plus, it was all overcast: the sky was gray, the sea was gray, the city was ugly. Frankly, I felt no desire to hang around after we did a drive around to look at the city.

We headed towards Le Canet, which is where the beach and port are.

What to say about Le Canet... It really represents the worst of French modern construction. It could have been any beach town anywhere in the world. Tacky, ugly, seriously depressing, yet enormously expensive. I don't think you could pay me to live there. I certainly feel no urge of any kind to go back for a day on the beach.

We headed back towards home, taking a different route, and as soon as we were back in the country our spirits lifted. We went through amazing combinations of vineyards and orchards with the Pyrénées standing as a backdrop that just took our breath away. The orchards were in bloom, most with simply stunning bright pink flowers. I think these may have been cherry trees, but couldn't swear to it.

Still, breathing in the fresh spring air and seeing those bright flowers in the late morning sun quickly washed the thoughts of Perpignan out of our heads.

It was getting on to lunchtime and we hadn't seen any restaurant signs along the side of the road, which is relatively unusual, to be honest. So we came to Vinça, a largish town, and decided to look there. They had an auberge that seemed perfect, except that it didn't allow dogs. What a shame, I'm sure we would have had a nice meal, but I wasn't about to make Maggie wait in the car after a three-hour drive. Instead, we found a small restaurant a little further into town. We decided to check it out.

Well, it wasn't a smashing success, to say the least. The food itself was very good, but *slow*! One waiter, one cook and everything cooked to order, which is nice. But someone hadn't done their preparation I think, because it took two hours to get two courses served. And, to be really honest, neither one was that complicated. I think the table that came in after us almost got up and walked out, and I wouldn't have blamed them. Still, not every discovery can be perfect, right?

When we finally finished the meal that would not end, we continued along our way. And then we made a wondrous discovery! We actually drove through *Rivendell*!

I'm serious, there was this beautiful, mountain spa town called Molitg-les-Bains, perched on the side of a cliff. It was really amazing. Unfortunately, the whole town was closed for the winter!

MOLITG-LES-BAINS

Molitg-les-Bains (the name is pronounced "Molitch" and means "Big Mill") is a small mountain village located in the department of the Pyrénées-Orientales, just south of the Aude, somewhere between the towns of Prades and Quillan. It is famous for its thermal station and even has its own website: http://www.molitg.com/

The entrance to Molitg's Thermal Station, off the Main Road.

The thermal station and the hotel are built inside and alongside the cliffs, nested in a hollow. The River Castellane crosses the gorge at the bottom of the hill.

The Road from Prades to Quillan crosses Molitg. Below is a photo of the old church, and the road leading to the village of Old Molitg, at the top of the hill.

As we continued up the mountain road, we saw vertiginous drops and magnificent views. It was quite a drive, with most of the road only being wide enough for one car, so when someone came the other way you had scootch over to the side of the road and hope you didn't fall down a ravine. Quite the tonic for one's nerves after lunch!

More contrasts came with every turn of this beautiful road. We suddenly went from spring, with green fields and budding trees, to the dead of winter with masses of snow still covering the fields and sides of the road. The temperature dropped down into the 40s again, then we would take another curve and like that, we'd be back to spring.

I couldn't help but be grateful to live amidst such beauty. There is nothing that a big city like Perpignan could offer me that would make me trade the forests, fields and mountains for even the largest and most modern house in town!

Tuesday, March 22

Yesterday wound up being a relatively quiet day, because I seem to have had a touch of food poisoning. At least I'm guessing that's what it was. Maggie was sick too and JM felt a bit unwell. My guess is that the chicken from Sunday's *sloooowwww* lunch was the contributing factor.

However, all appears back to normal today, so life goes on.

Also, yesterday, we got our Sky TV installed. There are companies who specialize in installing it in places outside of the U.K., and I don't like to ask too many questions about the "where" of the whole thing. I figure since I'm paying the official price, and therefore not pirating, that I should be able to live anywhere that I want to watch television. Heck, if the curvature of the Earth didn't get in the way, I would have been darned pleased to have continued paying for DirecTV!

Now, the big challenge is to not watch too much TV again! Since we've been here, we really haven't been ruled by the tube, watching only an hour or so a night. I definitely want to continue being more social and less tube-ish! There's a good side to not always having it on, life seems calmer and quieter, which is a good thing.

Speaking of "social," I stopped in at the flower shop today. Lily (what else *could* she do with that name?), who works there, is an absolute doll and we hit it off right away. She handpaints the most beautiful glasses and coffee cups, etc. I wanted to buy a present for Bernadette because on our last visit there, the dogs had played a little rough and destroyed the Japanese fountain that had been her Christmas present from Philippe.

It turns out that Lily, who lives in Camon, is the head of the tourist bureau there. I offered my services for translation assistance both there and here in the shop. Then she told me that, next Monday, which is a holiday here, Camon is hosting a tour of the medieval Cabanes above the village, followed by an omelette lunch next Monday, which is a holiday here. I think we'll probably go. On the poster, it reminds participants to bring their own cutlery!

Lily and her husband have lived here for 15 years. They had come for a vacation when they lived in Paris and fell in love with the region. They've been here ever since. I think there are quite a few of us who feel that way. Maybe that's why we all get along so well.

THE GORGES OF SAINT GEORGES

Returning from Molitg-les-Bains through the Col du Jau, crossing the mountains separating the Pyrénées-Orientales from the Aude, on the road from Prades to Quillan, we drove through the Gorges of Saint

Georges, a narrow road stuck between two huge, rocky walls and the river Aude, leading to the village of Axat.

Wednesday, March 23

OK, I now have proof. The people in Chalabre notice me because of my dog!

In the Gorges, there is a Spring that comes out of the rock by the roadside.

Seriously, I just came back from buying a few things at the Huit-à-8, another, small local supermarket, and strangers were stopping me on the street, asking where Maggie was! I hadn't taken her with me, because she can't come inside and it's too close to the road for me to safely leave her outside.

A woman inside the store started talking to me and said she thought she recognized me from somewhere. It seems she remembers seeing me walking Maggie around town.

So, I guess I do need to keep spoiling the Diva, since she has clearly been the one opening all the doors in town.

It's a strange dichotomy that exists in France. Most people here adore animals. Yet, at the same time, there's a large group of people who will get a dog or a cat, then simply abandon it because they're going on vacation and don't want to be bothered. In August, when most people take their holidays, there are vast numbers of animals found abandoned at rest stops and along the highway. It's simply horrible.

I find it hard to come to terms with these two opposing sides of human nature. I suppose that those with whom I get along the best are the people who, like us, are simply gaga over their pets. Several of the older people in town have now taken to talking to me in glowing terms about their beloved, but deceased fur-children. I suppose they see a kindred soul.

At any rate, if Maggie is indeed bringing out the kindness in the local citizenry, it's a good thing and should be encouraged.

Friday, March 25

Light. Sunlight. Cloudlight. Electric light. Thursday was a day of light.

We started out early, because our friend, Peter, needed a lift to the Carcassonne airport: the long holiday weekend had begun! We were happy to take him, both because it was fun to have a chance to talk, but also because we needed to go to the Centre Commercial to buy lamps.

The sky was quite overcast and there was a bit of drizzle as we got to Salvaza airport. Everything is starting to turn green in the countryside, but with the cloud cover, only the pink buds of the fruit trees gave any real color.

Before the lamp buying expedition, we stopped at France Telecom to sort out the arcaneries of our various phone services. Luckily, they really seem to know what they're doing there and are able to get around the safeguards set up in the system. We should now be saving a ton of money, since we don't need the super expensive services like the Orange PC card and 20 hours a month of cell phone time. It is definitely cheaper to use the DSL and Skype service when possible.

We retraced our path to the Solea lighting store in the shopping center. It's vast! And there are lamps, chandeliers, etc. of every color and taste. To be honest, it's pretty overwhelming. Of course, as always, we found things we wanted and discovered that if we needed two, they only had one and it would take three to four months to get the other one, etc. I never knew, for example, that lamps are in some ways like women's clothes: there are new models each season, so the old models just disappear and are no longer available. Weird.

At any rate, we made our purchases, drove back and discovered that (i) we hadn't bought enough of certain things and (ii) we'd bought two lamps that were the wrong size/shape for where they needed to go. After trying to switch things around, we realized we needed to go back to Solea and exchange them.

By this point, the sky had cleared and was that brilliant blue that you really only see in the South of France. It was broken up by large, fluffy clouds and this created the most extraordinary lighting as we drove. The green fields looked like emeralds in the Sun. The dramatic beams of sunlight highlighted certain of them, making us feel as if we were driving through some magnificent painting. It almost hurt to look at the beauty of the entire panorama. How can we be so lucky to live in a place that looks like this?

Back in Carcassonne, Carole, the sales clerk from Solea, dealt with us with the patience of a saint. JM and I couldn't agree on certain of the lamp fixtures, so she kindly came and gave her opinion, explained why some would work out better than others, etc. Finally, we wound up with the right number of lamps, in a style that we both liked and were able to head back home.

The Sun was starting to set, giving us yet another perspective on the countryside. Sunlight, cloudlight, moonlight. It's all good in our little corner of paradise.

Sunday, March 27

Easter weekend and another pre-conception went out the window.

I'd always assumed that Easter was a quiet day where everything is closed and no one would be around. I was clearly wrong, at least as it applies to Chalabre!

When I went to the bakery on Saturday, I asked them if they would be closed today, Easter Sunday. They looked at me as if I was bonkers. No, it's one of their busiest days of the year. I had thought that everyone would be in buying his or her chocolate on Saturday. Instead, there was a steady stream of customers all Sunday morning, not only buying the house chocolates, but also pastries by the boxload. It will be the same thing tomorrow morning, Easter Monday, another holiday here in France.

I also noticed dozens of people wandering through town yesterday and today. I have no idea where they're all coming from. Are they villagers I haven't seen before? Are they families visiting residents? Are they some of our holiday home owners who have come for the long weekend? I may never know. But there is constant activity in the streets, people going by the windows, children playing everywhere; we're a real beehive of activity. There were even people riding through town on horseback yesterday!

Then, last night (and tonight as well, I understand) there was a big, live music concert at the Café de la Paix! They billed it as a "rock" concert, but it sounded more like Spanish/Flamenco/Pop to me. It was great, whatever it was. We walked past as we took Maggie on her last outing of the evening. The weather was not too cold, lots of the people on our street were sitting out on their doorsteps, just listening and having a fine time, you could hear the music all over town. It made us realize, once again, how lucky we were in our choice of villages. It never occurred to me that we would not only have a great place to live, but free music to listen to as well!

Happy Easter to all and don't eat too much chocolate.

The Café de la Paix in Chalabre

Tuesday, March 29

We've got holes!

Why am I excited about that? It's because the holes are further examples of us making progress in the restoration of our little nest.

Manu, the mason and cousin to Stéphane the electrician, came by yesterday, Easter Monday, to make our first hole. He took a big chunk of plaster off of the someday-to-be dining room to see if the stones could be revealed. The great news is that they can! So, our new plan is to do the whole dining area, from the fireplace forward, in restored stone. On the other side, we'll remove the formica display case and restore the stone there with an archway, to make a stone display case for teapots, etc. From the chimney back on one wall, and the archway back on the other, we'll do *provençal* style plaster with a light yellow color. We'll put rustic tile on the floor as well.

All of this means that for everything to go together, the plasterwork on the ceiling has to go. We'll be able to restore the original beams and have exposed beam ceilings, probably with plaster in between the beams. I can visualize the whole thing now.

Today, Jacques, the roofer/carpenter, came by with his crew to make further holes. We've already discovered that the hobbit ceiling in the kitchen can be removed to expose the beams in there! You can see the wood from the floor above in between the beams, so I'll have to see if we stain that or paint it white afterwards. By the way, JM and I sealed off the ceiling holes with duct tape, because there were also *spiders* in there!

We've also just had holes dug in the two bathrooms. Strangely, the beams in the first floor bathroom are laid in a 90 degree angle to the beams on the ground floor! That's really strange, but, okay, so be it.

It turns out that the best solution is to remove the whole floor/ceiling and build a new one. With that, we can make the level whatever we want it to be and have a flat, straight floor for the upstairs bath. It really does make the most sense. We don't have to move out while they're doing it, since, although we won't have a ceiling in the bottom bathroom, the fixtures and plumbing will remain in place and functioning.

I love the fact that all the workers not only give you a choice of several solutions, but they give advice about what they would do if it was them and also, they totally clean up after themselves so that there is very little dust and crud left behind.

Plus, since we live here, they are happy to stop by and say, "Hey, I'm free this afternoon, so would it be all right to come and do such and such." It's great, because we get things done more quickly that way.

So, even though we're going to have all these holes hanging around until June, we are all set to go then and I can see that we'll be in a totally different place by fall.

Friday, April 1
Sorry that I've been quiet. I've had a killer migraine for the last two days and couldn't stand looking at the computer screen.

The headache was caused by the chemicals used to treat the little wood-eating beasties in the attic. Not termites, as we don't have them around here (hard concept for a California girl to grasp), but something called *capricornes* and *vrillettes*. We didn't have a lot of them, but since they were munching away on the beams in the attic, they needed to be dealt with. Most of these old houses have them, so it wasn't unexpected. Eventually, as we uncover some of the beams and floors in the other rooms, we'll have to treat there as well.

The chemicals are harmless to humans, but jeez, do they smell! We opened up all the windows, but since it was raining, I couldn't keep them open all day. The smell kind of creeps up on you, and by the time I woke up in the morning, the headache was there for the duration.

Of course, it's my own fault that I let myself run out of migraine medication. When you don't have a headache, you're always convinced that you'll never get another one. You always *do* get one, but by then it's too late. I really do have to make a doctor's appointment.

Luckily, the pharmacists in town are very nice and I was able to get something a little stronger than aspirin to help me cope. It's not gone yet, but I can live with it until it decides to leave.

Headache or not, last night we entertained our first guests! I had gone across the way to the butcher to get some ground beef. I don't know why, but I'd been dying for meatloaf, which doesn't even have a name here, as no one makes it. I chopped up some lardons (a bit like bacon, but meatier) threw in some eggs, garlic, salt, herbs and breadcrumbs, then put some French barbecue sauce on top. I made spinach with *crème fraîche* as the vegetable.

When I asked if they had any, Mireille ground it right in front of me. You can't get any fresher than that. Then, while it was cooking I saw our neighbors, Jane and David. They're a very nice British couple that owns the house two doors down from us. They only get to come on their holidays, so I hadn't met them before, although Nicole had mentioned them to us.

They've been hard at work on their house, which has not been lived in for 40 years! I thought they might be able to do with a hot meal. Besides, I needed someone who could serve as guinea pig for my culinary experimentation! The poor fools agreed to come over and I hope they didn't wind up regretting it.

We actually had a lovely evening talking mostly about U.S. politics. I think it's always a bit of a shock when our European friends hear some of the stuff that does not get reported much in the press over here. I think it's also a bit depressing. I know it depresses me!

It really does feel like home now.

Saturday, April 2

Today is market day again. However, it is so windy, I don't know how anyone is holding their stuff on the tables. I had to close all the upstairs shutters, because they're blowing shut on their own and I was worried that we'd get broken windows!

When I went out to the post office, Roxie was across the street, faithful as ever to his post outside the butcher's shop. His eyes lit up when he saw Maggie, and before we knew it, he'd come running to see us. But, for some reason today he brought Maggie a present. He brought his old, clearly favorite toy and dropped it at Maggie's feet as an offering. She doesn't really play with toys, but she did give it a poke, just to be friendly. I think he was disappointed that she wouldn't take it and play more though.

We're taking our rental car back this morning. Lizzie has kindly offered to follow us to Laroque d'Olmes then bring us back. After that, we'll be carless until at least next Thursday. We did a big shopping at Carrefour yesterday, so between that and the local shops, we shouldn't even notice. The only thing that might be a problem is that I'm running out of Maggie's Mastery dog food, so I may try to scrounge a lift to Limoux at some point during the week.

Speaking of yesterday, we waited all morning for our electricians to show up. It's most unlike them to not appear and not come by to say why they aren't going to be working. We had received a large box of our latest *Robur* graphic novel at the post office, so I decided to go fetch it with the car, because it was way too heavy to carry back on foot. As I drove up the Cours Reynaud, I spotted Arnaud Molini, one of our electricians, coming towards me on crutches! He apparently did something to his ankle either playing rugby or out with the firemen (the story is unclear) and will be using them for three weeks! No wonder he wasn't here putting in wires.

Poor Stéphane Montoro was running around like crazy, trying to handle all their regular work as well as several emergencies. He hadn't stopped by because I'd parked the car out behind the garage and he had thought we weren't home. When I saw him go past the house, I ran out to find out the plan and he came in to pick up some tools. Now, we're not sure if they'll be back Monday or at some point later in the week to finish hooking everything up. Ah well, without a car, it's not as if we'll be going anyplace!

The car return went off without a hitch. No extra charges or anything, which was nice. Plus, they're close enough that if we *need* to rent another car for any reason, we can get there with no problem. Much, much simpler than going to Carcassonne.

After Lizzie dropped us off, we had a nice lunch. So easy to whip something up here! A couple of scrambled eggs, some cream, a little ham and you've got a true feast. Then, this afternoon, we visited a bit with neighbors David and Jane. They showed us through their house, which is great. Only two doors down, but a totally different layout than ours. They don't have heat or modern plumbing, but in the main, I think most of their work is redecorating and not structural. We convinced them not to lay concrete down over the dirt-floor in the cellar. The dirt cellar really acts as a great insulator for these houses, keeping them warmer in the winter and cooler in the summer. Plus, they absorb the damp, which is very useful.

Now, it's going to be a quiet evening of just the two of us (well, three of us including Maggie!), having a simple dinner and watching television. I don't think there's anything to beat that!

Monday, April 4

My antique mirror is fixed! Gabriel, the *ébéniste*, called to say he'd fixed it and dropped it off yesterday. You absolutely can't tell that it was ever broken. I don't think we'll want to use it as a baseball bat, but sitting nicely on a shelf, it should be fine.

Gabriel also dropped off the estimates for restoring the buffet and bookcase, so we are definitely going to go ahead with those. But not before June, since at this point, they're the only things we have in which we can store anything! That will certainly change, but not too rapidly. June suits him as well, because he's quite busy. Now that I've seen some of his work, I can understand why!

I discovered that weathermen in France are just as bad at predicting the weather as weathermen in the States. Yesterday, they called for storms in the late afternoon, but instead it was beautiful. So, we took Maggie and went for a long walk along the Hers. We even got to see some sheep, which, needless to say, made Maggie's afternoon!

David and Jane had invited us over for dinner last night and we spent another great evening with them. We're all really sad that they're heading back to England tomorrow. I wish they could find a way to live here all the time. They do too. You can't beat the commute for getting together for dinner. I think the walk from our door to theirs is less than 50 feet!

Today, we've already taken care of getting Beanie insured. Our insurance will cost us less than $300 a year, which is a huge saving over our L.A. rates. Then, at the post office, we had another surprise. Our official *"carte vitale,"* or medical card, had arrived. Since I had planned to make a doctor's appointment, it couldn't have come at a better time.

I had to make a choice of one of the four doctors in town, and wound up picking one of the women doctors who is also a homeopath and pain specialist. I'm going to see her on Thursday. I have to admit that I kept putting off calling, mostly because I still get nervous making phone calls in French. I know that's silly, but I'm always worried that people won't understand me! Now I sympathize more with the way JM used to feel about making calls in L.A. Somehow, the telephone is far more intimidating that talking to people face-to-face. I have to get over it though.

Before I go, we've just had exciting news. Beanie and the rest of our possessions are being delivered on Friday! I actually don't care about the furniture, but I will be thrilled to have our Greenie Beanie back again. I will take a picture of her and her California license plates in front of the house as soon as she's here.

Tuesday, April 5

I realized today that I'm a foreigner. It's really the first time in my life that I've had to think about it more than in a passing way.

It started when our friends David and Jane stopped by for a coffee before they have to go back to England this afternoon. I started thinking that everyone with whom we speak English here is actually from the

U.K. I'm the only American that I really know. So, I'm, in fact, the only person here with an accent that is different.

When I speak French, I speak it well, but I speak it as a foreigner. When I speak English, I speak with an American accent. I'm truly the outsider.

It's very odd, as an American, to think about that. We're so used to being in our own country. We automatically assume that we fit in everywhere. And, I can't complain, I *do* fit in here. I have both French and English friends, with a smattering of Dutch ones thrown in as well. But, I'm still odd woman out.

All in all, I believe that's a good thing. It helps in understanding how others feel when they travel to a new place. It's a wonderful way of expanding your empathic horizons.

So, here's to all the foreigners amongst us. May we all find happiness in our new homes.

Wednesday, April 6

Today was a day for talking, cooking and hammering.

In preparation for the replacement of our garage door and the arrival of our furniture and car, we've got electrician and plumbers working away. What with one thing and another, the noise level in the house has not been conducive to contemplative thought. Still, it all needs to be done and there's no way to accomplish that in silence.

Maggie likes all the guys, but she's less than convinced about the noises they make and the tools they carry around with them. She likes them to pay attention to her, but also spends half her time hiding under furniture or glued to my leg.

So, we used the noise as an excuse for socializing. Peter is back from London, and came over for lunch and to watch the episodes of *Doctor Who* that we taped for him while he was gone.

Lunch gave me another one of those great opportunities to really appreciate life in our small village. We decided on a simple lunch of tomato salad, scrambled eggs with lardons, my homemade apple-pear-raisin compote and vanilla ice cream.

I went to the small vegetable store where I bought some amazingly good local tomatoes. While I was there, one of the local women came in with eggs that she'd gathered this morning! So, of course we had to have those. Back to the house where I made a quick vinaigrette, scrambled the eggs with some fresh cream and that was it. Very simple, very fast and a true feast. I love the fact that I can just run out and in ten minutes be back with food that is fresh and delicious. No need to keep things in the refrigerator for days at a time or try to figure out on Monday what I might want to eat on Wednesday!

At the end of the day, when the plumbers were finished, I wound up having a lovely conversation with Christian about cooking. Both of us are passionate about it and we shared recipes for some of our favorite dishes. Now, even though we won't be having dinner for another two hours, my head is filled with thoughts of all the wonderful things I'll be able to cook in the months to come.

Arnaud Molini working on rewiring the house

Thursday, April 7

Some days, there really isn't much to write about and others I hardly know where to begin.

Thursday was my introduction into the French medical system for myself. I decided to try the village homeopath, Dr. Cornic. She's extremely nice and I would really like to be able to control my migraines with something that didn't rely on major drugs, if it's at all possible.

First, Dr. Cornic referred me to an osteopath for my neck and back, because most people seem pretty convinced that the headaches are related to an old neck injury. Then, she gave me some homeopathic prescriptions.

Those turned out to be quite interesting, because the local pharmacist actually had to make me a bunch of capsules from scratch. I just think that's pretty cool. It's so rare that you see that kind of thing in the States these days.

At any rate, we'll see how it all works out in the coming days.

Most of the rest of the day passed quietly, with Arnaud working more on the electricity and getting it ready for what would turn out to be our *big* day on Friday.

Tuesday, April 12

I'm really behind on my blog because we've been so busy, but I *have* to tell you this story! I promise that I'll get to the details on the last few days next time.

We got our car on Friday along with everything else. However, the creeps at U.S. customs had kept our license plates.[10] Everyone here said, "You can't drive a car in France without number plates." I told JM this and he said, "The customs agent here said we could as long as we have all the papers."

I wanted our friend, Peter, to drive us to the Police Prefecture to do the correct paperwork and leave Beanie at home until all was legit. JM insisted that we go on our own. I didn't feel like arguing, so I said, "fine."

On Monday, we got to Carcassonne and I parked in one of the municipal lots. We had a meeting at the Chamber of Commerce, which turned out to be a waste of time anyway. However, when JM put money into the meter, he'd only put in enough for an hour. I went back while he finished the boring meeting to put in more money so we could go to the Prefecture.

When I got to the parking lot, there were cops sitting and waiting in front of Beanie! I decided to be brave and go to put the new parking ticket in the window. When I had the car door open, a policeman came over and asked if it was my car. I answered that it was and he told me

---

[10] As it turned out, they hadn't, but that's a story told later.

that were impounding it! I tried to explain about it just arriving on Friday and us getting the paperwork, American customs, etc. No good. He insisted that I give him the keys and asked for my passport. Then, I ran off to get JM.

We got back and I was practically in tears. JM talked to the cops and the upshot was that they didn't write us a ticket because we were in good faith, but they *did* insist that the car be impounded until we have some type of license plate!

We're waiting for a piece of paper from French customs which *will* allow us to get a temporary plate that will be good for four months, until we go through the process of getting the car registered in France. Then, we'll be able to liberate Beanie from prison.

The tow truck driver took us with him to the impound lot, which was right next door to the place where you go to get your car inspected for accreditation. We had a good chat with the guy who is responsible and it seems we should be able to get what we need to be official.

Still we were stranded about 45 miles from home! Luckily, I was able to call our friend Peter, and he came to pick us up, sweet man. I made him dinner when we got back to Chalabre. It was the least that I could do!

So, that was our day yesterday. Wasn't that special?

Thursday, April 14

Last Friday was the Big day. Our furniture was scheduled to arrive sometime after 9 a.m.

But that wasn't all. It was also the day that the new garage door was to be installed.

Also, Arnaud was coming to keep working on the electricity.

But wait, there's more! Christian had promised to come by and fix the shower so that the wall didn't keep getting more and more soaked, because the plaster was starting to come off and fall into the tub.

Hectic? You bet.

The first hint that it would not all go smoothly was when we got a call from the driver of the truck that was hauling the container. He had gone to the disused Chalabre rail station, because they needed a place where the truck could be on one level, while the opening was at street level. This was so that they could drive the car off the back. Apparently, containers do not come equipped with ramps!

The truck driver was not authorized to unseal the container. Only the guys from the moving company could do that, and they had not yet arrived. To make matters more complicated, his cell phone wasn't really working all that well so he couldn't call them to find out what to do.

Luckily, we were able to coordinate everyone and soon, the movers themselves arrived and headed out to the *Gare*. I had to go to meet them there, because they weren't allowed to drive Beanie due to insurance reasons, and therefore I had to drive her home. It's a ten-minute walk, which in nice weather is a pleasure. As I mentioned, the weather wasn't nice. However, Christian was leaving and kindly offered to give me a lift.

The Gare de Chalabre

The Bram to Levelanet railway line that included villages such as Laroque, Chalabre and Camon on its route, was sadly decommissioned in the 1960s, but the station remains, a mute testimony to an era when the train was still a link with the outside communities. It is used today mostly as a warehouse and by the local firemen.

Another reminder of those days is a beautiful ironwrought railway bridge over the river Hers which now functions as an ordinary bridge.

Being an idiot, I dressed for the weather we'd *been* having, not the weather we *were* having. After standing out in the cold and drizzle, I was totally frozen. But, I was heartened to see my Beanie, safely arrived. That was when I discovered that, to my great disappointment, that the U.S. Customs people in L.A. had *kept my license plates*! I was so ticked off. I had wanted to take pictures of Beanie as she visited France. Also, I thought they would be majorly cool to hang on the wall somewhere in the house. Still, I guess it's a small price to pay for getting her here at all. Of course, our later troubles all stemmed from that little incident as well.

If only this had been the end of the moving trauma. But alas.

Because of the rain, the station platform was a sea of mud. The container truck was seriously heavy. With Beanie out of the back end, the weight was unbalanced and they couldn't get the container truck out of the mud. So, for about five hours, it was totally stuck. The movers had to start unloading the boxes, etc., putting them into their smaller truck, then bringing that into town to unload into the house. By the time they got the second truckload out, though, the container was light enough that a nice farmer with a tractor was finally able to pull it out of the mud.

We had about 300 cartons in total. And here we'd thought we'd done such an excellent job of getting rid of stuff in Reseda!

Most of the moving in process went astonishingly smoothly. However, when it came time to bring the big leather couch that also doubles as a guest bed, up to the library, there was a bit of a problem. With the excellent wrapping job that the L.A. movers had done, the couch was a couple of inches wider than it had been pre-wrap. It also weighs a ton! Seriously, between the couch itself, the metal bed frame inside and mattress, I would hazard a guess that it is something over 500 pounds.

The library is on the second landing of the staircase, which meant that they had to get it around two narrow turns. But, they managed that fine. The real trauma came when they actually tried to fit it through the doorway. It was about two or three inches too wide! They tried several times and actually wound up breaking one of the bars of the banister! In spite of that, no success. They had to take it back down to the dining room.

The end of that story came yesterday afternoon. Arnaud, one of our wonderful electricians, brought over five of his volunteer firemen friends and a huge tractor with a platform on the front. The platform rises on an arm and they loaded the couch onto that, then lifted it in through the window! It was most impressive to see. They wouldn't even take a cup of coffee afterwards. So, following Arnaud's advice, I went out to buy a bottle of pastis to give them in thanks.

At any rate, back to the moving in.

I would have to say that moving in has proved more tiring and complicated than moving out. Probably due to the fact that we didn't have to pack the boxes, but we *do* have to unpack them! Still, a little less than a week later, I'm starting to appreciate the compensations.

I had forgotten how comfortable our furniture is! It's wonderful to be sitting in my leather recliner, keyboard on my lap, computer on a table, feet up, typing all this to you in amazing comfort. Maggie is happy to have rediscovered things that smell "right" to her! I have enough dishes, knives, forks, etc., that I can cook more easily. And, our house is starting to look as if we live in it, not just squat in it.

So, for all the minor trauma of last Friday, things are getting better. The next big step will be having the wall knocked down in our bedroom so that we can set up our bed and stop sleeping on the BZ! Won't that be wonderful!

Friday, April 15

Whatever happened to spring? It was here for about six hours yesterday, but now seems to have gone back into hiding somewhere and doesn't appear to be ready to return in the near future. Arnaud told me not to count on it until May!

When it went away yesterday afternoon, it was replaced by a horrible thunderstorm, causing Maggie to try hiding everywhere she could think of to escape its evil. She was unsuccessful and looked exceedingly miserable.

Luckily, it didn't last long and although it wasn't warm or even clear, it at least stopped making noise.

I took advantage of the weather to make a "comfort" dinner and invited Peter and Lizzie to join us. We wound up having a very nice time and it was fun to entertain without having to wash and reuse the plates between courses!

Today, the rain has been going on all day, which is unfortunate as it was the day the roofers chose to replace the skylight. Poor Mikael, who actually was working up there, looked miserable. I wonder if he's re-evaluating his career choice.

Still, they're almost done and the new skylight will be clear and won't leak.[11] At the same time, they built the wall extension (I can't think of what else to call it) in our bedroom. This is to make the wall behind our bed all the same thickness, to compensate for the chimney sticking out about 12 inches from the original wall. If we hadn't built something like that, our bed would not have been able to be against a solid surface.

All of this wood work caused a bit of a scare around lunchtime.

JM and I had gone up to see make sure we were all in agreement about the way the wall would look. Of course Maggie had to follow along to see what we were doing. Then, we went back downstairs to work until it was time to eat. When I called Maggie over from her place under the table, I saw that the inner eyelid in the corner of her eye was horribly swollen! It looked as if some sawdust or other bit of wood or plaster has gotten into her eye.

This was the first time I really felt bad about not having a car. If I needed to take her to the vet, it would be impossible without someone to

---

[11] Ha! If only! Note to all interested parties: it is a law of nature that as soon as you put any opening in your roof, it will leak.

drive us. I called Peter, who graciously said he would do it if we needed to go. When I called the vet, they suggested rinsing her eye with saline and seeing if whatever was in there would wash out. Before I could do that, though, it started to clear up on its own. I guess we'll never know what caused it, but I'm glad it turned out to be nothing serious.

As the week has gone by, we've made more progress on clearing up boxes. Arnaud kindly loaded a whole bunch into the back of his pickup and took them to the dump for us. He told me that we should just keep loading them down to the garage and he'd take care of them.

I think I'm going to need to make some chocolate chip cookies to give him next week...

Sunday, April 17

I think the nasty winter bug that has been dropping the Chalabrois like flies has finally hit me. I'm still hoping that I can fight it off, but don't know if I'll succeed. Cross your fingers that my sore throat and mild fever don't hang around!

Last night, before I realized that I was coming down with "the thing," we invited Peter over for *Doctor Who* and pizza. However, the cooking fever hit me before the viral one, and I decided to play in the kitchen.

Peter used to live in the U.S., so he has fond memories of certain American comfort foods. It was cold and rainy yesterday, the perfect comfort food kind of day. I looked around the kitchen to see what I could concoct.

You may laugh at me, but I *did* ship over several essentially American ingredients that I was pretty sure I wouldn't be able to find here. One of them is that wonderful classic, cheddar cheese soup. That stuff is so useful for making all kinds of casseroles, and as far as I can tell, has no real French equivalent. I decided to use it to make a Frenchified version of macaroni and cheese casserole.

I mixed the soup with *crème fraîche*, grated *gruyère*, garlic and herbs. Then mixed it with curly short spaghetti, knacks (which are like the *best* hot dogs you've ever tasted!) and *lardons*. As a marriage of two cuisines, it worked great. I know it will be too expensive to have friends send me cans of that soup when my meager supply is gone, but it is one of the few ingredients (along with real maple syrup and peanut butter) that I'll miss.

Still, the rest of the dinner was 100% local, and that was terrific as well, so there will be definite compensations for the cheddar cheese soup!

I'm off to wallow in an afternoon of American DVDs and vitamin C.

Monday, April 18

A major achievement in the renovations today. Manu came and demolished the wall in our bedroom. It's just amazing what a difference that makes. The room is now huge! It gives a real sense of what things will look like when the work is all done.

It also seems as if we may get the stone done a month earlier than expected. That will be really exciting to see take shape. The only thing is that we'll need to have some of the electricity connected in the guestroom/library, so we can move up there to work while the stone work is being done. Not a big deal, but important.

Still no paperwork from customs on our car, which means we are still without wheels and Beanie remains in prison. Poor Beanie. Two months in a container and now she's in the hoosegow! Will she never be freed?

Perhaps I need to put up "Free Beanie" posters around town? At the very least, I should get a t-shirt made...

I'm glad we like our house and village so much, otherwise I could see that we'd start to go stir crazy. As it is, my only problem is a soon-to-be pressing need to get Maggie some new dog food. I had a sample of something that she liked, now to see if that agrees with her so I can work on getting more of it.

I like feeding her a blend of dog and human food, as it seems to work well with her allergies. The problem is finding dog food that doesn't contain any of the "no-nos" that she absolutely can't have. Always a dilemma, even back in the States.

Still, with all this being at home, we're getting a fair amount of work done. For me, it would be easier to type if my cold would go away, since I have to keep stopping to grab another kleenex!

I need my mother's chicken soup!

Tuesday, April 19

I was sitting in my recliner chair in the library, with the window open, trying to catch the fleeting rays of the sun in this weirdly changeable weather that we're having.

I had my eyes closed and just sat there, listening to the sounds of the village. I was struck by the difference between here and Reseda. It was actually ironic, as Reseda is smack dab in the middle of one of the biggest cities on Earth, and Chalabre is a small village in the middle of the country.

Yet, in Reseda you barely heard a sound (except for the gardeners and their hideous noise-making machines), while here, there are voices of young and old, and the non-stop sounds of activity: at least until it's time to stop for lunch.

How odd then, that I find the music of the voices here as soothing as the sounds of suburban solitude in Reseda. Perhaps it's because the voices outside my window in Chalabre remind me of the sense of community that reigns here. It is wonderful to listen to an unknown neighbor discuss the produce picked up at the store this morning, or what they are planning to make for lunch or dinner.

It is the sound of village life and is so vastly different from anything I've known before.

The voices lull me with the knowledge that I have found true happiness in this place. There is the realization that if I step outside my front door, I, too, can take part in one of the conversations of the village and will no longer be alone in my chair in the library.

Thursday, April 21

This has been a quietly weird week. Quiet, because except for Manu knocking down our bedroom wall on Monday, we haven't had anyone here doing work since. They're all busy finishing a roofing job over near the Hotel de France. They could've picked a better week for that, as we've had rain almost every day. But, once they started, there was nothing to do but keep going.

It's been weird, because besides having a cold, I wound up tripping on my clod-hopper feet yesterday. I'm bruised but not broken, and actually don't hurt as much as I thought I would. I found out that my mother fell yesterday too. So, I guess we were "communicating" to each other. We should have picked something else though!

We've profited from the quiet to get some serious unpacking done. Yesterday, we got both the offices sorted out. This afternoon we're tackling the library. We open each box, see what's in there, mark them in detail, then move them so that the right things are together in the right room. If you're planning on moving, I would seriously suggest *not* collecting books. They are wonderful to have but a major pain to move.

Still, as we progress, we can start picturing how things will look when we're all done. Each day convinces us that we chose the right house for us.

Today is an important day for us. It is the 7th Maggieversary! Seven years ago, Diva Maggie first stepped across our threshold in Reseda. When I look at the video footage we shot of that first step, I see a worried, insecure creature. Today, the dear Diva is confident, happy, joyful and proud. It makes our hearts sing to see the change in her.

As I said to friends yesterday, our girl really has changed our lives as well. I've made so many good friends around the world because of her, including so many of the ones we have here in Chalabre. When I walk through the village as Maggie's companion human, I know that people remember me because of her. I think that "first contact" with a lot of our neighbors was much easier with her as an icebreaker.

So, here is to our wonderful Diva Maggie. May you have many more years of health, happiness and wonderful French food!

Friday, April 22

I don't know if it will last, but suddenly this afternoon, spring seems to have sprung!

We're not sure where it came from, because all the predictions were for rain and this morning it was chilly and gray. But we looked out the window and *pow!*, there it was. So, since we'd spent a fair part of the day inside working, we decided to take a pre-dinner promenade and enjoy the sun.

I've noticed before that as soon as there is any sun and warmth here, everyone comes out and starts walking around, visiting, finding any excuse they can to be outside. We're clearly no different from the rest of the village in that respect.

We walked up to the post office to drop off a letter, then took the long way around, past the church, past the *crèche* and over to the large field behind the *crèche* where there's going to be a circus this weekend!

I don't know if I've mentioned it before, but the historical society in the village–*Il était une fois Chalabre* (Once Upon A Time Chalabre)–has signs up on lots of buildings and walls, explaining the historical significance of the various places. The field has a wall around it and was the site of the original Gaul village in 407 AD. It's amazing to be walking around a place that has been here since 407!

So many of the buildings have numbers carved into them showing that they date from the 1500s, 1600s, etc. Funny to think that *our* house, which dates from around 1840, is a *new* house by village standards.

I hope the weather holds out for the weekend. I don't expect the circus to be much of a big deal, but I still want to check it out and doubt I'll feel like doing that in the rain.

Saturday, April 23

Travel. Something we humans do all the time. But since we've been unpacking boxes, I've come to realize how many of our belongings have voyaged far as well.

Not just the things we bought in L.A., of course. It's logical for those things to be here with us. What's funny is looking at how many of our belongings started their lives here in France, traveled to L.A. and have now returned here, to Chalabre.

When we were first married, we had dinner with JM's cousins, Jacqueline and Jean-Paul. Jacqueline used a cute little silver crumb sweeper: it looked like a mini-carpet sweeper, to get the crumbs off the tablecloth after dinner. For some reason, it fascinated me. She insisted that I take it with me, which I did. Now, here it is, back in France, sweeping the crumbs off our table. The crumbs, by the way, are on a *Provençal* tablecloth, which *also* began its life here in France. It was purchased from Tissus Michelle in Le Mourillon in Toulon many years ago.

I uncovered several of my favorite kitchen tools this week and a number of them are things I've had since the early days of our marriage, gifts from my mother-in-law, and obviously of French origin. Why should one spatula be better than another? I don't know, but my favorite one is French and I've had it for 25 years!

Today, I came across my absolutely favorite of all my cookbooks. It's a small book meant for young housewives called, *Apprendre à Bien Cuisiner*, and abbreviates as *ABC*. It has practically every recipe you could want, in simple terms, easy to prepare and understand. If I could only keep one cookbook in my kitchen, this would be the one. It's the most unfancy cookbook I've ever seen. No illustrations of any kind, but nothing I've made using its tips has ever failed. I will be happy to see it back in a French kitchen where it belongs.

Tuesday, April 26

Well, I'm pleased to say that we have finally unpacked everything that can be unpacked. Everything that has to remain in boxes (books, extra kitchen stuff, towels, etc.) has been opened, catalogued and moved to the proper rooms. So, until we actually have the redecorating done, I guess we're as moved in as we're going to be.

It was very satisfying, if a little tiring. It's amazing how heavy boxes of books are. I think anyone could save a ton of money at the gym if they just started schlepping boxes of books up and down multiple flights of stairs. JM has said that he's going to miss the extra exercise.

Amazingly, everything seems to have come through the move unscathed, although one of our couches seems to make a noise that we don't remember it making before. Of course, it was on carpet there, so that may account for it.

Now, we're impatient for the work to continue so we can start getting things really organized. We seem to have fallen into a temporary workers black hole. No one has been in to do anything in over a week, so while we're enjoying the peace and quiet, we've got half-finished projects everywhere.

Next week, Manu has said he's coming in to do the stone in the downstairs walls. That means that either Arnaud or Stéphane *has* to come to connect electricity in our library so we can work while downstairs is out-of-bounds. I haven't seen either of them around town either, so I'll probably have to call.

On the other hand, Christian saw me as he was driving into work this morning. All our plumbing supplies have arrived and he took me over to his storage garage to show me. That was cool, seeing things that I *know* will be installed in another month or so.

That time should pass quickly. Next week will be three months since we arrived here. It's hard to believe. I feel torn between remembering what it was like to live anywhere else and truly grasping that we *do* live here now. Weird, I know.

The *platanes* are blooming, the birds are singing, the sky is blue and it's warm enough to go out without a jacket. I'm going to leave you all to stroll in the sunshine.

Wednesday, April 27

Since we've moved to Chalabre, every time my mother-in-law calls, she asks JM if I'm happy here. She worries that I won't be able to adjust to the lifestyle.

In answer to her and to everyone else who wonders if a lifelong, big city girl from L.A. can make the leap to a community of 1,000 people and really find happiness, I point to this recent headline from the *Los Angeles Times*: "*Copycats Feared in Freeway Shootings, CHP says car-to-car violence that's left four dead may be creating its own momentum.*"

How can anyone miss that?

When I went on to read that article and the related ones, I learned that in the last two weeks, four men have been killed on L.A.'s freeways, while another was wounded. The ever-increasing commute times are making people tense and angry. This is the result.

With Beanie still in prison, I haven't driven in close to a month. I have walked in the rain, the cold, the sun and the warmth. I have carried my little basket of groceries, walked Maggie, held hands with JM and not felt overly stressed, tense or angry a single time.

What could make me miss the anger and tension of an L.A. freeway? What convenience could possibly make up for the beauty of the countryside in which we live? What could take the place of the friendliness of my community? The conversations with my neighbors? The relaxed atmosphere of a life in a peaceful village?

Am I happy here? You be the judge.

Thursday, April 28

Sun! Glorious Sun! It was 27 C (80 F) here today! I was at last able to pull some of my summer clothes out and wear them without freezing to death.

The nice thing is, that so far, even if it is warm outside, the inside of the house stays fresh and cool. Like being air conditioned without paying an electric bill. It will be interesting to see if that remains the case when the temperatures are hot for several days on end. I'm still unclear about how hot it does get here in the summer. Is it more like L.A. or Philadelphia? Only time will tell.

At any rate, we made lots of effort to go outside and walk. It was wonderful. Just feeling the Sun warming our bones was heaven.

There is also news on the Beanie front! In theory, the paper from customs is in the mail to us. We should have received it today, but so far, nothing. Hopefully it will arrive tomorrow at the latest. Peter has promised to drive us to Carcassonne as soon as it does arrive, so we can proceed on freeing Beanie from her Hellish prison. I have no idea how long that will take once we start the process, however, so stay tuned.

And, Stéphane was good to his word and is back at work on the electricity. It's really a shame for his sake that this wasn't the week they were working on the nearby roof. It would probably be a lot nicer for him to be working outside with this weather. Still, selfishly, I'm happy to see things happening.

We had a surprise visit from our friend Philippe and his son Mikael this afternoon. The only sour note was Diva Maggie. They brought sweet little Leila, the Bichon Frisé. She likes Maggie, but is a bit afraid of her, totally understandable due to the size differential. Well, Maggie was *odious*! She started her shrill, BC bark and would pretty much not stop the whole time they were here. Also, if Leila went near her bone that has been lying around the house unwanted for three days, Maggie kind of snarled at her. My Diva is *not* a good hostess! I was so embarrassed.

Tonight, the visits continue. Peter is coming over for pizza. We haven't had pizza from Stella's for over a month, so that will be a nice treat. But, I'm still going to marinate some strawberries in *Crème de Pêche*. Can't beat that as a dessert with a little vanilla ice cream or *crème anglaise*.

Sunday, May 1

Beanie is free!

Yes, friends, the happy day finally arrived and Beanie is now home.

Friday morning, I went for my usual post office run and there was the eagerly awaited Chronopost with the famous form from customs. As soon as I got back, JM called the Prefecture de Police in Carcassonne and spoke with Mme. Corbieres, who told us to come in before 3 p.m.

Peter had already said he would take me to the Super-U on Friday, and while JM was on the phone, he called. We immediately changed our plans and he drove right over to take us to Carcassonne. Honestly, I don't know what we would have done without him. Because, as usual, things always take longer and are more complicated than you expect.

Although everyone was very nice and helpful, there were several steps that had to be taken and each one of them was in a different place that needed a *car* to get to! Without Peter, I think we would have been making the taxi drivers of Carcassonne into millionaires.

First, JM went to the Prefecture and got the temporary license plate number and *carte grise* (French equivalent of a California pink slip). These were the documents that we had wanted to get the day that Beanie was "taken."

With the temporary tag numbers, we immediately went to a local shop that does keys, etc. They make instant license plates and made up the set we needed for Beanie. In France, you have to have a yellow plate on the back and a white plate on the front. The back plate can be square or rectangular, but the front one has to be rectangular. The back plate fit perfectly in the existing spot for an American plate, but the front one was a bit trickier and required piercing to be attached (ouch!).

At any rate, plates in hand, it was lunchtime. Peter and I had passed a Vietnamese restaurant after parking his car, and we both thought that would be nice to try. It was called Restaurant Hanoi, and if you're in Carcassonne, I recommend it. The best nems I've had in ages. Plus, they were very dog friendly and brought Maggie a bowl of water without my even having to ask.

The funniest thing I've ever seen in a restaurant happened while we were there. The owner went out and a few minutes later came back in carrying a pizza box from the Italian restaurant next door! That just cracked us up! I guess he got tired of his own cooking!

Lunch over, we went to find the impound lot. That was a bit trickier, because it was in a big industrial park and we didn't have the exact address or directions. But, after a few false starts, we managed to locate it. The only problem was that Beanie was blocked in by a truck that they were in the process of repairing. Since the truck couldn't be driven, they couldn't pull Beanie out. We had to go away for an hour, then come back.

When we got back, we discovered that there was yet *another* paper that we needed from the local police station. The impound lot sent someone to get it, but they wouldn't give it to him. So, we still couldn't get Beanie back. Eventually, we drove back into the center of Carcassonne and JM went into the police station. They gave him the paper and we drove back to get Beanie. This time, everything was as it needed to be and we were able to drive off, happy as clams.

I have to say that Beanie handles the back roads of the Aude like a dream. She seems made to take the curves and hills. Plus, with her air conditioning, she's perfect when the weather is too hot for the open windows to do their job.

To thank him for spending his day helping us, we invited Peter for dinner at Le Commerce in Mirepoix. We hadn't been there in over a month, due to not having wheels. The beautiful summer-like weather had continued and we had dinner outside beneath the platanes.

As night fell, the sky turned to velvet blue. The platanes were lit with golden lights and we sat there, unable to believe how lucky we are to live in a place as perfect as this.

ROUVENAC

About 10 miles east of Chalabre, on the road to Esperaza, lies the peaceful village of Rouvenac, pop. 150-200. JM's great-grandmother on his father and grandfather's side of the family was originally from Rouvenac, which we didn't know when we decided to move to Chalabre.

The town square of Rouvenac features an excellent restaurant

RENNES-LE-CHÂTEAU

A Google search for Rennes-le-Château finds 1.3 million sites. No need, therefore, to recap here the story of its colorful priest Bérenger Saunière, his mysterious wealth, the as-yet-undiscovered treasure, and the village's historical connections to the Merovingians, the Holy Grail and other famous Mysteries, which recently inspired Dan Brown's best-selling Da Vinci Code. *Rennes-le-Château stands proudly atop a hill in Languedoc about 20 miles east of Chalabre and we drove there on a beautiful Saturday afternoon.*

The mysterious tower erected by Bérenger Saunière is now emblematic of Rennes-le-Château

Bérenger Saunière's house

Wednesday, May 4

Before I get started, I've been taken to task for not letting everyone know that we've got new pictures up on my website. These are the ones that we took last week, after we got Beanie back, when we explored Rouvenac and Rennes-le-Château.

It's a big holiday weekend here: Ascension. It starts tomorrow, most people take Friday off from work, so it continues through Sunday.

Here in Chalabre, this particular date is known for the last cold weather of winter. Even though it was gorgeous all last week, the temperature turned cold and grey today. It's supposed to continue at least for tomorrow. It's known here as *les Saints de Glace*, or the Ice Saints.

It's also the big village fair, with rides, stands, etc. The fair sets up on two of the *Cours*, rotating each year. This year, it's on the Cours Reynaud and Cours Sully. Next year it will be in front of our house! Needless to say, parking is at a premium.

Beanie has a prized spot on the street, but they are already few and far between. I'm pretty sure that for at least half of the weekend, our garage door is going to be blocked by cars, in spite of our shiny, new no-parking sign. "What sign? Where?" It's a shame, too, because Arnaud finished attaching the switch yesterday and we can now open and shut it from both inside and outside. We moved things around so that there's enough room to park in there as well. Although Stéphane Montoro seems to think that there's no way I'll get Beanie in there. I will need to prove him wrong!

Based on the fair we saw in Mirepoix last Friday when we were there, my guess is that Maggie is not going to have a happy weekend. It's going to be loud and crowded, two things that do not make for a happy Border Collie.

From my conversations with many of my neighbors, I get the feeling that it's not actually something that most of the adults particularly like, but it's very good for the local cafés, and I hope the Hotel de France and Stella's pizzeria. Although, when we talked to Stephanie yesterday, she told us she still hasn't received the money from the insurance company, so she hasn't been able to start repairs on the big dining room. That's a real bummer for her with summer coming up fast.

I promise a full report on the fair. I'll need to go out and take some pics as well.

Thursday, May 5

Not only was today a holiday, but it was also JM's and my 26th wedding anniversary! It was always a holiday in L.A., because it's *Cinco de Mayo*. We were just lucky that it was one in France this year as well.

Unlike in L.A., though, where the weather is usually beautiful, it was not particularly nice yesterday. The rain and cold weather continued. We left Chalabre around 11 a.m. to have lunch with Philippe and Bernadette in Pamiers.

We had a lovely time, as usual, and came back to the village around 5 p.m. Since it was even colder and rainier than it had been when we left, we expected that the fair would be a bust.

Boy, were we wrong! I guess people around here are pretty used to this time of year being yucky, so they don't let it stop them from playing outside. The village was packed! With two of the Cours shut down for the fair, parking was at a serious premium. Not a legal spot in sight.

No problem. We have a garage. So, we drove around to the Rue du Presbytère, ready to slip Beanie into her private parking space. Honestly, it was a great idea. Unfortunately, the "no parking" sign we'd so carefully installed didn't seem to have worked any better yesterday than it had the day before! Some idiot had once again parked in front of the garage door.

As much as it goes against my nature, I was forced to do what everyone else around here does and park illegally. I parked directly behind the two cars in front of our house, figuring that when they were ready to go, they'd make themselves known. It didn't come to that, however, because I noticed someone across the street pulling out of a prized legal space! I called for JM and we ran outside. He stood in the spot while I got Beanie into position and we pulled right in. Now, she's staying there for the rest of the day, I think.

I went into the bakery to ask Nadia if she had any strategies for keeping people away from our garage door and she just laughed. It should be an interesting summer, parking-wise!

With the nasty weather, we never did brave the fair. Somehow, eating fair food in the rain did not seem an appealing prospect. But today (Friday) has dawned cold but sunny. I think we may attempt it when things get rolling this afternoon.

Monday, May 9

The village fair is over. Chalabre is breathing a sigh of relief.

Once the weather cleared, it was pretty packed. Most of the time, there were no parking spaces of any kind in town, unless you were willing to park illegally. Which, this being France, most people were!

We did manage to keep our garage door clear, but instead of parking *in* the garage, we parked in front of it. We were kind of worried that if we went inside our handy-dandy wheelbarrow would not suffice to keep the door unblocked and we wouldn't be able to get out.

Word is that as summer arrives, this is going to be an ongoing problem. I've purchased an orange cone at the Gamm Vert and hope that this, coupled with the wheelbarrow, will serve as a sufficient deterrent. But, there remains a tinge of skepticism.

We were relatively unbothered by the fair itself. When we were working in the library, especially if we had the windows open, it was pretty loud. But when we closed the doors and went into the television/temporary bedroom, we really didn't hear a thing. Most of our neighbors didn't seem to be so lucky and complained about the loud, booming music going on until all hours.

Much worse than the fair was yesterday's rugby match. This whole area is into rugby in a *major* way. Chalabre's team had an away game yesterday and the local supporters started gathering early in preparation for taking a bus to the game. They were a colorful sight, to say the least. White and blue bike shorts, t-shirts and some kind of very silly hats. JM swears that the men were all wearing fishnet stockings, but I have to admit I didn't notice that part myself.

Not only were they loud to look at, they were loud to listen to as well! Lots of airhorns, drums, shouting, whistles, etc. Maggie was enormously stressed out, as airhorns are one of her big "devil" sounds! She spent most of the morning hiding in closets.

Luckily, we were having lunch with Lizzie and her friend Sally, so we got to leave before the match actually started. That meant a much more tranquil afternoon. While we were seated at Le Joug having lunch, two of Lizzie's other friends from Rivel, Maggie and Martin, joined us and we wound up having a wonderful time. Diva Maggie was able to rest under the table, while eating about half of my steak and part of Sally's lamb chops.

Things started to wind down at dinnertime, and by half-past eight, the fair was folding its tents in preparation for its next stop, somewhere down the road.

Wednesday, May 11

Dust? You think you know dust? You know *nothing* about dust!

We, on the other hand, have learned that dust created by uncovering stone walls and beamed ceilings can move from room to room, invade closed and covered cupboards and turn a black dog white.

For the last two days, Manu has been doing an impressive job in the dining room to be. The walls, even unfinished, are really amazing to look at. We've even had a discovery! Hidden in the wall to the left of the fireplace was a lovely little alcove! We expect the worst of the mess to be over by Friday night.

Something we hadn't planned to do, but which I see now absolutely must be done, is to replace the mantel of the fireplace. Right now, it's a kind of ugly beige fake marble that doesn't go with anything. We're going to replace it with flat stones so that it goes with the rest of the walls. I think it will be a huge improvement.[12]

Once Manu has all the plaster removed, Arnaud and Stéphane will do the wiring so that it's hidden in between the stones, then there will be new mortar put everywhere. The new tile won't be done until *all* the work in the house is finished, since there's no sense putting it down, then having it all messed up and scratched.

I think I need to buy some wine to offer my neighbors as a peace offering, too. We may have dust, but *they* have the noise vibrating through their houses as well. At the end of the day, we'll have a nicely done house. They'll just have been inconvenienced!

Friday, May 13

The work is progressing nicely on the stone walls and beamed ceilings. But that's not all that's happened this week in Chalabre!

Wednesday afternoon, one of our neighbors from across the street, Monsieur B., came to the door and said he needed to speak to us. When

---

[12] Actually, we wound up replacing it with a beautiful wood mantelpiece created by extraordinary cabinetmaker Gabriel Chevalley.

we went outside, he walked over to Beanie–not a good sign. Indeed, he'd smashed in her back bumper! Poor Beanie. All this distance traveled, only to be ignominiously wounded while standing still and minding her own business.

To make matters even stranger. Monsieur B. doesn't even drive a normal car. He has a little mini-electric car. These can be driven on the streets without a driver's license! It seems clear why he doesn't have one. Cours Colbert is a very wide street and his tinker toy is the smallest car in the village! It appears he got confused between the brake pedal and the accelerator. A fatal flaw in the plan.

M. Hervas' garage

JM went down the street to get M. Hervas, the local mechanic. He said he would look at Beanie today and see what he could do. Monsieur B. said he would pay for the repairs. We all decided there was no reason to involve the insurance company.

That over, I took a walk to the Huit-à-8 to pick up a few things. Every once in a while, if I'm standing in one place for too long, my blood pressure suddenly gets very low. That happened while I was in line at the *superette*. Of course, a couple of my neighbors were there and they, as well as the wonderful Huit-à-8 ladies were all making a huge fuss over me. They all agreed that I wasn't allowed to walk home and my groceries were whisked away to M. and Mme. Roget's car. I wasn't even allowed to bring them into the house myself.

A strange day, to be sure. On the other hand, there were several positive aspects to the whole thing. The Beanie incident gave the whole village something to talk about. Which, of course, they did. Everyone was very indignant on our behalf.

Then, I was pleased to learn that many of the villagers really do accept us as being a part of things here. Mme. Roget was telling someone in the Huit-à-8 what nice neighbors we were and how glad she was that we'd moved in. We feel exactly the same way about them, so it was very pleasant.

Sometimes, things that start out looking negative, really do turn into a positive at the end of the day. Both of Wednesday's events seem to have done that.

And, as for Beanie, M. Hervas has repaired her so that she is almost as good as new!

Saturday, May 14

Cherry season! Yaaay! I always look forward to the first cherries of the year. This year, because of the unusually cold weather, they came later than they normally do. But, wow, were they worth the wait! I haven't had cherries this good in many, many years. I'm probably going to eat myself sick, but I'll enjoy every minute of it!

The weather has still been a bit on the changeable side: beautiful one minute cool and cloudy the next, but I am assured that by next week we should at last be full blown into spring. I will believe it when I see it. My Gamm Vert sandals are ready and waiting to be worn so that my little tootsies can enjoy the sunshine.

Tonight is the town party to celebrate the big rugby win last weekend. It was scheduled to be on the Rue de l'Abattoir, behind our house. Luckily, there are so many people going to it, that they moved the whole thing to the school gymnasium. However, this morning I saw M. Roget. He told me that he was a little concerned that I had Beanie parked out in front of our garage. He thought that with the night's events she risked being damaged yet again. I explained that I had parked there to be out of the way of the market this morning, but promised I would try to find street parking this afternoon, since our garage is too filled with boxes at the moment for me to park there. He explained that he was going to Mirepoix this afternoon, so I should take his spot if I needed it. What a sweet man.

It is amazing how quickly we've come to feel part of the village life. I know this is not the experience everyone has when they move to a new town. I really do think we had almost miraculous luck in finding this place. We realized that we have no desire to go on vacation, because for us, we're already living in our own, personal paradise.

Sunday, May 15

We had a great time last night. Three of our British friends (Maggie "the human," Martin and Peter) came over for dinner and cards.

There is a great French card game called *Tarot*. Now, this is *not* the tarot with which you tell fortunes, although the card decks are similar. The closest English-language equivalent that we've been able to come up with over the years is Hearts. The tarot deck has the usual 52 cards; however, there are extra cards. First, there is an extra face card, the *Chevalier* (or Knight) in each suit that fits in between the Jack and the Queen. And there's an extra suit of cards: 22 trumps, called *atouts*.

The game can be played with three, four or five people. It's the least fun with three and great fun with four or five. The rules are not super complicated, and Peter, who hadn't played before, was able to do very well after a trial round. It's one of those games that can be as addictive as eating potato chips, and we wound up playing until past midnight.

It has been years since we've had anyone to play with, as Tarot players in L.A. are few and far between. But I know that we'll be getting lots of games in now that we're here. The next thing to do is to take our boules down to the boulodrome so that we can play *pétanque*. We really suck at it, but it's still great fun.

Hmm... When are we going to fit work in?

Tuesday, May 17

Yesterday was an interesting day here in France. It was *Pentecôte*, which is normally a big holiday weekend. However, this year, it was an occasion for confusion and protest.

Some of you may remember that two years ago there was a hideous heat wave across Europe. Hundreds of people, mostly elderly and handicapped, died here in France, because there weren't enough emergency rooms and visiting nurses to handle those who were overcome with heatstroke.

The government came up with a plan to get some added revenue that is, theoretically, supposed to help the situation. Everyone in France who works is meant to give up a day's salary that will go to help the elderly and handicapped.

The theory sounds good. In practice, they took away the Pentecost holiday. This has been a huge miscalculation on the part of the government and has resulted in a backlash of protest.

Yesterday, there were strikes across the country. Many people simply called in sick and kept their kids out of school. Businesses that usually make a lot of money on the three-day weekend wound up with seriously reduced revenues, partly because it wasn't a holiday and partly because the weather across the country was miserable.

If I've learned one thing about the French in the 26 years I've been coming to France, it's that you don't mess with their holidays!

People feel as if they've fought hard to get what they have and do not want it being taken away from them on a whim. The anger over this entire thing looks like it's even going to affect the vote on the European Constitution, with many voters feeling that they need to "punish" the government by voting "no."

Today, life is back to normal, although the news is still talking about yesterday. Overall, I've seen that France or America, when the media get a hold of a story that they see as "popular," they will run with it until the viewers are ready to throw a shoe at the television screen.

The more things change...

Thursday, May 19

After all the rain we had over the last few days, today's astonishingly beautiful weather is even more appreciated here in Chalabre. We all keep finding errands to run and it seems as if everyone in the village has opened their windows.

When Nicole (Mme. Poole) arrived two weeks ago, she put a bench outside between our two houses. I find myself sitting on it to drink a coffee, or read a few pages of a book, whenever I have a couple of spare minutes. As I sat there with Maggie after lunch, I realized that in the 20 years we lived in our house in Reseda, I hardly ever sat outside.

That struck me as odd, because certainly in L.A. we had many, many glorious days. Yet, somehow, there was a feeling of isolation in sitting outside there, whereas here, even if no one else is around, I feel that I'm part of the community, even if I'm simply sitting on a bench.

Maggie also seems enjoy it when we're out there, perhaps because she can no longer just go and lay in "her" yard the way she could in L.A. And, of course, there's lots more to see when we're outside here: cats, dogs, people, cats, and then, there are the cats...

I really need to find a second bench to put under our dining room window, so that when Nicole stores hers back inside, we'll still have a lovely place to sit and enjoy the sunshine and cool breezes. I finally understand the concept of people sitting on their "stoop" in the spring and summer.

Sunday, May 22

Before I forget, I must tell you about my recent "invention." I was looking for a cocktail that I could serve guests before dinner. Most people like a *kir*, which is *crème de cassis* with white wine. I didn't have any *crème de cassis*, but I did have *crème de pêche* (peach), which I like to use in recipes. I mixed one third *crème de pêche* with two thirds *rosé* wine. The resulting concoction has now been dubbed a "Pink Possum." Try it, I think you'll like it.

By the way, if you mix it with sparkling white wine (of course, I use *Blanquette de Limoux*), it becomes a "Rabid Possum," and if you use regular white wine, it is then a "Pale Possum."

We're in a small "quiet" period with the work in the house. Manu Montoro has finished the first part of the restoration of the stone walls and wooden beams in the downstairs room.

Next week, Arnaud Molini and Stéphane Montoro will come back to finish up the electric work in that room; then, in June, the really major work will start through the end of July. I wonder if I'll ever be dust free again?

Yesterday wound up having its own share of strangeness. Being Saturday, Peter was coming over for dinner and *Doctor Who*. While we were waiting for him, I went downstairs to sit and chat with Nicole outside on the bench. One of the more colorful local residents came by and insisted on taking us to the Café de la Paix for a drink. So, I suddenly found myself swept away for a *kir*! The goal of the exercise was apparently to introduce me to a very nice single friend. Which was a bit strange as I am most definitely *not* single! Still, we had a nice conversation before I managed to make my excuses and come back to start dinner.

Then, before much dinner progress could be made, Yves and Hélène, the nice couple who live on the other side of Nicole stopped by to see how the stone walls had progressed. They live in Perpignan; this is their vacation home, so they only get to come visit it on weekends. They took us in to see their place, and I have to say I'm really impressed with the work they've done. They've done it all themselves, and it is lovely. It gave us a couple more ideas of what to do with the downstairs fireplace as well.

Today, the gloomy weather is back. I took Maggie for a long walk, hoping to get some exercise in before it starts to rain. Once again, I was struck by how friendly the people who live here are. I spoke with half-a-dozen villagers, all of whom are really interested to know how we're settling in and whether we like it here.

Silly question, because for us, it's paradise.

Tuesday, May 24

Yesterday we had a rather unpleasant experience in Carcassonne.

We had gone with Peter and Lizzie to pick Coral up at the airport. We left early so that we could have lunch at Hanoi, the wonderful Vietnamese restaurant we found there last month.

We sat at our corner table and noticed that the two girls at the next table were speaking English and having trouble communicating their order to the waitress. Being the busybody that I am, and over JM's protests, I offered to help. The waitress, who does speak some, but not much, English, was very grateful.

In spite of my help, the girls' order was a bit confused and when it arrived, they asked again for my assistance. A couple of times during the rest of their meal, we noticed them being a bit harsh in their dealings with the waitress, who is a lovely, sweet girl. They did the usual "if we speak louder, she'll understand us better" thing that English speakers often do in foreign countries. Finally, they got up and left. They did not utter a word of thanks to me for having helped them.

Now, I don't help people to get thanked. But, really, shouldn't there be a modicum of politeness in a situation like that? I suggested to JM, Peter and Lizzie that perhaps they didn't want to interrupt us when they left. But they pointed out that I was being too nice and it was just rudeness their part.

JM felt relieved to learn that they were Australians and not Americans, which he had thought they were at first. This was not typical Australian behavior, as all of our Aussie friends in L.A. are unfailingly polite and nice.

No, this was just genuine rudeness and made us feel very bad about the impression they must be leaving in their wake.

Friday, May 27

Maggie's courage left her last night.

We went out for our evening walk, and there was a guy on an absolutely gorgeous grey horse, standing and talking to a couple of people. As we walked towards him, the Diva was all proud of herself as she busily looked for cats to chase. She looked up and there was this huge creature that was clearly *not a cat*!

Somehow, instead of staring at it the way she looks at the ponies up at the castle, she decided that flight was the safest option. Her tail went down and she dragged me as far away from the "thing" as she could possibly get. When it stamped its hooves, she looked totally terrorized. I guess this means we won't be out herding horses anytime soon!

We are enjoying our period or relative dust-freeness at the moment. Nobody in the house doing work until next Monday. I almost don't know what to do with so much freedom. We did go into Pamiers yesterday and found a nice bench to put outside the house. Unfortunately, it's a bit big to bring home in Beanie, so Peter has kindly offered to take me back there to get it tomorrow.

When I told M. Gimenez across the street about it, he advised me to lock it to the bars on the cellar window with a bicycle lock! He worries a lot about people stealing things. I suppose after the great Orange Cone Theft Caper [13] last weekend, I should be more worried about it too.

---

[13] Yes, the Orange Cone we had bought at the Gamm Vert mysteriously disappeared one day. The ever-helpful M. Roget reported having seen it in the street leading up to the Castle, but by the time we went there looking to reclaim our property, it was gone, never to be seen again.

M. Gimenez told me that he and his wife had been raising ducks and chickens on their garden plot at the edge of town. They had 20 of each. When he went to get a duck yesterday (I leave why to your imagination) *all* of the ducks and the two biggest chickens had been stolen! I was really shocked by that. Of course, there's nothing that anyone can do, and like everywhere in the world, no one saw a thing.[14]

How sad that even in a place the size of Chalabre, there are those who will ruin things for everyone else without a second thought. My illusions were a bit battered, to be perfectly honest...

Tuesday, May 31

I was going to write all about our new garden. However, now it looks like we're not getting one after all.

Since most of the houses here are surrounded by streets, very few of them have actual gardens. Instead, the outside of town has a long section of garden plots that are owned by various villagers. Some of them are mostly grass and trees, others have a lot of flowers, but the majority of them are real kitchen gardens with greenhouse, garden sheds and lots of vegetables.

Our next-door neighbor, M. Martinez, wants to sell his because he can't work it anymore due to his arthritis. We worked out a price, which seemed quite fair to us, and were about to close the deal. Then, we took a walk to see it. It's a *real* market garden: loads and loads of carefully planted vegetables, about 50 or 60 yards long by 50 feet wide, shed, greenhouse, well, etc. JM totally freaked out because there's no way we could ever work a garden like that. I thought it would be horrible to tear up all that careful work.

I spoke to M. Martinez, who said we should plow it all down and he wouldn't be the least bit upset. But JM is still super-stressed out over the idea of it, so I've decided not to push the issue for now. I do feel a bit sad, because I really like the idea of having a "green" space where Maggie could roam around and we could sit out and barbecue, etc. But it's not worth having an argument over. So, I guess we'll remain totally town-dwellers for now, unless I come up with a workable plan.

---

[14] It turns out that I misunderstood the time frame here. The "duck incident" actually occurred something like 15 years ago!! Clearly, it was painful to be spoken about for so long.

THE GARDENS OF CHALABRE

Traveling south, we cross the bridge over the river Blau. Then, we walk down the first street on the right, lined with fine houses with colombages.

Just at the end of this street is a small canal (mostly dried up now) that used to carry water to the mill. To the right is the road that crosses the Gardens of Chalabre.

The Gardens are plots of land owned by various residents. There are plots on both the right and left sides of the road, until it curves right towards the river Hers.

At the river, the road curves again, left this time, and becomes a dirt road that follows the Hers. Below is Mr. Martinez's garden; there is some serious agriculture going on there.

This, above, is the garden we would have liked to buy, just fruit trees and grass, ideal for picnics. Then, the road goes on, towards the stadium and the campsite.

Chalabre from the Gardens

Yesterday and today were pretty quiet around here. Sunday was Mother's Day, which is a really big event here. The weather was lovely and everyone had family in town visiting, which made it pretty lively. We went with Lizzie, Peter and two new friends, Cathy and Sean,[15] to have lunch at Lac Montbel, then to walk around the lake.

Cathy and Sean's dogs got to run along the path leash-free, but I'm afraid the Diva was not so lucky. I was going to give it a try, but she heard some little creature in the woods and was ready to run off and give chase. It was clear there was no way she would come back if I called her, so she stayed my prisoner. She knew she wasn't getting the same treatment as Maggie (another Maggie!) and Molly, the two lurchers. I felt guilty, but I couldn't take the chance. It would have been horrible to have lost her in the woods.

So, for now I'm making an effort to let her walk on a long, lunge line when we're walking in the country, and she'll have to be satisfied with that.

---

[15] Cathy and Sean bought Lizzie's renovated *Café* in Rivel; Lizzie then moved to another nearby village, Léran.

Thursday, June 2

Still no news on the garden front, I'm afraid. Even though we've decided that M. Martinez's garden isn't the right one for us, we're still convinced (well, *I*'m convinced) that we need some green space of our very own.

Yesterday, we stopped over at Philippe and Bernadette's place for a visit. As soon as we got in the door, Maggie ran out to the back garden where she ate grass, ran around and generally seemed more than pleased to be there. It's clear that, despite all the long walks and companionship, she would still like to have her own little patch of green.

I've actually picked a garden that I really, truly covet. Unfortunately, it doesn't appear to be for sale right now. I hope, however, that if the current owner does decide to sell, that he will let us know so that we can make an offer.

This particular garden is filled with grass and trees. It resembles a mini-forest and is exactly what we need. I suppose that I will just keep walking past it and dreaming, hoping that, one day, it will be mine.

Speaking of trees, we are now into the time of year when the cherry trees are heavy with fruit. Bernadette and Philippe have a lovely cherry in their garden, however they don't eat much fruit! So, yesterday, Bernadette and I picked a ton of cherries, which she insisted I take. Who could refuse such an offer?

As I sat contemplating this wonderful bounty, there was a knock at the door. It was M. Roget, who brought me an even *bigger* bag of cherries from his garden! I am now contemplating more cherries than the two of us can possibly eat before they spoil. We did share some with our friends Peter and Margaret, but we are still quite cherry-heavy. I have told JM that if he helps me pit them, I will make him a variety of cherry-based concoctions. I think I know how we'll be spending our evening tonight.

Sunday, June 5

Apparently herding horses is not something that Maggie plans to do.

Now that the weather is nice, we see lots of horses coming through town for various reasons. The Château is gearing up for tourist season and they do jousting recreations. When they're not practicing, they ride the horses through town all the time.

Plus, there are people all around who own horses, so they ride them through the village as well. We've been out several times when there are horses here and Maggie is just not convinced about them. First, they are much larger than cats, so they clearly aren't cats. They don't smell like dogs, so they're not those either. And they have too many legs to be people. Whatever they are, they are very big and scary, so she is not particularly interested in being their friend.

She did like staring at the ponies up at the Château, but they were almost the same size as she and were behind a fence. Much safer. One of the locals has invited me to visit his horses, so we'll see if there's a change of heart when she gets to know them.

On the human front, we've now been out to the Boulodrome twice to play *pétanque*. I'd forgotten how much fun it is. So far, it has been me and Peter versus JM. He's beaten us, but only by a single point or two, so we don't feel totally humiliated. We tend to go out when no one else is there, which is probably better for my self-esteem. I don't think anyone is going to be asking us to play competitively in the near future.

The Boulodrome (left) overlooking the intersection of the Hers and the Blau

Yesterday, JM went to Perpignan for a book signing. I decided to stay home, since I wasn't sure if the bookstore was dog-friendly and I didn't want to have to try to find a place to hang out for five or six hours.

The day was pretty gloomy, so I wound up cleaning and studying for the French driving test. I am determined that I *will* pass the exam and am really cramming for it. It's not as if the *Code de la Route* is that complicated, but they use a slide show that can be a little sneaky. Also, there are things that you see people do all the time (mostly parking), which you assume must be legal, but which turn out to be illegal! I wonder how many of the folks out driving on the roads could pass their own drivers' test if they had to retake it?

Tuesday, June 7

This is one of those quiet weeks that periodically occur. Not a lot of excitement either *chez* Lofficier or in town itself. No complaints, of course, it's nice to have those now and then.

During the day, the village seems to be buzzing away. I suppose that we're really into early summer mode now. Lots of people out doing errands, kids all over the place, people sitting outside and chatting on the terraces of the cafés, etc. I find that for me, it's almost impossible to do any errand without being gone for at least 30 or 40 minutes. Not because it takes me that long to do any specific thing, but because there are so many people to talk to! And, the longer we're here, the more people I know, so it seems that's not going to change any time soon!

I'm even able to lure JM away from his computer in the afternoons. I don't know how hot it will get here later in the summer, but for now it has been just about perfect. Sometimes, the locals complain about the heat, but for us, compared to most days in L.A. during the summer, it feels like perpetual spring.

This afternoon, we took a three-mile walk, going down the path between the gardens and the river, then along to behind the rugby stadium. From there, you can cross over to the main road that runs from Chalabre to Lavelanet. As we were walking along it, back towards the Huit-à-8, an elderly lady crossed over to talk to me. She was concerned because we were walking along the "main" road and told me that the road by the gardens was safer because there weren't any cars. Of course, she was also walking on the main road, but she was only worried about us, which I thought was sweet.

It's nice to have these gentle days to lead us into summer. I hope that we never begin to take them for granted.

Thursday, June 9

Today, we got our window screens installed! They're great and a really practical idea. Because the windows open into the room and we have to close the shutters, which are on the outside of the house, there is no way to have the typical, American-style fixed screen window. Instead, these work like a roll-up window shade. There are metal tracks on the sides to hold it firm, and it locks in the down position so the wind can't blow it around.

We had three put into different rooms, and I have to say it creates a great cross-breeze, plus no worries about little beasties getting inside. I think that, eventually, we'll have them put in the rooms that are currently "screen-less" so that we can get air throughout the house.

It was quite hot today, I'd say around 85 F or so, but inside, with the breeze blowing through the whole house, it was perfectly cool and comfortable. If the summer stays like this, you will hear no complaints from me!

Yesterday, Lizzie finished selling her house to Cathy and Sean, who moved in right away. Today, Lizzie's movers finished getting her stuff out and their stuff started to arrive. We had Cathy, Sean and Peter over for lunch, just to give them a bit of a break from moving. It made me feel positively giddy to realize that even though our work is far from finished, we don't have to wait for any more boxes to arrive from anywhere.

As we sat there, chatting while the cool breeze blew through the dining room, I started to imagine what the house will look like when the remodeling is finished. It will be a real pleasure to entertain people here, as the house has a wonderful atmosphere to it.

Of course, right now it seems as if we will be living with unfinished walls, floors and plumbing forever, but I remain positive that one day, this, too, shall pass.

Sunday, June 12

Excuse my relative silence, as I have been busy studying for my French driver's exam!

Only eight U.S. states have treaties with France, allowing their licenses to be easily exchanged for a French *Permis de Conduire*. Unfortunately, California is not one of them. For a while, I had hoped that I could resurrect my Pennsylvania license, but I just don't think that's a viable option, given the rampant paranoia in the States since 9/11. I decided that the best thing to do was to simply bite the bullet and take the French test.

Most people here, when I say I'm doing that, tremble in fear. I'm not really sure why, as it seems to me to not be any more complicated than taking the test in California or Pennsylvania. The biggest difference in the written test is that they show you slides and ask questions, so it's not just a matter of trying to memorize things. You really have to *look* at the slide, because there are occasional sneaky bits that affect the way you answer. And, of course, I need to think metric, which I'm starting to do anyway.

Most people go to driving schools, which would have cost me about 200 euros. However, there are some pretty good courses on CD that you can get. The one I bought has 3,200 questions and is, I think, good method of training for the test.

I'll probably also have to take a road test. But, after driving for 36 years, I don't think I'll be too bothered by that. I try to be a careful driver and hope that will work in my favor.

Tomorrow, we're going to go to Carcassonne to see about taking the next step to making Beanie an "official" French vehicle and, on the way back, we'll stop at the Sous-Prefecture in Limoux to get the necessary documents to apply for a driving test.

Send me good thoughts. I want to pass this the first time out!

Tuesday, June 14

On Sunday, we took another drive through an area we hadn't seen yet. We went to Ax-les-Thermes, which is up in the mountains on the way to Andorra. We saw some simply stunning scenery, especially since the day turned stormy and the clouds over the mountain vistas are always breathtaking.

Then, today I bought a magazine about the Tour de France. The map showed that the Tour is going to go right through there! In fact, it will go through Esperaza, which is about 15 miles away, then make its way up to

Ax. What a coincidence that our first year here, the Tour is coming through as well.

It will be Stage 14 on Saturday, July 16. Last year, the Tour was being shown on OLN in the U.S., as well as some on ABC. If you're interested in seeing a bit of what our area looks like, then try to catch some of the television coverage. JM and I are planning on going to the mountain portion with a picnic and will do our best to get as many pictures as possible. I can't believe how excited we are at the prospect. Of course, any of you who know us, realize that for us to get excited about ANY kind of sporting event is pretty odd! But, this is kind of special.

Small parenthesis here: I spoke with our painter, Joël, and his wife Vivienne [16] a few minutes ago and they told me that the Tour comes through here almost every year! It actually comes right *through* Chalabre most times. Last year, there was a time trial between Sonnac and Camon. We probably even watched it without realizing that soon, we would be living here. How weird and ironic is that?

I hope we don't have weather like we had yesterday, though. *Big* thunderstorms all afternoon. The lights were flickering and we wound up turning off the computers, just in case. The house has surge protectors, but why take a chance?

Before the weather hit, we went out to Limoux and Carcassonne. I got all the necessary forms and ugly photos to apply for my driver's license. At one point, after all is processed, I'll get notified of when I have to go in to take my test. Gulp! Lots of studying left to do.

Guess I should stop and get to it, then.

Thursday, June 16

Wild things. Certainly the Diva doesn't qualify, but last night we saw several of them as we went to and came back from dinner.

Our friends Cathy and Sean had a backed-up sewer pipe, so we told them we would take them away from all that and whisked them off to dinner in Mirepoix. On the way there, a beautiful, young deer was standing in the middle of the road. He wasn't the least bit concerned about our presence, either. He looked at us, than casually wandered back into the woods.

---

[16] Who operates the local hairdressing salon.

We had our usual marvelous meal at Le Commerce. I know we should try other places, but it's always so wonderful there, that the temptation to explore just isn't all that great.

On the way back, a huge hare hopped across the road. He looked almost as big as Maggie, although I'm sure that wasn't the case!

What surprised us was that we hadn't actually seen any wild creatures on the road up until now. But, having seen these two, I realized that the signs warning about their presence are there for a reason. I definitely drove prudently. I have no great desire to run smack into a deer in the dark. Somehow, I don't think that either the deer, Beanie or we would come out of that unscathed.

Sunday, June 19

Summer is in full swing here in Chalabre and environs. Not only have we been having lovely, warm weather, but also there seems to be some event happening just about all the time.

The nice surprise has been that, even when it is close to 90 (F) outside, the inside of the house stays pleasant and comfortable. I don't miss air conditioning in the least. Even when we're out in Beanie, we only seem to use the A/C when we're in the middle of a town and just let the air blow through the windows in the country.

Last night, we went to Puivert, where they had a special market and music festival. You could buy dinner from start to finish from the local "producers" and listen to *very* loud music. We had already eaten, so just had dessert: yummy ice cream made from local sheep's milk. Absolutely outstanding. Then, I bought a jar of apricot/lavender preserves. Probably the best preserves I've ever had.[17]

Today, there was an equestrian circus here in town, but it was too hot to go sit outside to watch it. However, there are all kinds of other events coming up, and the Château opens up in two weeks with their medieval recreations. I can't wait to see those.

Every day, I feel more and more a part of the community here. When we were in Puivert last night, cars kept honking at us as several of our neighbors drove by! Today, people asked if we had a good time. It's so nice to be part of that.

---

[17] I notice I say that a lot! But, I'm always amazed by how good simple things taste here.

Tuesday, June 21

Poor Sean had to go back to London yesterday. We drove him and Cathy to Carcassonne and had another wonderful lunch at the Hanoi before dropping him at the airport.

Cathy hadn't driven her right-hand-drive care in France before and hadn't actually been to Carcassonne, so we didn't think dropping her husband off at the airport was the best way for her to start. I promised to ride shotgun with her today on her first trial run though.

Then, Peter came home from his reconnaissance mission to Spain. He was shocked that the housing prices there (in the south) were higher than here in France. Also, the heat was apparently brutal. I hope that means he's convinced he should stay here now. We stopped in to say hello, then picked up Cathy and went over to Maggie-the-Human and Martin's for dinner.

Martin is doing all the renovation of their place himself, and I have to say it's beautiful and impressive! Makes me jealous that we can't do that kind of thing on our own. But, wisdom is knowing to stick with what you *can* do!

We had a lovely meal sitting on their patio out in the garden. Diva Maggie enjoyed their garden immensely, although she has some weird little green plant bits stuck in her coat that I've spent most of the day removing. Once again, I was struck by how wonderful summer is here. It was light until 10 p.m.! You just feel like sitting up and enjoying it, because it's so beautiful and peaceful. We even saw a bat flying around, which was pretty cool.

Speaking of wildlife, Cathy told us that Claude, one of the Rivel neighbors, had approached her Sunday night while Peter was away. He was concerned because one of the lights in Peter's house was on. Then, he started moving his arms about and making noises as he tried to explain what he thought was going on. Cathy got all upset, because she thought Claude had told her that Peter's house was haunted! In fact, he was telling her that an *owl* might have gotten inside! Now, the entire village thinks she's terrified of owls! We all thought we would die laughing!

When we got home, JM and I couldn't stop talking about how our lives have changed. It's so easy to be social here, when you only have to drive five minutes in no traffic to get to someone's house for dinner. The stress of planning has simply disappeared. Traffic is highly overrated as a lifestyle choice.

Saturday, June 25

After 27 years in Los Angeles, I forgot that summer means something different in most of the rest of the world.

In L.A., except for a bit of what we call "June Gloom," summer is hot and dry. The weather people have trouble coming up with different ways of saying it, so weather broadcasts are filled with various cutesy features to fill up the space.

Here, in the Aude, summer means several hot days followed by rising humidity and thunderstorms. Last night, we went out to Le Commerce for a late celebration of JM's birthday [18] with Peter and Cathy. There had been a storm before we left, but the sky cleared up and the sky was blue by the time we got in the car.

However, as we sat on the terrace having dinner, a massive storm broke out! Maggie clearly thought this was something we'd come up with to make her suffer. We stayed out there though, because we were in a nice, protected spot. Cathy and I started to get a little damp when the wind changed, but otherwise it wasn't bad at all.

The Commerce has a lovely black lab that comes to visit the tables. She clearly realized that Maggie was terrified and kept trying to get through our legs to the spot where our poor Diva was cowering. When she got to her, she started licking her face, clearly telling her that it was all right and she didn't have to be afraid. I need to take her a special treat the next time we go for a meal.

As we drove home, the display was impressive. The sky was completely lit up by the lightning. I don't think I've ever seen anything quite like it. Oddly, Maggie was not afraid while she was in the car. I don't know if it was the sound of the engine blocking the storm noise or the motion of the car, but she curled up and went to sleep. To bad I can't just take her for drives whenever there's a storm.

We had left several windows open when we went out, so were a little nervous. Luckily, nothing was damaged, but I guess we have to pay a little bit more attention to the weather from now on.

---

[18] June 22.

Surprisingly, the storm didn't really drop the humidity any. Some of my neighbors think we're going to have another one today. No sign of it yet though. I guess I better keep my flashlights handy...

Sunday, June 26
The benefit of darkness is severely underestimated in our modern times.

Summer has definitely arrived here in Chalabre. It gets to the upper 80s, low 90s outside. The difference from L.A. is that we also tend to be a bit more humid, although it's far from unbearable.

Because of the thick stone walls of our house, inside stays quite cool and comfortable as long as we deal with the windows properly. This means opening the windows to air the house at night and in the early morning, but closing both shutters *and* windows as soon as it starts to get warm outside. It's amazingly effective, basically turning the walls into a very low-tech swamp cooler.

For several nights, therefore, we decided to sleep with not only the bedroom windows open, but the shutters as well. The downside of this is that instead of sleeping in a room that is in total–and I do mean total– darkness, the lights from the street, the Moon and the stars make the bedroom pretty bright. I hadn't realized that I was sleeping so well because of the total darkness.

I hadn't seen total darkness in L.A. since the night of the '94 quake when all the power in the city went out. It was easy to navigate through the whole house in Reseda without ever using a flashlight or even a nightlight. It also seemed normal to me to wake up every hour or so most nights. I just assumed I didn't sleep well, but in reality, the light was keeping me awake.

Here, I fall asleep almost immediately when we go to bed, and even if I wake up for a bathroom break during the night, I fall right back asleep until dawn. It is clearly the darkness that does it, because those nights where we had the windows open, I couldn't sleep. I was up constantly, totally unable to fall deeply asleep. When we went back to closing the shutters, boom, I was out like a light.

I don't think there's really a solution in our modern world. Without shutting our houses totally to the outside, we will be assailed by light in most places. I wonder if the stress of life as we know it isn't caused as much by poor sleep due to light pollution as to any other cause...

Wednesday, June 29

It has been a while since I've talked about food, which is actually pretty criminal, considering where we live!

'Tis the season of amazing fresh produce. Everything is so full of flavor that sometimes, I have trouble controlling my purchases when I go to the little fruit and vegetable shop owned by my friends Jean-Paul and Hélène. Jean-Paul goes out each morning to buy whatever is fresh from various local sources. He loves to talk about what he's selling and gives great advice.

Besides the produce that I buy, my neighbors the Gimenezes and M. Martinez also give me things that they've picked in their gardens. It's amazing how good something as simple as lettuce and zucchini can taste when they've been picked fresh that very morning.

I've had melons here that are so good, you want to eat until you burst. The same with the strawberries and peaches. I can hardly wait for grape season, although that's kind of a bad sign, because it means that summer is over and the time for the best variety of produce will be gone.

All of these wonderful products make it so easy to whip together a healthy and heavenly meal. We're eating more fruit and vegetables than we ever did before and not missing things like rice or pasta, which only take up space that could be filled with veggies. Something as simple as a quick ratatouille just adds so much flavor to any main dish that the pleasure of eating is more than doubled.

Of course, we've eaten out as well, with wonderful meals at Le Commerce, as well as good experiences elsewhere.

One of those other restaurants caused us quite a few laughs on Monday. We went with Peter and Cathy for a quick lunch in Limoux. It was very hot and muggy, so we sat outside a local brasserie, under an umbrella and looked at their salad menus. They had "translated" the ingredients for the salads and had clearly used an online translator to do the work. One of their salads contained "lawyer" as an ingredient. Of course, with Cathy being an ex-barrister, we all had quite a laugh over that. What could it have been, you might ask? Why *avocado*! In French, the word for avocado and lawyer are both "*avocat*!" The dangers of relying too heavily on technology!

Friday, July 1

Summer has taken a holiday. Not that I mind, really. After all those years of never-ending sunshine in L.A., it's rather nice to have "weather" for a change!

We went from the low 90s last week, to mid-seventies this week, which has been quite pleasant. However, we've also had some thunderstorms and drizzle. Now, normally that wouldn't be a problem, but tomorrow is the *big* Chalabre street festival! There will be a variety of vendors during the day (including us!), various demonstrations of sports and cultural activities, and at night, a giant communal dinner at the covered market. It sounds like loads of fun. But, rain will not make it hugely enjoyable for any of us.

JM and I have taken out a table to sell books. I've got no idea how well we'll do, but it will be fun to have a place to hang out to watch the world go by. Of course, we're going to the dinner and are being joined by Peter, Lizzie, Cathy and Sean. I'm sure most of our other village friends will be there as well. I have been guaranteed that the dinner does *not* include tripe, one of Peter's biggest fears!

Everyone in town has assured me that we will have sunshine tomorrow. I checked various weather sites and they all seem to predict nice weather as well: sunshine and 80 degrees. Hard to ask for a nicer day than that.

We'll just have to wait and see. Of course, I will take lots of pictures. The village is already getting prepared; the Café de la Paix is even building a beach on its terrace! Keep your fingers crossed that it doesn't all wash away.

Sunday, July 3

Sunday, a day to recover from Saturday!

Yesterday was an absolutely perfect day. Not too hot, the sky that beautiful blue that you only seem to really see in the south of France, a nice breeze but not too windy. Just the day that was needed for the Chalabre *Festival des Rues*!

In the morning, there was the usual Saturday market, only instead of being on the Cours Colbert, it had to be moved to the parking lot next to the Maison de Tourisme. If not, the entire town would have had to be closed down to traffic, which is not practical in the least.

The festival itself was scheduled to start at 2 p.m. Of course, being the South of France, that really meant that hardly anyone was even visible walking around until after 3 p.m.!

Our table was in a nice, shady spot on the Cours Sully, right across from the Mairie. The *frites* and *crêpes* concession was directly in front of us, which was pure torture. I had to give in and have a bit of both, of course.

It wasn't what you would call a huge financial success for any of the vendors, apparently. People here just don't seem to have a lot of disposable income. I think we've got one of the highest unemployment rates in the country, so buying books, trinkets and luxury gourmet items is just not happening for most people. Probably most purchases were made by summer people. But, the festival was a couple of weeks early to benefit from large numbers of tourists. School holidays don't really start here until next week.

Still, it was a great way for us to see lots of people that we know and visit a bit.

Peter, Cathy and Sean joined us for the communal dinner around the Halles (the covered market), which began around 7 p.m. For the first hour it was aperitif and lots of speeches. The rugby team was given its cup and everyone milled around and visited. We were all starting to get really hungry, but dinner wasn't being served until 8-ish.

I had tried to leave Maggie at home, but unfortunately, the local kids were setting off lots and lots of firecrackers. I went back to the house to check on her and she was hidden somewhere in the upper reaches of the house. When she came downstairs, she was drenched because she had clearly been drooling in terror. I decided that she was better off with us, even if it was probably louder outside. At least, she didn't feel abandoned.

I had taken silverware along with us as requested, but didn't realized that we also needed to bring our own plates, so we had to come back to the house one more time to get fully "kitted" out! Next time I do this, I'll get a supply of paper plates for everyone. It would have been loads easier.

Still, it was all worth it. The various local enterprises contributed the food. We had pizza and salad for an *entrée*. Then, dinner was a superb beef *daube* (stew) with potatoes, made by Didier and Mireille Antonio, our excellent local butcher and his wife. Dessert was a terrific Brie and fruit. Of course, there was wine as well, an excellent local red that I tried in spite of worrying about getting a migraine.

Afterwards, we couldn't resist and went back to the crepe stand for another of their yummy offerings. I think I need to run up and down the stairs a few extra times today!

Monday, July 4

Peter rang our doorbell this afternoon while I was up on the first floor. I went to the window to say I'd be right down and Maggie was, of course, right next to me. Since we're still in the midst of all the renovation work, there are odd things set up in places they aren't meant to be.

One of them is a half-moon-shaped table that we had near the front door in L.A. It has very spindly legs and really needs to be attached to the wall in order to be stable. Because I plan on selling it, right now it isn't attached to anything. Somehow, Maggie bumped into it and it fell over, right on top of my foot!

I think poor Peter thought I was dying in here, because I started screaming in agony! It is much heavier than it looks.

We called the doctor who said to ice it, then see if I could walk. I can, sort of, as long as I don't put any pressure on the front of my foot. It's pretty swollen and purple right now, but that could just be bruising and not anything broken. We're going to wait until tomorrow morning and see how things develop, then, if it's not better, I'll go and see Dr. Croesi. Luckily, he's a sports medicine specialist, so it's right up his alley.

It really doesn't matter if it's broken though, because there's not much you can do for a broken foot. It will be damned inconvenient, however. I did wonder what we'd do about all the steps if one of us got injured. I guess I'm going to find out.

Tuesday, July 5

Good news on the foot front: it's not broken!

Everything (including my leg) is still bruised and swollen, but after a visit to the doctor this morning, the verdict is probably no break. If it isn't mostly better by next week, I can get an x-ray, but I don't think I'll need to bother.

The offending table is now turned upside down so that it can no longer fall and damage anyone else. Tomorrow, I'm thinking of taking it to the *"Depôt Vente"* in Mirepoix to put it up for sale.[19] I found a set of lovely dishes that I'd like if they manage to sell it.

Meanwhile, with all the foot events, I forgot to write about another weird occurrence yesterday. I have this amazingly cheap, but comfortable, polar fleece jacket that I lived in all winter. Yesterday was cool and rainy, so I decided to wear it. I cannot find it anywhere! I've searched the house from attic to cellar with no success.

I decided to look in the car, just in case I'd left it there and hadn't noticed (considering that it is bright red, that seems hard to imagine, but still...). I took everything out, but no jacket to be found.

What I *did* find was Beanie's *California license plates*! Absolutely amazing! They were under the floor mat beneath the driver's seat. Now, I am positive that I've looked under there several times and not seen anything looking like a license plate. Peter has sat back there several times and he also claims to have never seen a license plate-looking thing.

Our only guess is that, when M. Hervas was looking around in the car for information he needed to fill out some of the paperwork to get her registered, *he* came upon the plates hidden under the rug in the trunk (covering the spare) and he put them on the floor in the back seat. I must ask him if this is the case, because otherwise I must admit the evidence points to me totally losing my mind.

Thursday, July 7

I needed to listen to music from a more innocent time today. I drove through Camon to the beat of the Beach Boys and came home from Lavelanet singing with The Beatles.

It didn't help to take my mind off of the ugly events in London this morning. How quickly you can go from thinking about paint colors and bookshelves to being in tears for all of those affected by the horror of an attack...

I hate the war in Iraq. We shouldn't be there and should never have gone. But the people riding the subway and busses to work in London today no more merited what happened to them than the hundreds of

---

[19] And sell it did, but we didn't buy the dishes that had gone up in price in the meantime.

thousands of innocent Iraqis have deserved what they've been living through for the last two years.

I will talk about life in Chalabre again. But not today. Today, I am sad for the world.

Sunday, July 10

Dirt, dirt and more dirt. This seems to be the theme of our lives.

The goal is for the kitchen/dining area to be completed by the end of July. Concurrently, Joël has started painting from the top of the house down. JM's offices are now painted and Joël will be installing bookshelves on Friday, which means that by next weekend, we will actually have two rooms emptied of cartons of books! Amazing. We then move everything from the library up to the offices while he paints and shelves that room.

I can almost envision a time when we will no longer be living out of boxes.

That time is still not here, however, as we have actually moved backwards a bit to enable the kitchen to be done. Everything that I had unpacked has had to be re-packed so that Jacques, Charlie and Mikael could remove the dropped ceiling from the kitchen and sand down the beams. They have also started doing the same thing in the first floor bathroom.

It's amazing what a difference that makes in the space and feeling of the rooms. Even though the objective space gained isn't a lot, the psychological space is amazing. Once the wood between the beams is painted white, I think it will all feel vastly opened up.

Another surprise was discovering that an extra wall had been built in the kitchen when they tiled it. This means that the kitchen is actually 20 cms wider than we thought! That means we will regain that space once the old tile and that wall is removed. We will have a much larger kitchen than I had expected. Bonus!

Of course, while all this is going on, there is a constant flow of dirt and dust. The sanding of the beams (which are all oak in the kitchen) is a filthy, filthy job. Everything has been moved down to the garage, which is really for the best, because otherwise I'm afraid the stove and fridge might have been permanently damaged. I've already lost two pounds running up and down the stairs between floors as I try to prepare meals with two levels separating the fridge from my temporary "cooking" area in the television room. (Peter generously loaned us a microwave so we don't have to eat out every night.)

I know it will all be worth it in the end. We just have to get to that point though, with our lungs intact.

Manu sanding a beam

Wednesday, July 13

Major traffic jam in Ajac today!

This doesn't sound like much, until you realize that Ajac is a tiny, hillside, medieval village in between Limoux and Chalabre. It shouldn't have traffic jams. But there is one mountain road that goes through it, and road crews have working on resurfacing it. The road runs between fields of sunflowers and vines, and there's just no way to avoid a road closure.

I know this because we tried! We wound through the little village streets that were barely wide enough to accommodate Beanie, then went off-road near a construction site, to take another eensie-teensie road that seemed to run parallel to the main road. Small problem there. It went through the vines, only to wind up at the dead end of the vineyard's main house! No way to get through back to the road.

So, we turned around and made our way back to the original starting point, where we sat in the traffic jam of *four* cars, until it was our turn to pass. Ah well, we had an adventure.

Our adventures in our own house continue, as Manu has now completely opened up the kitchen and installed a beautiful, new beam to hold up the ceiling! "New," is, of course, a relative term. While the beam is in a new place, it was actually an ancient, oak beam that had been sitting in our cellar! It is in perfect condition, and now that it's sanded down, it looks as if it has always been right there in the ceiling. How lucky for us that it was sitting down there and no one thought to cut it up for firewood!

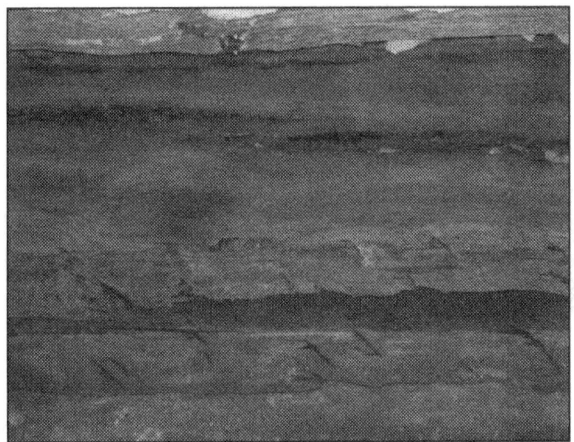
Close-up of one of the oak beams

We're still having one slight problem, which is that Manu does not think he can tile the bathrooms before the end of October. That means the new bathroom fixtures can't be installed until after that. But, we discovered today that the leaking from the bathtub is more serious than we thought. We will need to talk to Christian to see what can be done to get us through the next few months. I do not want my beautiful new kitchen water damaged before we even start using it!

Tomorrow is July 14, the French national holiday. You would think that everything stops for that, but we have plenty of work to do, nevertheless. No rest for the wicked when you're renovating a house.

Saturday, July 16

Work progresses, although we've had a few upsets both in the timetable and emotionally.

Downstairs (kitchen/dining area) is going to be amazing when it's done. At first, I was sad that we couldn't have the archway into the kitchen that we'd planned on. However, with Manu having used the original oak beams that were in the cellar to re-create the *colombage* on the wall, it is so astonishing looking, that I'm now thrilled beyond belief.

This just goes to prove that when you're working with an old house like this, you just have to be flexible.

Many of these houses were actually built onto already existing structures. For example, what is now our cellar, garage and ground floor were built behind the old ramparts of the wall that surrounded the bastide (the center of the original village). That would mean that those parts were done in the middle-ages. Then, the upper floors were added on in the 1800s,

It also appears possible that the front of our house and the back of our house were, at one point, two separate structures, which were then broken through to create one house.

Another thing that makes these complicated is that people were concerned with having a structure that kept them warm in the winter and protected from the weather. They weren't too worried about what it looked like. So, if walls and floors weren't totally straight, it wasn't that big of a deal.

All of this is what, today, gives the houses so much character. They were massively well built, but quirkily done. You need to always go slowly, as different generations of residents did their own "thing," over the years, so you never know what you will discover.

Unfortunately, this quirkiness proved a small problem yesterday. The leaking bathtub problem was made much, much worse by the removal of the false ceiling in the kitchen. This was probably due to the vibration caused by both the work in the bathroom itself, and the polishing of the kitchen beams.

At any rate, it meant that whenever we were taking a shower, water was literally cascading through the kitchen ceiling. Not a big problem while there's nothing in there, but as soon as it's all finished, not something that can be allowed to continue.

So, we tried to find a solution, based on the fact that Manu has had to take more time with the groundfloor and can't attack the bathrooms until this fall! Unfortunately, that caused its own set of emotional problems with feelings getting hurt, etc.

It all wound up being resolved, with a temporary fix that will hold things until all the work can be completed. But, it made the atmosphere a bit tense, to say the least.

It's good to remember that most of the artisans we work with are doing this work out of love for what they do. Many of them had other careers and chose to give them up for this. Indeed, they are often not artisans, but, as in Manu's case, true artists. There's emotional baggage that goes along with that, and its importance in the final result can't be underestimated.

Wednesday, July 20

I meant to write yesterday, but the usual sty-like nature of the worksite: a.k.a. our "home," has deteriorated even further.

When the bathroom fixtures were removed to allow the floor to be worked on, we discovered that the bathroom wall had absorbed enough water to irrigate a small field. This meant that the plaster had to be removed a.s.a.p. and the wall taken down to the stone. This had not been part of the original "master plan."

Luckily, Manu's cousin, confusingly also named Manu, was coming to help with jointing the stones downstairs. He was immediately changed to repairing the bathroom. Then, Manu's uncle and Stéphane's father, a retired stone cutter, was roped in to help with the walls and replastering the downstairs ceiling in between the beams.

Since Joel had already brought in his stepson to help with painting and restoring the hardwood floors in the library/guestroom/office, we are now pretty much a full house.

Of course, since we no longer have a bathroom of any kind, JM and I can't actually sleep in the house. We are bunking in the little house that lives between Cathy and Peter in Rivel. Diva Maggie is confused.

Although the watery wall was a bit of a shocker, it's all turning out for the best, as Manu-2 is staying on board an extra day to actually tile the bathroom floor, something we had thought we'd have to wait for until sometime this fall.

I suppose this means that tomorrow or Saturday at the latest, we'll actually have a working bathroom again and will be able to move back home. I think there's light at the end of the tunnel.

RIVEL

Rivel is a small village located about 5 miles south of Chalabre. It is very pittoresque, and today is mostly inhabited by a mix of retired French natives, British expatriates and holiday home owners from other parts of France and the U.K.

The "little house" between Café Rives and the Boulangerie in Rivel where we stayed during our time of "no water!"

Rivel

The Sainte Cécile Chapel on a hilltop overlooking Rivel

The Old Epicerie (Grocery Store) by the Town Square

Friday, July 22

No driver's license as of yet. However, not because I failed the test.

The driver's test here has a slide show and you answer a multiple choice question based on the slide. The fatal flaw in the plan was that the projector wasn't working properly this morning. After fiddling with it for an hour, they decided to try to go through with the test and see if it worked. However, I was the only one there who hadn't come through a driving school. That meant that I was the last one to get registered.

Registration was going to take over an hour, and with the hour or more that I'd already spent waiting, I decided that I'd had enough. So, I told the monitor that I would call for a new date and left.

Tomorrow is another day, as Scarlett O'Hara liked to say.

So, back we came to the worksite, which is progressing beautifully, if noisily. Everyone in town can hear when we're having work done! Still, the stone walls will be finished by tonight and tomorrow the bathroom floor will be tiled. Theoretically we should have a bathroom at the beginning of next week and a kitchen at the end.

Meanwhile, master painter Joël Brochet has finished my office/library and it is just lovely. Honey-colored antique pine floors, pale lavender walls with darker lavender and white highlights. I'm looking forward to moving back in there tomorrow, after the floor is completely dry.

I think Maggie has given up trying to cope with all of it and spends most of her time in the house hiding out in the television room. She doesn't even bother following me around, because she can't stand being around the noise and dust. Not that I blame her, mind. Poor baby. She has no idea that this, too, shall pass.

Saturday, July 23

So, here I am, all moved back into my office. I must say it is great to be back here. Although it does seem oddly empty without all the boxes and, of course, JM, who is now in his very *own* office upstairs. He's been busily sorting books and putting them on the shelves. The last of the wood and hardware is due on Wednesday, so we can actually start doing that in the library as well then.

The walls downstairs have been jointed and brushed. The stone is just beautiful. Manu is working on the kitchen walls today, then will give the beams a final polish tomorrow and treat them with a product to kill any lingering wood-eating beasties.

Cousin Manu is tiling the bathroom floor, which should allow us to actually have the bathroom fixtures put back in on Tuesday or Wednesday. Could it be that our house will soon be livable again?

I don't know how we could have coped with all of this without our wonderful friends and neighbors. They've all been terrifically generous in allowing us to stay (thank you, Cathy!) and also use their toilet facilities during the day (thank you, M. & Mme. Gimenez, Nathalie, Mme. Roget, Hazel & John!). We really do live in a great village.

I'm hoping that once all this work is done I can have a bit of a house party to thank all of them for their kindness. It will be nice to have a kitchen where I can prepare something like that.

Monday, July 25

The big subject of conversation in these parts of late has been the amazing lack of tourists this season.

We had been led to believe that the village would be swarming with visitors during most of July and August, but that has not turned out to be the case. We've spoken with the owners of the *buvettes* (snack/restaurant) in Le Cazal and Puivert, as well as M. Roget who gives pony rides in Mirepoix, and a variety of others in the area. Everybodt says that it is absolutely empty this year.

The reasons seem to run from the economy, not a big surprise, to people just living in a general state of fear. Now, clearly, if there is one place where fear of terrorism should be put to rest, it's Chalabre and the surrounding area. I doubt pretty strongly that there's a terrorist anywhere in the world who would think we were worthy of their attention, even if they had ever heard of us.

But, it's an interesting psychological study. That unreasoning fear that takes hold of people when they read the news or watch television can have widespread, rippling effects.

Of course, the irony is, as I told my GP today, that most of the folks who are staying home out of fear, probably smoke and drive after a few drinks; two activities that are far more likely to impact their lives and safety than a terrorist attack. Indeed, I was at the doctor's office today to get a tetanus booster, something that poses a *real* risk in an agricultural environment like this one.

Just some food for thought on this quiet Monday in July.

Wednesday, July 27

Yesterday we escaped... I mean, we went out for the day. We drove to meet up with our friends Philippe and Bernadette, then followed them to Gourbit, a small village in the Ariège. Philippe's father grew up in Gourbit and wrote a fascinating book about life there throughout history. We helped Philippe to publish it and were all invited to the Musée des Pyrénées to discuss that as well as general issues of micro-publishing.

We had a wonderful time and were given an amazing feast by Philippe's mother before the conference.

However, yesterday wound up being a scorching hot day, and although we were higher up in the mountains than Chalabre, it felt hotter to us than it does here. People felt like they were melting. Thank goodness for Beanie's air conditioner!

Speaking of Beanie, we had another funny experience with her today. We drove to the Toyota dealership in Pamiers to show them the paperwork we've filled out to get a French registration. Of course, no one there had ever seen an Echo before. We had salesmen coming out to look her over in admiration and one even told us, "I've only seen one of these in a movie before!"

The heat is back today and we have the shutters all closed up trying to keep the house cool. It's unfortunate too, because all of our artisans are here working like mad, trying to get everything done before the end of next week. It's wonderful to see the progress being made, but they are all suffering in the heat. It would be nice for their sakes especially, to have things cool off some...

Saturday, July 30

Although we're still bunking at Cathy's in Rivel, we now *do* have our very own toilet! Woo hoo! Who knew that could get anyone this happy?

The theory was that we would also have our new sink and water heater today, but so far that hasn't happened. I still am holding out hope, however.

Meanwhile, Manu has been working like crazy, getting the downstairs tile finished so that he can prep the kitchen and install the tile in there tomorrow or Monday. All downstairs tiling has to be finished by Tuesday night so that our countertop can be installed on Wednesday. If we miss that date, we wouldn't be able to have it done until September!

Eating out is starting to get a bit old. It's frightening how quickly the cost of restaurant meals can really add up, even if you are careful and try to pick inexpensive dishes. It is ever so much less expensive to cook at home. Still, with no running water, it really isn't possible to do much in the house. Wet wipes can only take you so far, after all.

But, I am learning that patience really is a virtue. And, even if I'm not particularly virtuous, it's not as if I have any choice but to be patient!

Monday, August 1

I've mentioned what a mess our house is right now. Everything that we're using on a daily basis is pretty much in one room. This includes food, dog supplies, etc.

Now, Diva Maggie has always been a fussy eater. She has never, except for what has come to be known as the "*foie gras* incident of 1999" stolen food or gone through the trash. Since we've been living here, I have to admit that I've been very bad about spoiling her. She has gotten to share morsels of food from almost every meal we've eaten. I had to experiment for a while to find regular food that she could eat, and I'm afraid that with all of that, possibly combined with the horrible dust and dirt, she developed a rather severe case of eczema.

I decided that the first thing I needed to do was to change her food to something that was lower in protein and fat, so I ordered Burns Chicken and Brown Rice from *La Maison des Animaux* knowing that it has a great reputation for clearing up food caused eczema. Unfortunately, Maggie had been scratching and biting at herself enough that I needed to put her on a small dose of prednisone to relieve the itching quickly.

I was worried that after her recent diet, the sight of dried kibble would not be a welcome one. However, the hunger caused by being on prednisone overcame any reluctance she might have felt about eating it. Yet, this hunger has been a two-edged sword! In spite of my feeding her the amounts recommended for her weight and activity level, she still seems to want to eat everything and anything! She even ate some bread yesterday, when one of the neighbor children gave it to her before I could stop him.

Today, there have been thunderstorms on and off. This is guaranteed to cause stress, so I put on her Anxiety Wrap and tried to just let her chill out. I realized I hadn't seen her for a little while, so went looking in her usual hiding places.

Imagine my surprise in finding her in the middle of the television/living room, her box of Avantix/HeartGard/Hairbrush and chewy treats knocked over and a guilty-looking Diva trying to hid the rawhide chew bone that she'd stolen! To top it off, there was an empty bag of smaller rawhide treats that I'm sure had at least six or eight pieces in it last time I looked!

I could barely believe my eyes. I have to admit that I did take away the remainder of the rawhide, because I don't want her to get sick. Now, I'm watching her like a hawk, to make sure she didn't eat enough to wind up with bloat. I don't relish an emergency trip to a vet, trying to explain that in French!

Thursday, August 4

Yesterday was one of those perfect days that made me feel as if I was in a novel or a movie.

Our friends, Margaret and Peter, two of the lovely people we've met due to our website and this blog (Hello, Stuart and Leslie!), invited us to a special lunch with their son and daughter-in-law, Tom and Colleen, as well as the owners of the Abbaye de Camon, Peter and Katie.

The restaurant was a wonderful, special place, open only on reservation for parties of eight or more. The host, André, was charming and convivial. We elected to sit outside in the garden, where the eight of us sat, talked and ate a magical meal of André's special house *foie gras*, tomatoes from his own garden, magret of duck grilled on an open oak fire, and confit of duck in mushroom sauce. Everything was perfect and delicious.

A giant beech tree covered us in its shade, the company was charming and delightful and almost three hours sped by as if they were mere minutes. It was the kind of day you want to preserve in your memory forever, and we're extremely grateful to Peter and Margaret for including us.

When we arrived home, it was to discover that my kitchen counter had been installed and was even more beautiful than I had expected. The work is now progressing rapidly and when JM and return from visiting the family in Toulon on Monday, I fully expect that life will be almost back to normal for the remainder of the summer.

Who could ask for any finer end to a simply perfect day?

Tuesday, August 9

We spent the weekend in Toulon, visiting with the family. Although it was nice to see everyone, I have to say that it did a fine job of convincing us that we were right to move to our little Shire, and not make any attempt to live anywhere near the *Côte d'Azur*!

It was hot. It was crowded. It was noisy. There was traffic everywhere. And, because there has been a drought in the region for four years and all the vegetation is dry as tinder, there were forest fires raging everywhere! It was like being back in L.A. and it was not wonderful in the least.

By the time we got back to our lovely Chalabre, we felt as if we never wanted to leave again. Just seeing all of our new friends, out beautiful hills and our village made us feel at peace. It is good to have had confirmation that we chose well.

Still, if there was a weekend when it was wise to go away, this past weekend seems to have been it. The annual Motorcycle Festival took place on Friday, Saturday and Sunday. According to all accounts, it was quite the experience. Loud (mostly bad) music was blaring till 4 a.m.! Everyone on the street told us that their windows were actually vibrating from the sound.

Then, there was a massive barbecue held on Cours Colbert, and the epicenter seems to have been directly in front of our house! That would have been an interesting sight to be sure.

Yet, part of me is sorry that I missed it. I'm sure it would have been loud and crowded, but it's all a part of life in our new home and I want to experience it all, no matter how strange it might be.

Much catching up to do, so *ciao* for now!

Thursday, August 11

I am happy to report that we once again have a fully functional bathroom. It's amazing how happy taking a shower in your own home can make you feel. I wanted to stay in there all day when I took my first at-home shower in our newly remodeled bath.

Everything is now zipping towards conclusion on this first stage of renovation. Manu finished up on Tuesday and Joel is almost finished with the downstairs. The weather has actually been the biggest hang up, as the cool temps and rain have kept the walls from drying enough for the color to be laid over the rough, white paint surface. Still, much is getting done everywhere else, which is great.

Arnaud is working on finishing the electricity, and tomorrow, if all goes well, my stove and refrigerator may be back in the kitchen where they belong.

It will be wonderful to have a bit of a breather from the work, although, depending on his schedule, Joël may actually be able to work on the television room next week. That would leave us with only our bedroom and bath to be completed in November, which isn't really too bad at all.

I think I'll miss everyone though. It has been a nice bit of socializing as well, having our various artisans/friends around the house. Still, I can't say that it won't be nice to be able to sleep in occasionally in the morning. We haven't had the chance to do that for a long, long time.

BEFORE

When we bought our house, our groundfloor dining room / kitchen looked like this. This was the view towards the entrance to the Cours Colbert:

And this was the opposite view towards the tiny kitchen:

DURING

We undertook the restoration of the stone walls. This involved removing the outer plaster walls, using a jackhammer to bring out the original stones beneath, then doing the same to the ceiling's wooden beams (oak and poplar), then using a powerful electric sander to polish them.

Manu and Arnaud at work

After the restoration of the walls had begun, the kitchen, however, was still closet-sized. So we decided to enlarge it. The walls to the right and left of the original door had to be knocked down.

But as it turned out, the doorframe was supporting the wall above it, so Manu needed to find a way to replace it, which he did by carving new beams made of ancient oak and erecting new diagonal supports.

A counter (also made of ancient oak) was built to connect the two diagonal beams; the open space at the bottom was filled-in with stone and masonry to match the wall. Stone steps were constructed to access the now-opened up kitchen space.

AFTER

As for the side facing the Cours Colbert, here is how it looks with its new tiled floors and restored stone walls. The only thing not depicted above is a painted vesselier *(dish cupboard) where the table on the left stands.*

Friday, August 12

I can't believe it. We've actually got a kitchen again! A sink, a stove, a fridge and a dishwasher, all in their own little spots, all connected, all raring to go! I keep standing there and looking at it in wonder!

Our wonderful painter Joël and plumber Christian (and his son!) practically killed themselves moving not only the appliances, but an extraordinarily heavy Louis-Philippe armoire, into place. Plus, they had to move our leather couch out of its normal place, so that Joël can start sanding the television room floor next week. It really was above and beyond the call of duty.

Christian and his darling wife, Nathalie, are then heading off at 4 a.m. tomorrow morning for a well-earned vacation with family in Normandy. I will miss them both while they're gone.

Various neighbors have been stopping by to check out the mostly completed downstairs. Just a few finishing touches need to be placed, but it's 95% there. It's hard to believe that in another week, we'll be done with everything but our bedroom and bathroom.

Right now, everyone's tomatoes are getting ripe. We've gotten a bunch from both Christian and our friends, the Gimenezes across the street. Tomorrow, I will celebrate our first meal from the new kitchen with those and I can hardly wait!

Monday, August 15

It has been wonderful getting back to living relatively normally with an actual kitchen. It has been hard, passing by Jean-Paul's fruit and vegetable shop, seeing all the lovely summer produce, and not being able to buy any of it. This weekend, we've been totally spoiled: fresh tomatoes from the gardens of the Gimenezes and the Drouins, beautiful peaches and nectarines and fabulous, fragrant melons from Jean-Paul.

Yesterday for lunch, we joined in at the Rivel community luncheon, which was quite fun. I love the fact that the villages do these kinds of things. The food is always great, you get to sit and chat with friends, and you just feel as if you are a part of something special.

Still, it was nice to come back home to relax and get to prepare dinner in my very own kitchen. Not that it was anything special, but good, simple ingredients can make a true feast. If you're looking for an easy vegetarian meal, here's what I threw together: about a pound of ripe tomatoes, peeled and roughly chopped, a handful of sautéed onions, salt, garlic, a bit of sugar and some leftover wine. Cook it on low to make a not too thick sauce, then roughly tear up half a loaf or so of bread (semi-stale works great) and mix that in with the sauce. Turn off the heat, stir in some grated parmesan and *voila*, you've got a kind of bread stew. It's filling, it's easy and it tastes wonderful.

We finished off the meal with a bowl of peaches and nectarines, marinated in a bit of *crème de pêche* liqueur and a little sugar. I don't think I've enjoyed a meal more in a long, long time.

Tuesday, August 16

Big excitement here in Chalabre yesterday.

To celebrate our once again having a kitchen, we invited David and Jane (who are back working on their house here in town) and Peter over for a simple dinner. I asked JM and Peter to take Maggie for a walk before we sat down to eat.

Peter came running back to the house, saying that there was an emergency. When he and JM had turned onto the rue Notre-Dame, which runs in front of the medieval church, they had smelled smoke. One of the houses across from the church was on fire and since no one is currently living there, there was no one to report it.

I immediately called the fire department, and they arrived surprisingly quickly, considering that it's an all-volunteer force and yesterday had been a holiday.

The fire turned out to be a huge one. It had clearly been burning inside the locked house all day, doing massive damage. Our friend Charlie has the house next door and had just finished redoing his roof. On the other side is the building where the village saddle-maker has his shop. So, we were worried about them as well.

The Gendarmes blocked off the bridge over the Blau, so no one could get in or out of town that way, which was a problem for Peter, since that is the direction of Rivel. We had at least five fire trucks, several from other communities and half the village was out to watch.

Although they did manage to get the fire under control, the house where it started is totally destroyed. The roofs of the two neighboring houses have suffered some damage, but nothing too severe from what I understand. It certainly could have been worse.

In a village of this age, fire is the thing that causes everyone to tremble. Even though our walls are made of stone, the inside structure is wood: floors, beams, etc., so while our walls would still stand, what would it matter if they contain nothing after the flames are gone.

A good reminder for all of us to keep watch on our electrical wiring and chimneys. From what I've heard, there is no definite answer about the cause of the fire as of yet. Possibly a rodent ate through some wiring, causing a short circuit. Others have speculated that "squatters" took over the house and caused the fire accidentally. In this case, it clearly wasn't caused by the chimney.

Still, whatever the reason, there was the chill of fear running through all the residents last night.

Friday, August 19

Last Sunday, we joined Cathy, Sean, Peter and several other friends for the village luncheon in Rivel. One of the "events" was a *Tombola*, which is a raffle for various prizes. Instead of having tickets, you picked a numbered square on a grid for each of entries. The drawing was held after lunch.

Because we had heard that the rest of the afternoon also included an interminable list of awards given out to the community children, we snuck out after lunch.

A day or two later, I ran into one of the people I've met from Rivel. We had often talked, but never exchanged names. When she asked our name she said, "Oh, *you're* the Lofficiers!" Apparently, we'd won several prizes at the tombola and no one knew who we were. I promised that the next time I was in Rivel, I would get in touch with one of the person who ran the tombola.

Well, as work has been progressing this week and there have been a variety of things for us to do, as usual, I never got to Rivel. Yesterday, we got a letter in the mail telling us we'd won a prize and could we please call. Mme. Salvat from Rivel, then stopped over this morning with our prizes: a tougnol (regional specialty, kind of a brioche with aniseed in it. Quite good), a rattan beach mat, a CD of French rap music (!) and two tickets to a night club in Pamiers. She explained that she'd asked the lovely Michelle at the post office if she knew us, and that's how she'd gotten our address. People here are adorable.

I am currently tracking down a Tougnol recipe, and if I find a good one, I'll post it for anyone interested.

We are making progress towards putting our house into living condition, and I have to say I will be grateful when I no longer have a single cardboard box hidden in any room or corner.

Monday, August 22

The premature change of seasons feels psychological as well as physical. Perhaps it's the gloom, but no one seems to feel as if it is still summer, even if there is a full month to go before the official start of autumn.

It's not even as if it's all that cold, but it looks cold when you peek out the window. I find myself wanting to drink hot chocolate and eat soup; definite cold weather cravings.

It was hard to notice the change of seasons in L.A. until the end of November. Perpetual sunshine will do that to you. You would think I would miss that, but I may be the only person in the village that is actually not bothered by the coming of fall. I am rather enjoying it, because to me it is a novelty. I'm even starting to plan how I'm going to deal with Thanksgiving! I'd better slow down it's too early for that!

Our good friends Christian and Nathalie were back from their week visiting family in Normandy today. We invited them to share our leftover daube for lunch. We were all wearing sweaters and everyone seemed to feel the urge to nest. Does this mean that barbecue season is definitely over?

We've now seen three seasons pass since we've been in Chalabre. Each one has had its charms and pleasures. Yes, even the snow of winter was fun in its own way. Now, we'll get to see the leaves turning color and, more excitingly, the grape harvest! That has always been one of my favorite times to visit France, and here we are, smack dab in the middle of it.

Sunday, August 28

Once again, we've had a massively hectic week. Joël finished painting our TV/living room, then we needed to put up shelves, hang paintings and *clean*! We've really been vacuuming, dusting, unpacking all the little tchotchkies for the shelves, etc.

The biggest challenge was getting the couch back up into its proper resting place. We knew it fit through the door, as it had been in there for several months. We'd seen Christian, his son Vincent and Joël move it back downstairs. So, it *had* to fit. Yet, somehow, getting it back up into the room proved challenging.

First, Matthew and his brother Vincent (a totally different Vincent!) tried to get it upstairs. They couldn't even get it past the downstairs doorway. Not a good sign. Later in the day, Manu, Charlie and Cousin Manu kindly came by to move it for us. I honestly thought that we were going to lose Manu 1 in a puddle of splat at the bottom of the stairs! That couch is damned heavy! Plus, it needs to be turned one way to get through the door at the bottom of the stairs, and a totally *different* way to get through the door into the room at the top of the stairs! We were very, very lucky to have such great guys to help us, otherwise I think it would have remained in the dining room forever!

We had multiple errands that all needed running, of course. I think that the people at Mico, our kind of mini-Home Depot, think that we come there like going to Disneyland. I wonder if they've ever had any individual come in and buy as many bookshelves as we've done?

Then, on Friday was Beanie's big day. We needed to take her to the DRIRE to be inspected for her official *"carte grise,"* the French equivalent of a California pink slip. We're lucky that, although she does need a few modifications, none of them are particularly serious and hopefully not too expensive. We hope that M. Hervas, our local mechanic and all around swell guy, can do them without too much trouble.

On top of all this activity, we've had people over for coffee, tea and dinner, been invited out for dinner ourselves, and generally found life to be a bit of a social whirl. Not that I'm complaining. It just makes the time fly by and with trying to also fit work in, sometimes I'm afraid that my blog takes a hit.

I hope that this week will prove calmer. And, of course, there's the planning for our first visitor from back in L.A. Our dear friend Diane is coming to see us next week! I can hardly wait to see what she thinks of our new digs.

Saturday, September 3

After an exhausting week, we are now totally unpacked for the first time since we left L.A., exactly seven months ago. Except for our bedroom and bathroom, the rest of the house is finished. Everything is in the room where it will be officially "living," and we've taken pictures to celebrate.

Although, to us, it feels like a long time, most people are impressed by how fast everything has gone. All I know is that I love having a kitchen again! I have been cooking like crazy, making up for lost time. Yesterday, I invited M. Michele, who owns the Cazalette, the restaurant at the stadium, over for coffee. We ate many meals there this summer and it was nice to return the service.

We are blessed to have so many great friends in the village, because without them, we would never have been able to move the hideously heavy furniture around. I felt extremely guilty this week, because Manu hurt his back and I thought it was our couch that did him in! However, he reassured me that we were not the cause.

When I look at the before and after pics on the website, I'm still amazed at how drastic the change has been. We always loved this house, but now, it feels truly like it is "ours," and is alive once again. Houses need to be lived in to feel happy, and I hope ours will be that way for many years to come.

In this week of tragedy in Louisiana and Mississippi, I am reminded of how blessed our life is. I look around our home and our village and feel grateful.

Sunday, September 4

The peasants are revolting, although not in a bad way!

Last night, I drove JM to the train station in Carcassonne. We had decided that the most expedient way for him to get to Paris for a meeting was by night train. After calculating the current costs of gas, tolls, hotel room (for us and Maggie), etc., it seemed absurd for us to go up together. Round trip Internet only fare from SNCF was 100 euros as opposed to over 500 euros for going with Beanie.

Of course, we hate not being together, but sometimes you just gotta do what you gotta do.

At any rate, I pulled back into Chalabre just after 10 p.m.

We had known that last night was the *Grand Paella*, hosted by the local rugby club. It was taking place at the Cafe de la Paix, and Cours Colbert was blocked off so that there was room for a bandstand and tables. Yves and M. Bernard had suggested that I put something in place to block off a parking spot in front of the house, so JM had moved our bench after I pulled out the car. It worked perfectly and I was able to park with no trouble.

Trouble, if you want to call it that, started later in the night. The music was really cranked up, rattling the windows on our side of town. I closed all the shutters, windows and connecting doors to the rooms on the Cours side of the house. Even so, I could still hear the pounding in our bedroom. Thank goodness for ear plugs, as I was able to sleep without too much trouble.

Unfortunately, I seem to have been the only one in town who managed it! This morning, everyone was complaining. The music went on until four am and *nobody* else got to sleep. They surrounded the Mayor this morning to complain.

Part of the problem is that beer was being sold to kids as young as 13, and there is no police presence to speak of. In comparison to a big U.S. city, it was pretty harmless. But out here in the boonies, it just won't do.

I don't know what the answer is, other than to ban these events. But let's just say that this isn't the week to propose a new street festival.

Monday, September 5

I've been sad, here in Chalabre, with JM away in Paris. However, I think I got the better part of the deal, because he tells me that the City of Lights has been hot and humid. Not my favorite weather there at all.

It has been weird here, with lots of humidity, grey skies, and finally major thunderstorms tonight. I understand that it will remain like this for the better part of this week, which is sad because our friend Diane is arriving on the train with JM tomorrow afternoon. I really wanted her to get to see our Shire in the best conditions.

Another minor event was that I threw my back out this morning. Not really sure how, unless it was because I kept the fan on in our bedroom last night and the cold air blowing on me caused it. I've been walking around like a 100-year-old woman all day. Of course, my neighbors and friends have all been concerned.

That concern is really touching. In particular Conchita and Mariano Gimenez have come to check on me several times, just to make sure that I'm all right. They were particularly worried because my shutters were still open relatively late and they came to make sure I hadn't fallen or something. It makes me feel secure here, knowing that even with JM away, I'm not really alone.

I have so many good friends and neighbors here that I feel quite spoiled. I see Louis, Nathalie, Bernadette, Christian, Mikael, and so many others each day that it never ceases to amaze me. I could go days in L.A. without seeing one of my neighbors. We all liked each other, we just didn't really interface all that much. Here, it is impossible for anything to happen without someone noticing. Perhaps it's not everyone's cup of tea, but for me, it is a pleasure. Not the place to live if anonymity is what one seeks!

I am going to hobble upstairs now, with the hope that my back will sort itself out by morning. I need to be in good shape to greet JM and Diane at the train station!

Monday, September 12

I'm sorry to say that we did not have the greatest weather to share with our dear Diane when she was here last week. It rained on-and-off for most of the three days, although we *did* have some lovely clear patches, so she actually got to see a bit of sun.

It was fun having her here, though, and I really didn't care what the weather was like because spending time together was the main goal of her visit. I have to say that she was really the hit of the village! One of our neighbors dubbed her "Madame Barbie," and meant it in a good way. It's true that Diane did add a bit of "glam" to the whole place while she was around, weather or no.

We did spend a lot of time driving places last week, thus my silence since then. We managed to get back to Molitg-les-Bains, which was still beautiful, although a lot more crowded than our first visit (when it was closed). We had an ugly experience of anti-doggism, as neither of the two "fancy" restaurants would accept Maggie. The nerve!

Instead, we first tried a café on the main drag. The people were very nice, but to say that they were a bit overwhelmed by the necessity of dealing with actual diners would not be putting it unkindly. After 45 minutes, they still hadn't taken our order. The table that had arrived just before us was getting their food, sort of. However, the different guest's plates were coming to the table separated by at least 15 minutes apiece, so that no one was able to eat together. We finally just got up and left.

That turned out to be a good thing, because we wound up in the village of Old Molitg, further up the hill. There, we discovered a wonderful little restaurant/*crêperie* called Les Marronniers, run by a very sweet couple originally from Brittany. Too bad they aren't a little bit closer, or we'd go there all the time. The experience was only marred by the Diva, who decided that she did not want the restaurant dog coming near our table! Luckily, after a brief "time-out" inside Beanie, she was once again her well-behaved self. I suppose the lure of crepes proved too strong for her to control her evil impulses.

Sadly, Diane had to return to L.A. all too soon. Friday night we had a last dinner at Le Commerce in Mirepoix, then a nighttime drive to the Medieval Cité of Carcassonne, where we enjoyed a burst of clear weather, enabling us to see the beauty of the medieval towers lit up against the night sky. Then, down to the station where we left our friend to take the night train to Paris.

One funny incident on our return home. The Gendarmes were doing one of their periodic vehicle stops. They pulled me over just after I turned onto the Chalabre road in Limoux and asked for my license. Since I don't have my French license yet (hopefully will pass the test this coming Friday!), I pulled out my California permit. The baby Gendarme (can't have been more than 12) called over a colleague and they both looked at it in wonder, before signaling me to back up and leave.

Maybe it will make sense to keep hold of it, even after I'm official in France?

Saturday, September 17

I was going to write one of my usual blogs today, until I read this on *Daily Kos* and got chills down my spine:

What did you do today? [20]
by
Betsy Driver

What did you do today?
I filed Chapter 7 bankruptcy today.
I had been trying to avoid it but I knew there was a deadline coming. Things would be changing soon.
It was one of the biggest, saddest things I did today, this month, this year, this lifetime. When I left my attorney's office today, it felt like I had been kicked in the stomach.
It wasn't credit cards that did me in. I never really used them. I keep one for when I need to rent a car, make hotel reservations, etc. but rarely ever used it otherwise. Even when I used it to guarantee the rental or reservation, I would pay cash.
It wasn't because I was stupid and didn't pay my bills. I did.
But I got sick. Real sick–sick enough to end up in the hospital. I had no insurance and the bills were beyond my means. And the hospital sued

---

[20] This article was published on *http://www.dailykos.com* on September 17, 2005, is © 2005 Betsy Driver and is reproduced here by permission of the author.

me, and they won. The bill was more than I make in a year. Then I got sick again and spent another three days in the hospital.

I don't have medical insurance because I can't afford it. It costs about 40% of what I make. I make about $100 more per month than I can to qualify for Medicaid. My job does not offer insurance.

I have some medical issues that require drugs each month at a cost of $78. These are life-sustaining drugs. If I don't take them, I die. I should see a doctor every 6 months but I can't afford it. It is also the reason I ended up in the hospital twice. If I was able to afford private insurance, it would exclude this pre-existing medical condition.

The bankruptcy filing listed $35,000 or so in hospital bills. Another $2,000 or so was other stuff–nothing major and out of control. The judgment on the first bill was limited to what Medicaid would have paid by the judge. The difference was enormous–thousands of dollars. They were trying to sue for retail because I didn't have insurance and which was way more than HMO and Medicaid reimbursements. That was the only bright spot... that they could not gouge me further because I am poor; the judge would not give them that amount One mistake I made is that I didn't show up with an attorney that day in court but my limited budget forced me to make a decision–I knew I would lose the judgment because I was in their facility and knew my dollars would be better spent on the bankruptcy filing. In our country, dead people can't even get out of medical bills... they will sue the estate according to my attorney.

It got bad after that judgment. My parents who live in another state started to get calls. At first I couldn't figure out why they were calling there. It turns out they got that number because she was listed as my emergency contact at the hospital. The night my mom was dying and ultimately died, a debt collector called repeatedly like it was a game. She called every 20 minutes or so. This was all by a hospital that is non-profit and receives government subsidies. In court, the attorney had with him my medical records; so much for HIPAA. I guess it only applies to those with insurance.

And finally, I gave in and decided, "Screw them.. It ultimately came down to those calls to my parents and then only to my dad where they would deliberately ask for my mom. I know this because they were told by him that she had passed away months ago.

When I went over the final filing today with my attorney before it was submitted (it's all done online these days), I was both angry and *amused that he knew the names and addresses of all the people I owed money to. He said it is always the same people.*

I know I am not alone in what happened to me. Most bankruptcies are due to medical bills

A national health care program could put an end to thousands of bankruptcies. But big business prevails these days and allows banks and credit card issuers to make a fresh start more difficult for those who did nothing to deserve it, other than getting sick in one of the few nations in the world that does not provide medical care to their residents.

My attorney indicated he has never been busier. Gee, I wonder why?

I'm lucky though. Those folks in NOLA who will be struggling (and think of those medical bills!) will not find it so easy. They need to got through income tests and credit counseling at their own expense. That is not right.

No one, anywhere, should every have to declare bankruptcy because they had the misfortune of becoming ill. What has happened to American society that a woman on her deathbed is harassed because her child can't afford medical care? Where is America going? What happened to the America that was supposed to take care of its neediest citizens?

I don't talk enough about how at peace I now feel, since moving to France. For the first time in years I'm not worried about going to the doctor for medical care, worried that I'll have some horrendous bill to pay, despite insurance. Talking to the doctor, going to the pharmacy, having a lab test, none of these things now feel like a luxury to me. I hardly abuse the system, but at least I feel that I can use it when I need it.

Certainly, access to medical care shouldn't be the number one priority when one moves to a new country, but it's definitely up there in the top five. But, isn't that wrong when the country you're leaving is the U.S.? Shouldn't the richest nation in the world provide at least that much for its citizens.

I feel lucky today. But I feel saddened for those I've left behind.

Monday, September 19

Not even the first day of autumn and it already feels like winter! I put the down comforter on the bed for tonight, and everyone in town is wearing sweaters and jackets.

Luckily, according to the paper, this little cold snap is scheduled to fade away by the end of the week. I don't mind a little cold, but I'd like to ease into it gradually, rather than fall into it head first.

Funny anecdote: I decided to make chicken soup on Saturday. I ordered a rotisserie chicken from our butchers, Didier and Mireille, figuring we could eat it for lunch, then throw the rest of the bits into the soup. I realized that on my morning veggie run, I hadn't picked up some of the fixings I needed for soup, so I grabbed my basket and went back to primeur (veggie shop). After grabbing the couple of things I needed, Helene looked at me and said, "Oh, you're making soup." Of course, I was astonished and told her she should be a detective. "It's not that complicated," she said, "With this weather, *everyone* is making soup today!"

Well, I was happy to have it, I can tell you. There are just days when you *need* to be eating soup.

It also seems that "crud" season has started. Elise, Christian and Nathalie's daughter, has been sick since yesterday. Nathalie thought she might be coming down with it as well. When she called the doctor's office, he said the waiting room was packed, so I guess they're not the only ones.

I'm thinking I'd better keep a pot of chicken soup in permanent boil on top of the stove.

Thursday, September 22

Now that summer is over, I've decided to see if anyone in town is really interested in learning English (well, American, to be accurate). A lot of people have told me that they would take lessons if I started offering them, so I'm taking them up on it.

I've put cards around the village, and now have to see if anyone will "bite." I do have my first guinea pig, my friend Nathalie. I started giving her lessons last week. But she already speaks some English, so it's not like we're starting from scratch.

Amusingly enough, I've had a few English-speakers tell me that they would be interested in my doing the same thing in French! It's always just been a question of helping folks to have enough vocabulary so that they feel as if they can comfortably speak to someone when the occasion arises.

Needless to say, I'm not expecting this to make me rich. But it would be good to pay a grocery bill now and then.

I also think it will be a nice way to have a certain amount of socializing going on during the winter months. Now that the nights are falling earlier and the weather has turned quite a bit colder (it was 3 C/40 F this morning!), no one is sitting outside in the evenings. It's amazing how used to seeing everyone we got during the summer. It's a little sad to not have that now. Funny, I never missed that in L.A.

On another note, I hope that the weather reports on Hurricane Rita are wrong. It sounds like things will be very bad in Texas if she hits the way things are predicted right now. Two massive hurricanes in less than a month are not a good thing, no matter what kind of spin you put on it.

Quick update on today's blog!

I was just outside and saw a few of the neighborhood kids. Didier & Mireille's middle girl was crying. She came over to see Maggie and get a hug. When I asked what was wrong, she told me that Caramel the Cat has been missing for two days. This is extra upsetting, because two days ago, there was a big splotch of blood on the street in front of our house.

Now, up till now, no one has found a dead cat. I didn't hear any screeching brakes or anything of that nature, so I told her that there's still hope. If Caramel isn't back by tomorrow, we'll help to make a few posters to put around town.

So, everyone, please put in a good thought for the missing Caramel.

Sunday, September 25

First, the bad news. I'm afraid that Caramel the Cat is no more. We had confirmation that she had, indeed, been hit by a car on Tuesday or Wednesday. Her young mistress, Audrey, is heartbroken, but will survive, as the very young do after these kinds of losses. I think there is a hamster in her future, as it is too difficult to keep a cat safely confined as a house cat here.

In Possumworld, we had our first, official "party" yesterday. We were joined by six writers who also live in the region. Since many of them came from several hours away, we did lunch instead of dinner, to make it easier for everyone to return safely home.

I took this as a signal to really cook up a storm and spent two days getting ready. I decided that even though most of the guests were strangers, I would experiment with some new recipes and hope for the best.

Once again, I discovered that when you start with fabulous ingredients, it's hard to go wrong, even with experimentation. I still had some of the wonderful tomatoes that my lovely neighbors, Conchita and Mariano (the Gimenezes) gave me. I sliced them down and made them into *tomates provençales*. Meanwhile, I made a pastry crust. Saturday morning, the experimental part of the recipe took place. I blended several kinds of cheese with a couple of eggs to make a kind of creamy mousse. I put that on the bottom of the tart shell, then layered the caramelized tomatoes on top, finishing off with slices of fresh mozzarella. Then, I baked the whole thing for about 40 minutes, until the crust was golden. It turned out better than I had hoped. I hope I can remember what I did for a future time.

We had the tomato tart with chickpeas in homemade vinaigrette followed by a variety of charcuterie. The main course was pork tenderloin that I made the day before, and two "American" side dishes a noodle kugel (OK, so it's a traditional German-Jewish dish, but who cares?) and a corn pudding that I've had success with in the past. I had no idea how any of these non-traditional French dishes would go over, but was pleased that everyone ate with hearty appetite! In fact, everyone had seconds and even thirds. The way to a cook's heart.

For dessert I made an apple crisp, killer brownies and fresh strawberries marinated in *crème de pêche*. Then, we exploded. I was quite worried about the brownies, since there was a certain amount of conversion in the recipe. Luckily, they turned out so good that there were almost none left after lunch. Lucky, I say, because I don't like to keep brownies around where I can easily get to them for too long!

It was a terrific afternoon. I was happy to give my kitchen a real workout, and we don't have too many leftovers to deal with.

Monday, September 26

It seems early in the season, but everyone I meet seems to have come down with some kind of nasty bug. It's only September! Shouldn't that be waiting until at least November before we have to worry about it?

I want to enjoy fall. It's my favorite time of year, and I think it's going to be spectacular here. The *vendanges* are underway, and there are tractors pulling huge truckloads of grapes everywhere you turn. Everything is starting to change color and the air smells like a combination of early frost and wood smoke. It's perfect.

Everyone has pulled their sweaters and jackets out of the closet. Knees have disappeared, as no one is wearing shorts these days. We all feel like cooking soups, stews and pot roasts. The light has taken on that soft, golden color that we only see at this time of year.

I always loved to come to France in late September for our vacations. Now, I get to enjoy it as a resident. I know it means that soon the weather will get colder, but I don't want to rush things. I want to enjoy these wonderful days for as long as possible. Maybe I'll go and have a hot chocolate...

Fall in the forested hills above Puivert

Tuesday, September 27

Today's blog is a gentle reminder to all my friends who live in cities and who find themselves too busy to see their friends or do things with their families. I've been reminded, since living in Chalabre, that life is more than working. Life is friends, and conversation and family. Life is more a question of quality than the quantity of "things" that we can each accumulate.

What good is working to buy stuff, when there is no time to enjoy it? Shouldn't the goal of work be to make only enough money so that we can live, not spend so many hours doing it that we are too tired for anything else?

I look around at the variety of friends that we've made since coming here. They are all ages, do many different things in life, have varied backgrounds. But the one thing that they all have in common is a desire to enjoy life with their loved ones. Many of them have left the rat race of big city life to relocate to this quiet rural area. Many of them had well paid jobs in other industries and have chosen to follow their passion as artisans. Most of them could be making far more money living elsewhere. But they have all realized that that is not the path to happiness.

So, for those of you who may not have the option of relocating, I say, think about what is important to you. None of us know how long we will have on this Earth. Take the time to appreciate what you do have, to love those around you, to sit and relax and eat a meal in friendship. You won't regret it.

Friday, September 30

This morning, while I was making breakfast, I started ruminating on privacy. Now, this may be more of a city vs. rural/village thing than a particularly U.S. vs. France thing. Hard for me to know, as up until we moved here, I've always lived in cities or suburbs.

I started thinking about it after a conversation with one of my neighbors this morning. She asked me not to mention something to another neighbor, because she was worried the information would spread before she was ready for that to happen. Of course, doofus that I am, it had never occurred to me that there was a problem, because these are two neighbors who get along.

Then, I realized how, when one lives in a city, nobody really knows anything about anyone else. But here in the village, everyone knows *everything* (or at least a version of everything)!

I looked around at the dining room/kitchen and thought about how much more concerned I am with keeping things looking presentable than I was in L.A. After all, there, unless we specifically planned for a visitor, no one really came to the house all that much. Here, our dining room not only opens directly into the street, but when it's dark outside and lit up inside, anyone can easily see through the windows. Since I don't want the whole world to know what a lousy housekeeper I am, I work twice as hard at keeping things under control.

So, is this a rural/city thing or not? I imagine that in small towns all over the world, things probably work on a similar basis. For some reason, it doesn't really bother me though. I guess if you're writing about your life on the Internet, you are pretty much accepting that everything about it is an open book. After all, if I really didn't want anyone to know about me, I wouldn't be posting all the boring details of my existence for the world to see.

Sunday, October 2

We had friends over for dinner again last night, which is one of the real joys of life here in the Shire.

Because my tomato cheese tart was such a success last week, I decided to make it again this week. Several people wrote asking for the recipe, so I will post it here for anyone interested:

Tomato Cheese Tart

Filling:
1 pot Boursin for cooking (about 2 cups of any Boursin-type cheese)
8 oz cream cheese
1/2 cup grated parmesan
1/2 cup grated emmental
2 eggs

Blend until smooth and creamy. Pour over the unbaked pastry shell.
Layer the tomato slices on top. Slice mozzarella over the tomatoes and bake until golden (about 40 minutes)

Pie shell:
2 1/2 cups flour
1 cup butter
1 tsp salt
1 tablespoon sugar
3 tablespoons sour cream
1/3 Cup ice water

Cut butter into flour/salt/sugar mixture (easiest to use food processor for this). Mix sour cream and ice water. Put half in food processor with flour. Pulse 3 or 4 times, if the dough is still dry, add a bit more liquid just until dough comes together. Pat dough into a circle and refrigerate for at least an hour. Can do this a day ahead.

Roll out pastry and place in a large tart pan (mine is about 12 inches in diameter). Any leftover dough can be re-rolled, covered in a layer of sour cream and brown sugar, rolled up and sliced to make pinwheel cookies!

Tomatoes Provençales
(I usually make these a day ahead)

3 or 4 good sized tomatoes
I slice them into 6 or 8 slices each, depending on the size.
Put them in a baking pan that you line with non-stick foil or parchment paper. (This makes them *much* easier to remove from the pan). Brush a little olive oil on the paper first.

Pour a bit more olive oil over the tomatoes, then sprinkle the tops with salt, garlic powder, a little sugar and any herbs you like. Sprinkle some breadcrumbs on the top. Put them in a 375 oven and cook until the juice has cooked down and they are starting to caramelize.

We had chicken, pan roasted vegetables (carrots, potatoes, onions, garlic and some beautiful fresh mushrooms–*girolles*, I think), and then I made one or our favorites, spinach with *crème fraîche*. Luckily, there are plenty of leftovers for today!

Dessert was basically evil incarnate. White Chocolate Cheesecake. This is something relatively unusual for France, so I thought I'd try it. When the recipe says that it serves 14 to 16, believe it! It is massively rich. My edition of Mastercook gives the calorie count at 768 calories per slice! You *don't* want to make this too often! For anyone not worried about their cholesterol or hips, here's the recipe:

White Chocolate Cheesecake

Crust:
2 cups Graham or chocolate cookie crumbs

1/4 cup sugar
1/3 c melted butter (1/3 to 1/2)

Mix together and press into a greased 10" spring form or cheesecake pan. Bake at 350 for 10 minutes. Meanwhile, prepare filling.

Filling:
4 eggs
1/4 cup sugar
2.5 lbs cream cheese
1/2 cup melted butter
2 tablespoons vanilla
12 ounces melted white chocolate

Place eggs and sugar into bowl of a large food processor. If your food processor is small, you will have to do this in two batches. Do *not* use a blender, it's not the same! You're better off doing it by hand, starting with the cream cheese and sugar, then adding eggs. Process until sugar is dissolved. Add cream cheese in 4 or 5 additions. Scrape sides of bowl often, and process until smooth.

With the machine still running, add remaining ingredients. Process a few more seconds. Poor over prepared crust. Bake at 350 for 30-35 minutes and no longer! It will look loose and under baked, but that is how it is supposed to be. Resist the urge to cook it until it is set, otherwise it will be dry and grainy. The middle 3 inches should still be wobbly. Let cool, refrigerate overnight. It will set, I promise. Bring to room temperature to serve, and use a hot, wet knife to slice. You can serve 14-16 people with this cheesecake-it's very rich and creamy.

Now, run around the block several times, so you don't feel guilty!

Monday, October 3

I've said it before, I love the fall. However, we seem to have jumped straight into winter without passing go! Nighttime temperatures are in the forties and it didn't get much above 50 during the day today. There was even snow a little higher up in the Pyrénées this morning.

Still, given that it's been in the upper 90s and low 100s back in L.A., with forest fires rampaging everywhere, I'm not complaining in the least. Give me sweaters and cozy blankets over that any day of the week.

Christian, who besides being a plumber, is also the main village heating system expert *and* chimney sweep, is going full-blast. For the next month, he's going to be doing practically nothing else, other than the odd emergency. He's even going to come to finish installing our bathroom at night, so he doesn't make anyone wait too long to have their chimneys looked at.

It seems like such an old-fashioned term, "chimney-sweep." I have to admit I never thought much about it before. I just assumed it was one of those things you should do once in awhile, kind of like cleaning behind the refrigerator. Since being here, though, I've learned that it's vitally important. Chimney fires are a huge danger in a place where many homes have no other kind of heating. And, if you do have a fire and you don't have an official certificate from an approved sweep, your insurance company probably won't pay you a shekel.

Clearly, it's something that one needs to keep in mind. Since I don't know when our chimneys were last looked at, and we built a lot of fires downstairs last winter, we've decided to not take any risks. Until Christian comes and does his chimney-thing, we're just going to stay bundled up and not go burning anything in the fireplace.

What a bummer that would be, to have finally finished the remodeling, only to have it all wrecked by a fire!

Wednesday, October 5

"Fire season" in Chalabre has a different meaning than it did in L.A.

Yesterday, our chimney was swept, so today, I just *had* to light a fire! I put an apple crisp in the oven, lit a fire, took my current book project downstairs and just sat there working and smelling the odors of baking apples and wood smoke. The room is so warm and comfortable with the fire that it's hard to concentrate, because you just want to daydream.

I think that with the exposed stone, the room stays even warmer than it did last winter, as the stone absorbs the heat from the fire, then radiates it out as the day goes on. In fact, the whole house feels warmer, just from that one fireplace.

There is a dark side to this, of course. Diva Maggie does *not* like the sound of a crackling fire. It is clearly the work of the devil. When forced to go downstairs by circumstances, such as going for a walk or eating, she walks as closely as possible to the wall opposite the fire, keeping her head turned so it won't "see" her. You just can't be too careful. I'm guessing we're never going to get to the point where she lays by the hearth, soaking in the heat.

Still, the humans are enjoying it. The flames even make the gloom of a rainy day seem somehow brighter. Even though we have central heat, I think that in the main, I prefer the fireplace. I think with the cost of oil going up this winter, we'll be using it as a heating source as much as possible.

Perhaps I need to roast some potatoes in the coals for dinner, just as a celebration of the change of seasons...

Saturday, October 8

A visit to the rheumatologist on Friday brought home, once again, the differences in how medicine seems to be practiced here and in the U.S.

My family doctor referred me to a specialist. No need for any approval from an insurance company. Just a letter with the information I needed to give to the new doctor.

I called for an appointment on Wednesday. The receptionist apologized for not being able to get me in to see the doctor in the next two days! She asked if an appointment the following week would be all right. The last time I needed to see a specialist in L.A., the usual waiting time for an appointment was a month.

When I got to the clinic, I assumed I needed to check in with someone. Nope, I was told to sit in the waiting room and the doctor would come to get me. There were a couple of people waiting already, but about half-an-hour or 45 minutes later (really not bad waiting time by any standard), the doctor himself came to get me!

That just floors me. I don't think I've ever gone to visit any medical office in the U.S. where the doctor actually comes to the waiting room for the patient and there is no assistant or other support person to ask you a bunch of questions that are then repeated by the doctor.

He entered my information into his laptop computer himself, talked to me, *listened* to me, examined me, all very personal, very relaxed. No sense of the doctor being superior to the patient. Then, he *asked* me if I minded having x-rays done! He wrote out a prescription for the x-rays and the medication that he will need to inject. I found the last really interesting, because I go to the pharmacy, get the medication, then bring it back to him to inject.

When I went to the radiology department to make an appointment, they made it for Monday morning. Again, I never got an appointment for anything like that so quickly.

The final thing that I find fascinating is that you pay the doctor directly. No coyness about it. No acting as if it somehow beneath the doctor to deal with money. He tells you how much it is, you pay him, he gives you the necessary social security/insurance form, and that's it. Really refreshing.

By the way, this specialist visit is more expensive than typical GP visit. The GP visit costs 20 euros, the specialist visit cost me 27 euros. Between social security and my private insurance, all of that is reimbursed directly into our band account. I took the insurance form to my local pharmacy and they send it to social security for me. No hassle.

Another interesting fact. The treatment that I went to talk about is something that my doctor in L.A. wanted me to have done about a year ago. However, in order to get it, the insurance company had to approve it. They didn't, so I didn't get the treatment. Here, *only* my doctor has a say in what care I get. No one else has to give their permission.

That's a big step forward, or maybe backward to a simpler time.

Sunday, October 9

I have a "posse!"

Of course, they range in age from about 6 to 10 or 11, but still, they're *my* posse, so I'm not complaining.

I think that the initial attraction, as always, was Maggie. She has an amazing appeal to kids and adults alike. Somehow, the attention lavished on her has spilled over to me. So, now Audrey, Aurélie, Marion and Paul come running whenever they see me.

Audrey and Aurélie are the children of Didier and Mireille from the butcher shop. Marion is the daughter of Philippe and Nadia, the bakers, and Paul is the son of our local dentist, Dr. Martinez.

Sometimes, I feel a bit like the Pied Piper. However, I refuse to have anything to do with rats, so the comparison will stop here.

They all seem fascinated by the fact that I cook a lot. I find that amusing, given that the come from families where food is a way of life. We've taken to exchanging samples of things we make. Yesterday, I made a meatloaf. I remembered how, when I was a little girl, my mother used to make little "meatloaf men" for my sister and me. So, I made two little meatloaf men for Aurélie and Audrey. They were a huge success. I'm sure it had as much to do with the form as with the content.

Today, Audrey wanted me to show her how to make an American dessert, because it's her mother's birthday. So, I invited her over to make chocolate chip cookies, using real Nestle Toll House morsels and the official recipe on the back of the bag! The Four Musketeers appeared at my door together, so I had them all in and we made cookies together.

I gave everyone their little package of cookies to take home, although I do feel a bit weird sending pastry home to the local baker!

But, besides being an afternoon of gluttony, I used the exercise to teach them a little English and the differences in American and French measurements. So, it was a little bit of a learning experience for them.

Time to go and play Tarot in Rivel!

Monday, October 10

We went to play cards with Régine and Laurent in Rivel yesterday, and took Maggie with us, of course.

It was a beautiful, Indian summer day, so we sat out in the garden for an hour or so. Maggie was definitely interested in "something," so after a few minutes, I let her off her leash. In spite of Régine having been certain that their cat was elsewhere, he was clearly in the garden. Maggie found him in about 1/2 a second.

The cat immediately ran up a tree, and Maggie started the obnoxious, obsessed, patented BC bark of death. And, of course, tried to leap up to the top of the tree with a hopeless lack of understanding about gravity.

After we played our little game of "ring around the rosy" as she deftly managed to elude my attempts at grabbing her and reattaching her leash, I finally won. I dragged her, and I do mean dragged, out of the garden and put her in the car, which by then was in the shade and cool. She continued the bark for about an hour, spraying bits of drool everywhere.

Finally, I took her for a walk around the village, letting her play with another friend's dog and hoping to tire her out, even a bit. We went back to play cards inside, where the cat is never allowed because of an allergic Laurent.

However, instead of settling down as she usually does, the next three hours were spent with Maggie trying to turn over the card table, rip my arm out of the socket and generally do anything she could to get back outside and get that cat! I let her wander and she went to the front door and started clawing at it.

I'm pretty sure she's never going to be invited back for another visit.

Thursday, October 13

The quiet season seems to be settling in. All the tourists are gone, people spend a lot of time indoors, the rain is falling.

Still, for us, life is becoming "normal" at last. Most of the work on the house is finished, just a few more days of actual work to finish up the upstairs bathroom, then the house will be quiet as well. Our artisans will visit us as friends, not workers.

I've actually been able to get back to work and have finished a manuscript that's been hanging over my head for months.[21] And, speaking of work, I've signed up with the unemployment office. I want to see if they can point me towards something that I can do which will actually earn me a few euros to help out with expenses. The problem is, I'm not sure what kind of work my skills suit me for. Not much, I'm afraid.

And, it's not as if opportunities abound in Chalabre either. I'll probably need to go to either Limoux or Lavelanet, which needs to be factored into any eventual salary, as driving will mean paying more money for gas, which is far from cheap here.

That reminds me that Beanie has finished another giant step on her road to a Carte Grise. M. Hervas finished all the requested changes today. Now, the only thing standing in our way is a document that we need from Toyota France. They are not hugely helpful though, so I have no idea how long it will take to arrive. I guess a bit of nagging is in order.

So, winter sets in and the administration rolls on and on and on.

Friday, October 14

I mentioned yesterday that Beanie has had all the work she needs to get her *carte grise* (registration), except for a document we need from Toyota France.

---

[21] Xavier Maumejean's *The League of Heroes*, ISBN 1-932983-44-9.

When we went to the DRIRE (which means something, but I can't remember what right this minute),[22] which is where you take your foreign car to have it inspected to see if it meets with the NF (*normes françaises*), we had a list of small, but vital things that needed to be done.

Our local mechanic, M. Hervas, used to be a Toyota mechanic, which was a really lucky break for us. He's got a great reputation in town and is always very nice, very good and super honest. We took him the list of items that needed doing and he said he'd have no problem.

The only hang-up was speed, as he is *always* busy. That's a good sign, of course, but you have to be patient if it's not an emergency, which this wasn't.

One of the really convenient things about having a mechanic half-a-block away, is that you don't have to worry too much about taking your car in then finding a ride home. I usually just leave him a spare key, and he comes to take Beanie when he's ready for her, then brings her back home again. That's a heckuva lot easier than in Reseda, I can tell you.

The list of things that Beanie needed were strange and varied. Some of them make sense to me, others, not really. For example, parking lights in France have to be white or yellow. Beanie's were orange and shared the same place as the turn signals, which *do* have to be orange. That made sense, because I think when people saw our orange lights coming at them at night, it confused them.

Also, it's mandatory in France to have at least one rear fog lamp, which we didn't have, but now do. That makes sense too, I suppose, but I have the feeling I'll never remember to use it. Plus, I don't really go out in the fog all that much anyway.

One of the things that I didn't see the point of, was the way that Japanese cars signal low break fluid. Apparently, the "low" level in France is higher than it is in the U.S., so we had to have a change in the way the sensor works. Since I'm used to the way our car works, I wasn't overly worried about it, but that was a "have to" for getting approved. Luckily, M. Hervas is a wizard at figuring out how to make stuff like that work.

A couple of other things had to do with the way identification info is shown on the car. We have lots of little stickers in the U.S., here, everything has to be engraved in metal, so we had to get that kind of thing done. And, the last thing was those rear reflectors that cars have as part

---

[22] *Direction Régionale de l'Industrie, de la Recherche et de l'Environnement.* A corps of State-trained mining engineers

of the rear lights. For some reason, ours were not in the correct place, so we had to get little stick on ones for the back.

As of now, Beanie is a unique vehicle. There is no other one like her in the world, as far as I know. She is, of course, worthless here in France, as I doubt she'll have any resale value at all. But she is priceless to us and definitely was worth the effort of bringing all this way.

How much did all this retrofitting cost, you may ask? That was the shocker. Yesterday, when M. Hervas dropped her off, he hadn't calculated the bill yet. We popped over this morning to pay and to get a new bottle of gas for the stove (very useful garage!). The grand total for all of Beanie's new thingamabobs came to 230 euros. Knowing what I do about the cost of *any* kind of repair in L.A., I came away vastly impressed. Vive Beanie! Vive M. Hervas!

Monday, October 17

I was thinking today how hard it is to get used to going to the doctor again. When we lived in L.A., even though we were *very* lucky to have insurance, I tended to censor myself on going to the doctor's office. I learned to do a lot of self-treatment, because even with insurance, there were always out-of-pocket costs that tended to be relatively expensive, either co-pays or prescriptions that never seemed to be covered by our insurance.

I've noticed since being here, that people tend to go to the doctor's office for relatively minor things. I suppose that isn't always a good thing, as the system here *is* in deficit, probably because of that. Still, there are times one should go to the doctor without hesitation.

I still have trouble bringing myself to do it though. There's this underlying feeling of "guilt" that is hard to pin down. I suppose that I'll get over it eventually, but haven't as of yet. One of these days, my attempts at self-treatment will probably get me into trouble, but for now, I'm still doing it. I guess there are some cultural influences that are hard to overcome, no matter how much logic dictates that we move forward.

Tuesday, October 18

Tonight I am going to try teaching my first "official" student. It's still one of my friends, but she has less of a base of English than Nathalie, so it will be practically starting from scratch.

I've had several more people suggest to me that I teach French conversation to native English speakers, so I may actually start doing that as well. I find that concept rather funny, to be honest. Still, I suppose it may be less intimidating to have someone to speak to who has "been there, done that." I'm certainly far from judgmental about things!

The problem with all of this, of course, is that it's really not a sound way of earning a living. Part of the problem is that I have trouble collecting money from friends. I know that's silly, but there it is. Somehow, if I buy something from a store owned by a friend, it doesn't bother me. But charging money for talking to people seems weird.

I will have to get over that, but I don't really know how. I haven't figured out if it's because I undervalue my services or if I'm just embarrassed to ask people for money. I lean towards the latter, to be perfectly honest.

Maybe I need an agent...

At any rate, until I'm sure that this actually helps anyone to really learn anything, I'm hesitant. Tonight will be a good test run. My original class of four is down to one though, since more and more people are dropping like flies with colds and virii. Their kids go to school and bring them home as presents. I'm still swilling vitamin C in an effort to hold the germs off here. Although, I should probably make a big pot of chicken soup and freeze it, just in case.

Saturday, October 22

We wound up having a busier than usual week.

On Wednesday, I went back to the Rheumatologist. I discovered that an appointment around 9 a.m. is much better than one at 4:30 p.m. I got in to see him almost on time!

After looking at my x-rays, he decided I should have an MRI. That will get done in a hospital in Foix, so as much as MRIs are uncomfortable to go through, it will still be interesting to see the new hospital in Foix. Hey, you always have to look on the bright side.

I decided that I should try to get my old MRI results from L.A., which was an interesting long distance phone experience. I was feeling extremely grateful for our new, France Telecom phone service, which gives me a monthly fixed rate price for unlimited calls to France, Europe and North America. Otherwise, I don't even want to think about how much doing that would have cost.

At any rate, the theory is that I will receive the copies this week by FedEx. Okay, so it will take slightly longer than if I was in L.A., but there's no driving involved!

On Thursday, we had a visit from an American friend, Michael, and were lucky to have absolutely incredible fall weather for doing a bit of tourism. This time of year can be absolutely stunning. The temperatures have been in the high sixties during the day, the sunlight is beautiful, shining on the vineyards and forests, which are now starting to be a riot of color.

I know I can't count on the weather holding out for long, but I'll take what I can get.

Next week life in the village will probably be on the quiet side. The All-Saints vacation week has started and most people with kids are taking off for mini-holidays. The butcher, the Hotel and probably several other stores will be closed.

I guess it will be a good time to hunker down and get some work done.

Tuesday, October 25

Chalabre is putting on its fall wardrobe.

The plane and chestnut trees are really changing color and losing their leaves. Chestnuts, themselves, sometimes attack passersby in the streets, as a sudden breeze knocks them out of the trees. The clocks don't "fall back" until this coming Sunday, so it is still night until sometime after 8 a.m.

As you walk around town, you see that the stores are starting to post their winter hours, which are shorter than the ones in summer. The kids are on their fall break for All Saints, and wander around during the day, soaking up the autumn sun and trying to find something to do.

Chrysanthemums are the flower of choice for All Saints Day, when people go to the cemetery to put them on the graves. I just walked past the flower shop, and the sidewalk in front of it is a riot of color because of all the pots of plants. Too bad we don't have them out all year, because it really brightens up the corner.

Christian and his team are working overtime, getting everyone's chimneys swept and checking out their heating systems. The first seasonal colds and flu have begun attacking people, old and young.

And, now that American culture has really invaded, the windows in the shops are even decorated for Halloween! The kids are all talking about what they will wear as a costume. I'm still not sure if they're going to go trick-or-treating or not, but I've gotten in a supply of candy, just in case. It pays to prepare.

Wednesday, October 26

I now have *four*, yes that's right, *four*, students who want to learn/practice English (or American, if I'm really honest about it).

They're at various stages of ability at this point, so I need to separate them into different groups. Mireille is much more at the beginner stage, even though she did study some years ago.

My other three, Nathalie, Anais and Thomas, are all able to have some level of conversation, so I've decided that the three of them should be in one group and poor Mireille, for the time being, has to remain alone.

This has caused me to look at the various language books I have. I've realized that most of them are just stupid. No wonder kids really don't like studying a second language. Yes, they will work for most people, but who cares? I've actually ordered a couple of children's storybooks, including on that has about a dozen *Dick and Jane* stories. I think it will be more fun for everyone to have something like that.

Plus, since I'm going to start reading to the pre-schoolers at the local library after Halloween, I would like to use them for that as well.

Audrey, Mireille's 12-year-old, is not scheduled to study English until next year, but she's asked if she could start learning now. Of course, I told her that would be fine. I think she likes the idea of being a bit ahead of her classmates next year.

Too bad none of this does anything to improve our financial situation, though. So, I'm signing up with the unemployment office this week and dropping my résumé off at various places in town. Not that I expect to make a great deal of money. No one comes to this part of France expecting that. But, it would be nice to find something local and part time that will help with our relatively moderate expenses.

The life of a writer is not a wealthy one in most cases! As I often point out to people, rich writers are the exception, not the rule.

Friday, October 28

OK, I admit it. I'm having a bad day.

It's not fair to do this blog if I only post about the positive things that happen. So, today I need to explain why I'm feeling so negative.

I took my driver's test (the *Code de la Route*) for the second time this morning and I failed it again! Now, I am not used to failing tests and I have to tell you that I don't like it.

I try to console myself with the fact that only about a third of the 40 or so others taking the test passed, and everyone there but me was from a driving school. But I have to say that it didn't really help my mood. After all, I've been driving since I was 16 and I am *waaaaayyyy* older than that now.

JM has tried to make me feel better by explaining that no one here feels the process is fair. But I really studied and that just doesn't help. I have ordered a different CD-Rom course to study in earnest before trying again next month. I *will* pass this thing. *I will!*

Part of me is angry that California is not one of the U.S. states with a reciprocal treaty for driving licenses with France. Really, what's the big deal? Practically anyone who isn't totally blind seems to be able to get a license in California. The test was something like 12 multiple choice questions. And they're afraid of giving licenses to someone coming from France? Seriously, give me a break.

I looked into getting a license from Pennsylvania, which *does* have a treaty with France. It is, after all, where I first learned to drive oh-those-many-years-ago. Unfortunately, it appears to be much more complicated to get them to give me one again now. I'd actually have to move there, not just pretend to live there.

So, for now, there is no other solution than to pass the bloody exam. Send this tired old brain good thoughts, dear readers. It can use all the help it can get.

Still, JM reminds me that I did have a major success today, proving that I'm not quite as stupid as I felt when I returned home. Our master electricians, besides upgrading our electricity, also added new phone jacks throughout the house. But to their, and our, surprise, except for the one in JM's office, where our modem resides, none of the other plugs appeared to work. Every time we would attach a phone, we would be rewarded with such horrible static that it was impossible to use any phone at all. It was puzzling and weird.

Suddenly, while making lunch, I had a brainstorm. The problem was the DSL connection. We needed to add filters to each of the plugs to separate the DSL signal from the phone signal. I had a spare filter, so I connected it to one of the "problem" jacks, then attached a phone. Voila, no more static! I was pleased about that, because not only couldn't our electricians solve it, but they consulted a Telecom engineer and he couldn't figure it out either!

Maybe there are a few functioning brain cells left after all.

Sunday, October 30

Saturday was the kind of day you wish you could bottle and keep for one of those miserable days in February when you are sure you will never again be warm or see the sun.

The temperature was in the upper 60s and the sun was golden. We decided to drive up to the Plateau de Sault to Espezel, where they were having the 28th annual *Foire des Eleveurs*, which is an agricultural festival celebrating the breeders of cattle, horses, sheep, etc. We didn't know what to expect, but thought it would make a nice outing.

JOUR DE FOIRE *IN ESPEZEL*

*Espezel is the largest town on the Plateau de Sault about 20 miles south of Chalabre towards the Pyrénées (*http://www.paysdesault.com*). To go to Espezel, we traveled south to Puivert, then took a small, winding road that cut through the foothills, still dressed in their beautiful Autumnal colors.*

The Plateau de Sault

First of all, the drive up to the plateau was spectacular. It's several hundred feet higher up in the Pyrénées than Chalabre, so the trees in the forest have really changed color. As we wound through the protected forest, we would suddenly come around a curve where the sun would be highlighting the golden foliage of a tree. It was so beautiful you felt as if your eyes ached from the glory of it all.

When we got to Espezel, there were already a fair number of cars parked at the outskirts. We figured we should park while we could, which turned out to be a good move.

Espezel is a larger village than Chalabre. Probably on a par with Mirepoix in size. I don't think I have ever seen such a huge market! The entire village was covered with stalls and teeming with people and dogs. I'm not sure if it would have been possible to see everything. Maybe if you were there for the whole weekend. Certainly, the two or three hours we walked around wasn't enough.

If ever there was a call to spend money and eat, this was it. There were bakeries, sausage-makers, cheese sellers, wine merchants, jams, herbs, vegetables, fruits. Anything and everything you could want.

The Plateau de Sault is known for its special gourmet potatoes. So, as well as being able to buy large bags of them (which we did), there were stands where they were stirring large pans of sautéed potatoes, sending the smell of golden brown frying potatoes everywhere. We didn't wind up tasting any though, because between carrying all our purchases and trying to control Maggie, who was going nuts trying to see all the dogs that passed us, it was just too complicated.

We detoured out of the main street to go towards the area where the animals were being displayed. I heard someone calling to me, and there was one of my friends from the Chalabre market! It was the clothing stand that is outside our front door every other week! Such a big fair, yet you still ran into people you knew. Really fun.

We looked at the various not-a-cats: horses, cattle, sheep, donkeys, goats. I thought that Maggie would enjoy the sheep. After all, when we'd taken her to try herding in L.A., she had loved it. She didn't want anything to do with those nasty sheep! They stared at her with expressions of great suspicion. She turned her back so she wouldn't have to see them! I suppose her fear of horses has now transferred to fear of all farm animals. At least I don't have to feel guilty that I don't let her herd them.

The local potatoes are a famed delicacy

Garlic and other fresh produce for sale

Another local delicacy: fritters made from nettles

Freshly baked bread for sale

Flags of all nations, baskets, etc.

Maggie's people: local sheep, ready for a herding demonstration

"Not-a-Cats"

Moo

The animals were all beautiful, especially the horses. They were especially displaying the large, farm breeds, which were magnificent. It awoke my lifelong desire to have a horse. I know that won't happen, but it doesn't hurt to dream.

Finally, we picked out some yummy things to eat as a picnic lunch and staggered back to the car (and I do mean staggered, because I had Maggie's leash in one hand and a 10 kilo sack of potatoes in the other!) and headed back down the mountain.

There was a feeling that we might have been enjoying the last truly glorious day of fall. But we felt as if we'd celebrated it in style.

Monday, October 31

Today was one of those "fun with the administration" kind of days.

Tomorrow is a holiday here, and since it's taking place on a Tuesday, many folks took today off as well. JM and I figured that would make today a good day to check in with our local unemployment office in Limoux.

As a returning French citizen, there is assistance available to help us reintegrate into the "system." We decided that I should be the one signing up for it, since, sadly, I'm the one who makes the least amount of money. (I don't think my 15 euro an hour for English lessons really counts as earning a living!)

It's one of those *Catch-22* situations. I needed to sign up with the unemployment office, who have rejected my claim for benefits, because I never actually earned any money here in France. With that rejection, I was able to go to the Employment office and have a file opened. With that, I will be able to go back to the unemployment office, and hopefully have the right to some kind of financial assistance.

Clearly, the Employment Office is *not* geared towards native English speakers who make their living as writers/producers/editors/story editors. Yes, it's true, the Aude is not a hotbed of literary activity. I *do* have other skills, but with one of the highest unemployment rates in France, there just aren't that many jobs available.

And, too, I've committed the cardinal sin in any job search these days, of being over 50. Might as well go out on an ice floe and wait for death. It seems to be the same the world over. Although, my interlocutor at the Employment office did tell me that many employers are now actively seeking "older" workers, because we actually *work* when they hire us. What a concept.

At any rate, as have been all our interfaces with the administration, it was a pleasant moment that was totally headache free. I now have the right to look for job openings online, so who knows what I might find.

As we were leaving, our friend Charles from the village came in to sign up for work as well. He recently got laid off from his job as a roofer. I'm guessing he'll have better luck finding something than I will.

Since we were in Limoux, we decided to kill two birds with one stone and head to the Leclerc for one of those big shopping expeditions where we buy exciting things like paper towels and soap powder. That was a big mistake. Apparently everyone in the Limoux region had decided to use their day off for a similar expedition. It reminded me of being on an L.A. freeway at rush hour! Still, we survived the experience and headed for home.

There will, of course, be big doings in the village tonight! Halloween has made its way here, and as with American kids, the French kids love it. We've already had some small Goblins at the door and I hope I don't run out of candy before the night is over. I wonder if they'll take I.O.U.s?

Wednesday, November 2

There are sad little faces around the village today. The holiday is over and school starts back tomorrow. Even though they've been bored half the time, they still don't want to go back to school. Complicated little critters.

The adults are all doing what they can to enjoy the beautiful, warm afternoons we're still having though. I'm sure the kids will all hate us tomorrow!

I've decided that, for me, there is no sense in moping over my driver's license set back of last week. I was not wild about the new software that I ordered. It keeps causing "runtime error 6, overflow" on my computer, which I've so far been unable to resolve. Rather than fight with it, I decided to return it and, instead, have joined an online *auto-école*, or driving school. Actually, I think it's pretty good, maybe better than the CD-Rom. I am making a concerted effort to train, train, train. Even if my writing has to take a backseat this month, I *will* pass my test next time. *I will!*

Of course, since Manu has been back at work demolishing our ancient concrete septic tank in the garage, concentration has been a bit limited. Somehow, the sound of a jackhammer vibrating through your entire house as well as your head, is not conducive to learning anything. Frankly, it's not conducive to much of anything! Still, after he left this afternoon, I buckled down for a good hour.

The kids might not want to go back to school, but I am going to study like mad.

Thursday, November 3

I can't believe it, yesterday was an important anniversary and I missed it!

A year ago yesterday, the day after George W. Bush likely "stole" a second election, I turned to JM and said that the time had come to leave the U.S. He asked me if I was sure, and I told him I was.

I immediately started looking into the various details online and less than a month later our house was sold and we were on a plane for France to look for our new home.

What an eventful year this has been. I am so grateful for the way things have worked out that I'm almost superstitiously afraid to think about it. As the months have gone by, the correctness of this decision has only been made more obvious.

Less than a year after moving to our new home, we have a totally new, and for us, better lifestyle. I have more friends and acquaintances than I would have dreamed possible. Our financial situation isn't any worse than it was in L.A., and it's better if you consider that we don't have a mortgage or killing healthcare costs. We eat better, we walk more, we socialize more. In every way that I can imagine, life is better.

Yes, I'm still looking for a way to earn a bit more money, but this would have been no different in L.A. After all, being over 50 does not make job searching particularly easy. At least here, I have health insurance. I do have some English students to start with, and this afternoon I'm going over to the local library to discuss reading to the pre-schoolers in English. Yes, it's volunteerism, but it will be fun and who knows to where it may lead?

So, even the black cloud of 2004 had a silver lining for the Possums of Chalabre.

Saturday, November 5

This morning's *Dépêche du Midi*, our local paper, has a big article predicting a very, *very* cold and wet winter. There has been a draught in much of France and the article states this winter will definitely put an end to it. Guess we'd better look forward to burning lots of fires around here.

Being cheap and earning very little money, we do not want to have to spend a lot of money on heating oil. So we only let our furnace run for two hours in the morning and three hours at night while we're watching television. During the day it's sweaters and blankets.

At least we have heat though. A lot of our friends still don't have their central heating up to speed. They will not be happy campers this winter.

And, it seems that winter was looking at the calendar and suddenly saw that it was November. This morning it decided that it was time to arrive. When I took Maggie out for her morning walk, it was cold. By the time we went back out to go to the post office a couple of hours later, it had actually gotten colder!

I just opened the windows to close the shutters and discovered that it is now simply freezing outside! Oh yes, winter is here.

Sunday, November 6

The Shire is calm and beautiful.

I'm sad to say that the same cannot be said about many other parts of France right now.

The riots that started ten days ago in Paris, have now spread across the country, coming as close to us as Toulouse and Montauban last night. The police say that they have never seen such young rioters. Clearly, this is as much a youth "event" as social unrest.

It's clear that the situation of the disaffected minorities is the root cause of this. With unemployment at 25% in some communities, it's not surprising that a feeling of, "we're mad as hell and we're not going to take it anymore" has exploded into fire and brimstone.

Of course, this kind of thing doesn't usually help to turn the tide of public sentiment no matter where it occurs. It can even have the unforeseen side effect of causing those who were once on the side of the rioters to turn against them. I'm sure that this round of violence will soon be gotten under control. The white hot rage always moderates after a first, blinding period. Still, the underlying situation is what needs to be addressed. I don't really see how at this point. It is a bad and ugly situation, no matter on which side you are.

Wednesday, November 9

Yesterday was my first "reading" day at the Bibliothèque Municipale (local library).

Once a week, the kindergarten and pre-schoolers (separately) are brought to the library for an hour to read, learn about a special subject, etc. It seemed like an interesting experiment to have me read them a story in English to see if they would like it. I think that, without really teaching them English, it's a good way for them to get used to the sound of the language while their little brains are in their most sponge-like state.

The first class was the kindergarten class. I have to say that they are simply adorable! How could I have ever been that small and cute?

Of course, Diva Maggie came along as my "helper," and I have to say she did an admirable job. She sat nicely, licked their little faces, let them pat her and prod her and never complained. She curled up to listen to the story, setting a good example for all.

Noëlle, the librarian, had made a photocopy of our first story, *Good Friends*, about a little rabbit who decides to share a carrot with his friends. Okay, so it's not Tolstoy, but the kids *are* only 5.

I read from the copy, while Noëlle showed the pictures to the kids. I have to say that they were extremely bright. They were really following the story and contributing comments in appropriate places. The method I chose was to read a paragraph in English, then translate it for them in French. I was surprised at how attentive they were during the whole thing.

Afterwards, they all wanted to tell me about their pets, or find pictures in the other books that showed they were interested. It was an a real delight and a resounding success. So, next week, we're going to try with the younger kids. I can't wait.

Friday, November 11

It's the 11th of November, Veteran's Day. We actually celebrate it on the 11th of November as opposed to the nearest Monday, like in the States.

Mostly, it's *not* an excuse for "Storewide Savings," although I noticed that a couple of the bigger supermarkets are actually open today, which surprised me. In fact, our little village stores were open in the morning, but as far as I can tell, they are open the morning of almost every holiday. Doesn't make being a shopkeeper sound all that appealing, does it?

For us, it was a quiet day. First, my dear friend Karine, who lives near Bergerac, finally got to come down for a visit yesterday. We haven't seen each other for six years, so it was wonderful to at last get together.

Unfortunately, she had to turn around and leave this morning, so it wasn't nearly enough time to enjoy each other's company. Hopefully we'll be able to do it again soon though. Or maybe meet halfway in Toulouse next time.

After Karine left, it was time to force Maggie into the bathtub to wash off the stone dust. I'm not taking any chances that she has an allergic reaction like she did during the summer. Not the best of times to bathe her though, as it didn't get above 10 degrees (around 50 F). To keep her from getting too chilled, I then had to subject her to the torture of the blow dryer. I'm not sure when she'll forgive me.

Still, there were *some* celebrations in the village. There was a Veteran's Day parade just before lunch.

One of the problems with being self-employed is that you don't really notice holidays all that much. We don't work the same kind of hours as the shopkeepers, but we are at our computers doing one thing or another while others are out playing.

No complaints though. We always try to take at least some time out of the day for a couple of walks around the village to appreciate how lucky we are here in the Shire.

Monday, November 14

Quiet and rainy in Chalabre. It's a bit like JM and I remember from our first visit here last December.

I took Maggie out *very* early this morning (6:30 a.m.!) and, except for M. Roget, I didn't see anyone in the street. Of course, no one should be out at 6:30 a.m. But, Christian was due at 8:15 a.m. and I had an appointment at the big new hospital between Foix and Mirepoix, so it seemed to make sense to get breakfast out of the way early.

We're on the last leg of renovation. Our second bathroom should be finished by tomorrow evening. The carpet can get laid after that, but since it needs to be brought in on the miraculous Mani-tout, I imagine it will have to wait for the rain to stop.

Tomorrow, I go back to giving English lessons to my beginning students (well, that's mostly Mireille at this point, but I have hopes of a couple more) and on Thursday it's back to the library to read to the 4-year-olds.

And, I'm still working on my darned driving test. I am making an effort to study everyday, so that the next time I go for the exam I pass. If positive thinking works, I should ace it.

Time to go down to the kitchen and take my banana/quince/raisin bread out of the oven. Nothing like a little experimentation on a cold, rainy November afternoon.

Wednesday, November 16

You would think after all this time that I would have learned *this* important lesson: if work is scheduled in your house, do *not* invite people to dinner that same night.

Clearly, I had a moment of brain fog when I invited fellow Americans Ellie and John to have dinner here tonight, even though Christian was scheduled to be finishing up the plumbing. I had not factored in the fact that my kitchen ventilator fan was being installed at the same time, as well as the final arrangements being made for connecting the gas bottles down where the septic tank used to reside.

Yes, I did give up on the idea of making a pot roast, as there were just not enough hours left in the day. But, I thought I could manage to throw together a lasagna and some dessert. Alas, when it came time for lunch, there was no gas at all! Panic set in and I was able to contact our would-be guests and rearrange for them to come next week.

Silly me. The gas bottle had been turned off while our carpenter installed the decorative thingy to hold the ventilator in place. My weak little hands just couldn't manage to turn the valve. How embarrassing. Still, it's better to be safe than sorry. It would have been worse to have guests walk in the door expecting dinner and have nothing to feed them.

Inexorably, though, progress is being made. Our second bathroom is now done and our bedroom carpet is set to install tomorrow. How will we cope once the final details are completed (a bit more painting and electrical work) and there is no longer anyone in the house but ourselves? Can you eat food that is not liberally seasoned with dust?

Joking aside, it will be seriously wonderful to finally have everything clean and relatively neat. The final challenge will be keeping it that way! Not for the faint-hearted.

After our cold lunch of leftover meatloaf, I'm pining for some comfort food for dinner. Time to descend and see what I can throw together in my semi-clean kitchen.

Sunday, November 20

Major news on the Beanie front to report: She is now officially a French-approved vehicle! We went for her latest inspection on Friday afternoon and she passed with flying colors. Special kudos go out to our local mechano-wizard, M. Antoine Hervas, for his superb efforts to comply with all the regulations. We need to wait until the beginning of December before all the paperwork will be at the Carcassonne Prefecture de Police, though. So, I still get to enjoy my easy-to-remember license plate until then.

Thursday was my second time of reading to the kids at the library. This batch was a year younger, four-year-olds. You can see a how big a difference a year makes in their attention spans. The boys, in particular, had a lot of trouble sitting still. But, they were all adorable and really seemed to enjoy the experience. We read the first of the *Dick and Jane* books. Perfect for them at that age. We're going to keep doing those and see how it progresses.

Maggie is really getting into the swing of the experience. She greets them, lets them pat her and kiss her, then lies quietly and "listens" to the story. She's totally in her element with the whole thing. I haven't decided if her presence helps the kids or interferes. I lean towards "helps" though, because it makes the experience a little more interesting for them.

I hope that everyone over there wants me to continue, as I quite enjoy doing it. After the group reading part, I hang around and get to interact with some of the kids. They seem to like having an extra adult there to read to them and talk with them, so it's nice for all of us.

We're inching towards Thanksgiving, but it's looking like JM and I won't be doing much that's traditional this year. First, you can't really have a fancy dinner on a day that, here, is just "Thursday." Friends are all busy working and carrying on with their lives. Plus, it's just about three weeks too early to find an actual turkey. While I can find parts, like boneless breast or a turkey roast, they are not the kind of "heritage" turkey that has the best flavor. Those are available for Christmas only. So, maybe we'll have a traditional Thanksgiving-Christmas dinner instead? What's wrong with making new traditions?

At any rate, dinner or not, we have a lot to be thankful for this year. Our new life here in Chalabre continues to get better with each passing week. Okay, it's a bit colder right now than in L.A. (Friends Diane and Evan report that it was in the upper 80s there last week, while here, it was -2 C / 28 F yesterday morning), but I don't really mind that all that much. In fact, I am reveling in my first real autumn in 27 years. I'd forgotten how beautiful it could be in a place that gets actual seasons other than Fire, Flood, Drought and Earthquake!

We have wonderful new friends, we feel as if we're a part of a real community, we aren't worried about losing our home if, God Forbid, one of us becomes ill. We feel surrounded by people we can call on for assistance; we know the system is there to care for us.

I'm not foolish. French society has plenty of problems, as evidenced by the rioting over the last few weeks. But *everywhere* has problems. You just have to pick which things you can live with and which things you can't. For us, we choose to live with this set, rather than those brought about by a right wing, conservative Christian, evil-empire that is trying to erode the precious freedoms that so many have died to protect for the last 200 years.

Wednesday, November 23

First and foremost, to all my U.S. family, friends and readers, have a very happy Thanksgiving! We have finally decided to make a small celebration here, even if I can't find a whole turkey to roast. But, it's the thought that counts as much as the food, right?

I had a bit of a surprise this week. I had not heard back about my next shot at taking the written driving exam. JM called and tracked down the head of the licensing department for our area and found out that the Prefecture had lost my file. He's going to look for it, and hopefully get me back on track to take the test in December.

The big shock came when I found out that I have to take the actual driving test. That wouldn't be so bad, except you have to bring your *own* dual control car. Of course, *everyone* has one of those just sitting around home. I was seriously bummed out, because in order to get one, it means signing up at driving school, which is seriously expensive here.

Instead, I decided to make another effort to see if I couldn't get a copy of my old Pennsylvania license. Although I spoke with some extremely helpful and nice folks in the PA DMV, the end result wasn't positive. I seem to have been "purged" from the system. The only possible way of tracking me down would be to have my original license number, which, after 28 years, I no longer do.

I even called the California DMV, hoping it would be on my file there. No joy with that either.

So, today, I bit the bullet and went over to the driving school to see what I would have to do. It turns out not to be too, too horrible. I will need to take only two lessons and they'll come with me on the day of the appointment. It won't be that expensive, somewhere around 100 euros, which is reasonable. I feel relieved. Now, I just have to pass the written test, which means study, study, study! [23]

On the positive side of things, we are now 99% finished with the work in the house. Only the ventilation to the exhaust fan to be connected to the outside of the house and a bit of paint to go. Then, a *major* cleaning. It's wonderful to feel as if we've accomplished something (well, as if our artisans have accomplished something!).

We also realized today that we have really come full circle in the weather department. I had an early morning appointment at the clinic in Lavelanet, so we were on the road before the sun was even fully up. The

---

[23] I finally passed both written *and* driving test and now have a French driver's license.

fields and forests were covered in a blanket of frost. The temperature was once again below freezing and we are expecting snow in the next couple of days.

We have now seen our shire go through each of its seasons, every one of them full of their own beauty. You would think that leaving the warmth of Southern California would make this cold a negative aspect of our life here. But, I find that I enjoy even that. Both JM and I have been flashing back to memories of our childhoods, and we realized that somehow, we had missed these seasonal changes more than we knew. The smell of frosty cold air blended with wood smoke is a far headier perfume than the smell of gasoline hanging in the air over the freeway. There's something wonderful about coming in from an icy walk to stand in front of the fireplace, as the friendly flames toast you back to warmth.

And, that brings us right back to Thanksgiving. We are blessed to have many, many things for which we are thankful.

Ciao for now!

Addresses

Real Estate

Lofficier Consultants, B.P. 22, 11230 Chalabre.
e-mail: consultants@randylofficier.com

Tourism

Office de Tourisme Intercommunal du Quercorb, Cours d'Aguesseau, 11230 Chalabre; Tel: 04-68-69-65-96; Fax: 04-68-69-65-95.
e-mail: office.tourisme@quercorb.com ; http://www.quercorb.com
Château de Chalabre: http://www.chateau-chalabre.com
Château de Puivert: http://www.chateau-de-puivert.com
Château de Montségur: http://www.montsegur.org/
Terres Cathares: http://www.terres-cathares.com/

Lodging

Le Falgas (*b&b*), 11230 Chalabre; Tel: 04-68-20-95-79.
Aux Fontaines (*b&b*)**,** 6 cours d'Aguesseau, 11230 Chalabre; Tel: 04-68-20-25. http://auxfontaines.com/
Château de Terre Blanche (*gîte, 2 apartments*), 11230 Chalabre; Tel: 04-68-69-38-51. http://www.le-guide.com/terreblanche/
Hotel de France (*hotel, 2 stars*), Cours Joseph-Reynaud, 11230 Chalabre; Tel: 04-68-69-68-60.

Restaurants

Le Commerce, 8 rue de l'Evêché, 09500 Mirepoix; Tel: 05-61-68-10-29. http://www.chez.com/lecommerce/ *Congenial, traditional ambiance, great service and great regional dishes. Wonderful 4-course, 11.50 euros menu on weekdays.*
Hanoi, 7 boulevard Omer Sarraut, 11000 Carcassonne; Tel: 04-68-25-21-72. *Friendly Vietnamese food in the heart of Carcassonne. The best nems we ever ate.*

Hotel de France, Cours Joseph-Reynaud, 11230 Chalabre, Tel: 04-68-69-68-60. *Chef Didier is a true artist with vegetables; excellent dishes, well-prepared; good, affordable lunch menu.*
Les Marronniers, 1 Carretera d'Els Banys, 66500 Molitg-les-Bains Village, Tel: 04-68-05-56-63. *Outstanding crêperie, wonderful regional dishes and warm, friendly service from a young couple from Britanny. Summer only!*
Pizza Stella, Rue de l'Abatttoir, 11230 Chalabre. Tel: 04-68-69-24-84. *Hearty Italian food; creative pizzas.*
Chez Esmée, Ste Colombe-sur-l'Hers; Tel: 04-68-69-22-57. *Hearty local dishes at a reasonable price.*
Le Pamir, 20 bis RD 117, Puivert; Tel: 04-68-31-28-73. *Afghani and Italian food.*

The Artisans

Joël Brochet (*painter, floors & decoration*), Le Bourdil, 11230 Chalabre; Tel: (off.) 04-68-69-36-80; (cell) 06-83-32-28-32. *A man of impeccable taste and dedication.*
Gabriel Chevalley (*cabinet-maker, carpentry & restoration*), Campsylvestre, 11230 Puivert; Tel: (off.): 04-68-20-78-06; (cell): 06-17-10-13-14. *Congenial and talented.*
Christian Drouin (*plumber & chimney-sweep*), Rue du Pont Vieux, 11230 Chalabre; Tel: (off.): 04-68-69-36-88. *Very reliable, always helpful and ready to pitch in.*
Serge Escande (*marble, granite & counter tops*), 11230 Chalabre; Tel: (off.): 04-68-69-27-17. *Friendly, resourceful, efficient professional.*
Georges Hamida (*cleaning & gardening*), 11230 Chalabre; Tel: (off.): 06-73-30-36-18. *Performed miracles on our 30-year-old linoleum.*
Antoine Hervas (*mechanic*), 13 Cours Sully, 11230 Chalabre; Tel: (off.): 04-68-69-37-59. *Helpful and generous beyond the call of duty.*
Arnaud Molini (*electrician*), 11230 Chalabre, Tel: (cell): 06-81-25-98-02. *Ingenious wizard of electricity who solves problems. (Arnaud was partnered with Stéphane Montoro when he did our house; Stéphane is now based in Toulouse.)*
Emmanuel "Manu" Montoro (*masonry & tiling*), Cours d'Aguesseau, 11230 Chalabre; Tel: 04-68-69-38-82. *A true artist of stone and wood.*
Viviane Coiffure (*hairdresser, men/women*), Cours Colbert, 11230 Chalabre; Tel: 04-68-69-20-66.

www.ingramcontent.com/pod-product-compliance
Lightning Source LLC
Chambersburg PA
CBHW030137170426
43199CB00008B/101